THE PROBLEM OF

THE JUDGMENT

Eleven Approaches to Kafka's Story

EDITED BY ANGEL FLORES

with a new translation of "The Judgment"
by Malcolm Pasley

GORDIAN PRESS   NEW YORK   1977

Library of Congress Cataloging in Publication Data

Main entry under title:

The problem of the judgment.

  Includes bibliographical references.
  1. Kafka, Franz, 1883-1924. Das Urteil. I. Flores, Angel, 1900-
    II. Kafka, Franz, 1883-1924. Das Urteil. English. 1976.
PT2621.A26U737 833'.9'12 76-48958 ISBN 0-87752-210-3

Contents

Acknowledgments

Indebtedness has been incurred to Secker & Warburg (London) for allowing me to include Malcolm Pasley's new English version of "The Judgment" from the forthcoming *Kafka's Shorter Works*, Volume II; to Schocken Books (N.Y.) for their numerous favors and generous help in my endless Kafka researches; to Cambridge University Press (London /N.Y.) for permitting me to reprint the essays by John M. Ellis from his *Narration in the German Novelle* (1974) and by Ronald Gray from his *Franz Kafka* (1973); to Winkler Verlag (Munich) for Hartmut Binder's study, originally published in German in his *Kafka-Kommentar zu sämtlichen Erzählungen* (1975); and to The Pennsylvania State University Press for James Rolleston's analysis from his *Kafka's Narrative Theater* (1974).

Foreword

It was the night of September 22, 1912 when at 10 p.m. Franz Kafka, not quite 29 years old, sat down at his desk in his bedroom and wrote steadily until 6 a.m. His creative effort resulted in the story he entitled "Das Urteil" (The Judgment) and this short piece, scarcely a dozen typewritten pages, marks the beginning of his most genuine expression. A veritable breakthrough, he was for once satisfied, even ecstatic. It was published in Max Brod's yearbook *Arkadia* in early 1913; later he was happy to see it in book form (actually a 29-page booklet in large type) in 1916 and again in 1920. He never condemned it to be destroyed as he did his novels and other writings.

A beautiful and extremely puzzling story, every reader seems to be curious to know exactly what happened and why! Kafka himself tried to explicate it, but his comments only compounded the mystery. It is possible that he himself did not fully understand what he had written. And to this late date, more than sixty years after it was written, critics—hundreds of them—are still admiring (or condemning) it, but forever seeking a satisfactory elucidation. Now in this year of 1976, when almost all of Kafka's writings are finally available, including his revealing diaries and letters (especially those to Felice Bauer, to whom the story was dedicated) I have asked a group of commentators for their latest judgments of "The Judgment."

"The Judgment" is Kafka's seminal story. It contains in miniature the essence of his themes and techniques as developed in his later work. What is most interesting, perhaps, is the diversity of reactions this powerful story arouses. Because the text is so very brief and the focus therefore so intense, this collection of essays constitutes an exposition of comparative criticism.

Angel Flores

July 1976
Palenville, New York 12463

Translator's Note on the Title

According to Kafka this work is "more of a poem than a story" (letter of August 14, 1916), and the difficulties of translating him appear here in acute form. The chief of these puzzles is how to deal with words or phrases of multiple reference, which appear typically at key points of his stories. One such key point is the title, and as with *Der Prozess* ("The Trial"? "The Law-Suit"? "The Case"?) the difficulty starts there. In accordance with the principle of preserving maximum resonance, of avoiding any reduction or narrowing of the meanings and associations which the original text carries, I have chosen "The Judgment," which is in any case the best-established English version of the title "Das Urteil."

As a legal term, "Urteil" means both the decision as to guilt or innocence and the determination of punishment in the case of guilt, that is, both "judgment" and "sentence." But it is not simply a legal term, for it is used equally to designate a wide range of authoritative, usually final, decisions. And it is obvious that Bendemann's condemnation of his son is not expressed purely in the language of the court-room. Before pronouncing the death sentence he judges Georg to be in some sense innocent, yet "devilish."

Among other earlier English titles "The Sentence" seems unsatisfactory, first because this is exclusively a legal term, and secondly because it directs attention to the form of punishment rather than to the condemnation itself. "The Verdict" (which has also been proposed) is quite wrong, since it suggests the idea that evidence of guilt has been assessed by neutral authority. It could be argued that "The Condemnation" is the best rendering, and I incline to this view myself, but since the arguments for "The Condemnation" and "The Judgment" are quite evenly balanced, the fact that the story is so widely known under the latter title has been allowed to decide the matter.— M.P.

THE JUDGMENT

Translated by Malcolm Pasley

It was a Sunday morning in the height of spring. Georg Bendemann, a young businessman, was sitting in his own room on the first floor of one of the small, flimsily built houses which stretched out in a long row beside the river, hardly distinguishable from one another except in height and color. He had just finished a letter to an old friend of his who was now living abroad, toyed with it for a while as he slowly sealed it, and then, resting his elbow on his desk, he looked out of the window at the river, the bridge and the rising ground on the far bank with its faint show of green.

He recalled how many years ago this friend of his, dissatisfied with his progress at home, had quite simply decamped to Russia. Now he was carrying on a business in St. Petersburg, which after a most encouraging start had apparently been stagnating for some time, as his friend always complained on his increasingly rare visits. So there he was, wearing himself out to no purpose in a strange land; his full, foreign-looking beard only partially obscured that face which Georg had known so well since childhood, with its yellowish skin that seemed to indicate the growth of some disease. By his own account he had no real contact with the colony of his

1

fellow-countrymen out there, and indeed hardly any social intercourse with Russian families, so that he was resigning himself to becoming a permanent bachelor.

What should one write to such a man, who had so obviously taken the wrong turning, whom one could be sorry for but could do nothing to help? Should one perhaps advise him to come home again, to transfer his business here, resume all his old personal connections—for there was nothing to prevent that—and rely for the rest on the support of his friends? But that would amount to telling him in so many words, and the more gently one did it the more offensive it would be, that all his efforts so far had failed, that he should finally abandon them, come back home, and be gaped at on all sides as a prodigal who has returned for good, that only his friends understood things and that he himself was a great baby who must simply do as he was told by these friends of his who had stayed put and been successful. And besides, was it even certain that all the pain that one would have to inflict on him would serve any purpose? Perhaps it wouldn't even be possible to get him back at all—he said himself that he had quite lost touch with affairs at home— and so he would just stay on out there in his remoteness, embittered by the advice offered to him and even further estranged from his friends. But if he really did follow their advice, only to find himself driven under on his return—not as the result of any malice, of course, but through force of circumstance—if he failed to get on either with his friends or without them, felt humiliated, and so became homeless and friendless in all earnest, wouldn't it be far better for him, in that case, to stay abroad as he was? Could one really suppose, in the circumstances, that he would make a success of life back here?

For these reasons it was impossible, assuming one wanted to keep up the correspondence with him at all, to send him any real news such as could be given unhesitatingly to even the most distant acquaintance. It was now more than three years since his friend had last been home, and he attributed this rather lamely to the uncertain political situation in Russia, which apparently was such as to forbid even the briefest absence of a small businessman while it permitted hundreds of thousands of Russians to travel around the world without a qualm. Precisely in the course of these last three years, however, Georg's own life had changed a lot. News of the death of Georg's mother—this had occurred some two years back, since when he and his aged father had kept house together—was something that had still reached his friend, and from the dry wording of his letter of condolence one could only conclude that the. grief caused by such an event was impossible to imagine at a distance. Since then, in any case, Georg had applied himself to his business with greater determination, just as to everything else. Perhaps it was that his father, by insisting on running the business in his own way, had prevented him from taking any initiative of his own during his mother's lifetime, perhaps since her death his father, while still active in the business, had kept himself more in the background, perhaps—indeed this was highly probable—a series of fortunate accidents had played a far more important part, at all events the business had developed in a most unexpected way during these two years, the staff had had to be doubled, the turnover had increased fivefold and a further improvement undoubtedly lay ahead.

But Georg's friend had no inkling of this change. Earlier on he had tried—perhaps the last occasion had been in that letter of condolence—to persuade Georg to emigrate to Russia, and had enlarged on the prospects that were open in St. Petersburg for precisely Georg's line of trade. The figures were minimal compared with the scale that his business had now assumed. But Georg had felt no inclination to write to his friend of his commercial successes, and if he were to do so now in retrospect it would certainly look peculiar.

As a result Georg merely contented himself with writing to his friend of such unimportant events as collect in one's mind at random when one is idly reflecting on a Sunday. His sole aim was not to disturb the picture of the home town which his friend had presumably built up during the long interval and had come to accept. Thus it happened that three times in three quite widely separated letters Georg had announced the engagement of some indifferent man to some equally indifferent girl, until quite contrary to his intentions his friend began to develop an interest in this notable occurrence.

However, Georg greatly preferred to write to him about things like these than confess that he had himself become engaged, a month ago, to a Fraulein Frieda Brandenfeld, a girl from a well-to-do family. He often talked to his fiancée of this friend of his, and of the special relationship which he had with him owing to their correspondence. "So he won't be coming to our wedding," said she, "and yet I have a right to get to know all your friends." "I don't want to disturb him," Georg replied, "don't misunderstand me, he probably would come, at least I think so, but he would feel awkward and at a disadvantage, perhaps even envious of me, at all events he would be dissatisfied, and with no prospect of ever ridding himself of his dissatisfaction he'd have to go back again alone. Alone—do you realize what that means?" "Yes, but may he not hear about our wedding in some other way?" "I can't prevent that, certainly, but it's unlikely if you consider his circumstances." "If you've got friends like that, Georg, you should never have got engaged." "Well, we're both of us to blame there; but I wouldn't have it any other way now." And when, breathing faster under his kisses, she still objected: "All the same, it does upset me", he thought it really couldn't do any harm to tell his friend the whole story. "That's how I'm made and he must just take me as I am," he said to himself, "I can't fashion myself into a different kind of person who might perhaps make him a more suitable friend."

And he did in fact report to his friend as follows, in the long letter which he wrote that Sunday morning, about the engagement that had taken place: "I have saved up my best news for the end. I have become engaged to a Fraulein Frieda Brandenfeld, a girl from a well-to-do family which only settled here some time after you left, so that you are unlikely to know them. There will be opportunity later of giving you further details about my fiancée, but for today just let me say that I am very happy, and that as far as our mutual relationship is concerned the only difference is that you will find in me, in place of a quite ordinary friend, a happy friend. Furthermore you will acquire in my fiancée, who sends you her warm greetings and will shortly be writing to you personally, a genuine friend of the opposite sex, which is not wholly without its importance for a bachelor. I know there are many considerations which restrain you from paying us a visit, but would not my wedding be precisely the right occasion for flinging all obstacles aside? But however that may be, act just as seems good to you and entirely without regard."

With this letter in his hand Georg had been sitting for a long time at his desk, his face turned to the window. He had barely acknowledged, with an absent smile, the greeting of a passing acquaintance from the street below.

At last he put his letter in his pocket and went out of his room across a little passage-way into his father's room, which he had not entered for months. There was indeed no call for him to go there in the normal course of events, for he saw his father regularly in the warehouse, they took their midday meal together in a restaurant, and while for the evening meal they made their separate arrangements they usually sat for a while afterwards in their common sitting-room, each with his own newspaper, unless Georg—as usually happened—went out with friends, or more recently went to call on his fiancée. Georg was amazed to find how dark his father's room was even on this sunny morning. What a shadow that high wall cast, rising up on the far side of the narrow courtyard. His father was sitting by the window, in a corner decked out with mementoes of Georg's lamented mother, reading a newspaper which he held up to his eyes at an angle so as to compensate for some weakness of vision. On the table stood the remains of his breakfast, not much of which appeared to have been consumed.

"Ah, Georg!" said his father, and rose at once to meet him. His heavy dressing-gown swung open as he walked, and the flaps of it fluttered round him. "What a giant my father still is", thought Georg.

"It's unbearably dark in here", he then said.

"Yes, it is dark", replied his father.

"And you've shut the window as well?"

"I prefer it like that."

"Well, it's quite warm outside", said Georg, as a kind of appendix to his previous remark, and sat down. His father cleared away the breakfast things and put them on a cabinet.

"I really just wanted to tell you", Georg continued, his eyes helplessly following the old man's movements, "that I've now written off to St. Petersburg after all with the news of my engagement." He drew the letter a little way out of his pocket and let it drop back again.

"To St. Petersburg?" asked his father.

"To my friend, you know", said Georg, seeking his father's eye.—In the warehouse he looks quite different, he thought, how he spreads himself out here in his chair and folds his arms across his chest.

"Indeed. To your friend", said his father with emphasis.

"Well, you know, Father, that I wanted to keep my engagement from him at first. Out of consideration for him, that was the only reason. You know yourself he's a difficult man. I said to myself, he may perhaps hear about my engagement from some other source, even though it's hardly probable in view of the solitary life he leads—I can't prevent that—but at all events he shan't hear about it from me."

"And now you've had second thoughts?" asked his father, laying his great newspaper on the window-sill, and on top of that his spectacles, which he covered with his hand.

"Yes, now I've had second thoughts. If he's a true friend of mine, I said to myself, then my being happily engaged should make him happy too. And so I hesitated no longer about announcing it to him. But before I posted the letter I wanted to let you know."

"Georg," said his father, drawing his toothless mouth wide, "listen to me! You have come to me in this matter to consult me about it. That does you credit, no doubt. But it means nothing, it means worse than nothing, if you don't now tell me the whole truth. I have no wish to stir up matters that don't belong here. Since the death of our dear mother certain rather distasteful things have occurred. Perhaps the time will come to speak of them too, and perhaps it will come sooner than we think. In the business there are a number of things which escape me, perhaps they aren't actually kept from me—I won't assume for the moment that they are kept from me—I'm no longer as strong as I was, my memory's failing, I can't keep track of so many different matters any more. That's the course of nature in the first place, and secondly the death of dear mother was a much greater blow to me than it was to you.—But since we're just on this particular matter, this letter, I beg you Georg, don't lie to me. It's a trivial thing, it's hardly worth mentioning, so don't lie to me. Have you really got this friend in St. Petersburg?"

Georg rose to his feet in embarrassment. "Never mind my friends. A thousand friends can't take the place of my father. Do you know what I think? You're not looking after yourself properly. But age needs to be treated with care. I can't get on in the business without you, you know that perfectly well, but if the business were to endanger your health I'd close it down tomorrow for good. This won't do. We'll have to make a change in your daily routine. A real, thorough change. Here you sit in the dark, and in the sitting-room you'd have plenty of light. You peck at your breakfast instead of taking proper nourishment. You sit with the window shut, and the air would do you so much good. No, Father! I'll get the doctor to come and we'll follow his orders. We'll change our rooms round; you shall take the front room and I'll move in here. It won't mean any upset for you, all your belongings can be moved across too. But there's time enough for that, just lie down in your bed for a bit, you really must have some rest. Come, I'll help you off with your things, you'll soon see how well I can manage. Or if you'd rather go straight into the front room you can lie down in my bed for the time being. That would really be the most sensible thing."

Georg stood close beside his father, who had let his head with its shaggy white hair sink on his chest.

"Georg", said his father softly, without moving.

Georg knelt down by his father at once, and in his tired face he saw the over-large pupils staring at him fixedly from the corners of his eyes.

"You haven't any friend in St. Petersburg. You always were a joker, and you've not even shrunk from playing your jokes on me. How could you have a friend out there of all places! I simply can't believe it."

"Just cast your mind back, Father,' said Georg, lifting his father out of his chair and taking off his dressing-gown as he stood there now quite feebly, "it must be almost three years ago that this friend of mine was here visiting us. I still remember that you didn't particularly care for him. At least twice when you asked after him I denied his presence, though in fact he was sitting with me in my room all the time. As a matter of fact I could quite understand your dislike of him, my friend does have his peculiarities. But then later on you got on with him pretty well after all. At the time I felt really proud that you were listening to him, nodding to him and asking him questions. If you think back you're sure to remember. He used to tell the most incredible stories of the Russian Revolution. For instance, how he was on a business trip to Kiev, and during a riot he saw a priest on a balcony who cut a broad cross in blood on the palm of his hand, and then raised this hand and called out to the mob. You've even repeated that story once or twice yourself."

Meanwhile Georg had succeeded in lowering his father into his chair again and carefully removing the knitted drawers he wore over his linen underpants, as well as his socks. The sight of these not particularly clean underclothes made him reproach himself for having neglected his father. It should certainly have been part of his duty to keep an eye on his father's changes of underclothes. Up till now he had not explicitly discussed with his fiancée what arrangements they were to make for his father's future, for they had silently assumed that he would remain on his own in the old flat. But now without more ado he resolved quite firmly to take his father with them into his future establishment. It almost looked, on closer inspection, as if the care he meant to devote to his father there might come too late.

He carried his father in his arms to the bed. During his few steps towards it he noticed with a terrible sensation that his father, as he lay against his breast, was playing with his watch-chain. He could not put him down on the bed straight away, so firmly did he cling to this watch-chain.

But no sooner was he in bed when all seemed well. He covered himself up and then drew the blanket extra high over his shoulders. He looked up at Georg with a not unfriendly eye.

"There you are, you're beginning to remember him now, aren't you?" Georg asked, nodding at him encouragingly.

"Am I well covered up now?" asked his father, as if he couldn't quite see whether his feet were properly tucked in.

"So you're feeling quite snug in bed already", said Georg, and arranged the bedclothes more firmly round him.

"Am I well covered up?" asked his father once more, and seemed to await the answer with special interest.

"Don't worry, you're well covered up."

"No!" shouted his father, sending the answer resounding against the question, flung back the blanket with such force that for an instant it unfurled flat in the air, and stood up erect on the bed. He just steadied himself gently with one hand against the ceiling. "You wanted to cover me up, I know that, my young scoundrel, but I'm not covered up yet. And even if I'm at the end of my strength, it's enough for you and more than enough. Of course I know your friend. He would have been a son after my own heart. That's why you've been playing him false all these long years. Why else? Do you imagine I haven't wept for him? And that's why you lock yourself up in your office, no one's to disturb you, the master's busy—just so that you can write your deceitful little letters to Russia. But luckily no one has to teach a father to see through his son. And just when you think you've got him under, so firmly under that you can plant your backside on him and he won't move, then my fine son decides to get married!"

Georg gazed up at the nightmare vision of his father. The friend in St. Petersburg, whom his father suddenly knew so well, touched his heart as never before. Lost in the vastness of Russia he saw him. At the door of his empty, plundered warehouse he saw him. Among the ruins of his stacks, the shreds of his wares, the falling gas-brackets, he was still just able to stand. Why had he had to go away so far?

"Now attend to me!" cried his father, and Georg, hardly aware of what he was doing, ran towards the bed to take everything in, but then stopped short half-way.

"All because she lifted her skirts," his father began to flute, "because she lifted her skirts like so, the repulsive little goose," and to demonstrate it he hitched up his shirt so far that the scar of his war wound could be seen on his thigh, "because she lifted her skirts like so and like so and like so, you made your pass at her, and so as to take your pleasure with her undisturbed you have besmirched your mother's memory, betrayed your friend, and stuck your father into bed so that he can't move. But can he move or can't he?" And he stood up quite unsupported, kicking his legs. He was radiant with insight.

Georg stood in a corner, as far away from his father as possible. A long time since he had firmly resolved to observe everything with the utmost attention, so that he should not somehow be surprised, outflanked, taken from the rear or from above. Just now he recalled this long-forgotten resolve, but it slipped from his mind again like a short thread being drawn through the eye of a needle.

"But your friend hasn't been betrayed after all!" cried his father, and his wagging forefinger confirmed it. "I've been representing him here on the spot."

"You comedian!" Georg couldn't restrain himself from calling out, then realized at once the harm done, and with starting eyes he bit—too late—on his tongue, so hard that the pain made him cringe.

"Yes, of course I've been playing a comedy! A comedy! Just the word for it! What other comfort was left to your old widowed father? Tell me—and for the space of your answer you shall be still my living son—what else was left to me, in my back room, hounded by disloyal staff, decrepit to the marrow of my bones? And my son went about the world exulting, concluding deals that I had prepared, falling over himself with glee, and stalking away from his father in the stiff mask of an honorable man! Do you suppose that I didn't love you, I from whom you sprang?''

Now he'll lean forward, thought Georg, what if he fell and smashed himself to pieces! These words went hissing through his brain.

His father leaned forward, but he did not fall. Since Georg failed to approach as he had expected, he straightened up again.

"Stay where you are, I've no need of you! You think you still have the strength to come over here, and that you're just hanging back of your own accord. Don't be too sure! I'm still the stronger by far. Perhaps on my own I might have had to give way, but as it is your mother has passed on her strength to me, I've formed a splendid alliance with your friend, I've got your clients here in my pocket!''

He's even got pockets in his shirt! said Georg to himself, supposing that with this phrase he could make him a laughing-stock in the eyes of the whole world. Only for a moment did he think so, for all the time he kept forgetting everything.

"Just link arms with your bride and try coming my way! I'll soon sweep her away from your side, you wait and see!''

Georg made grimaces as if he didn't believe it. His father merely nodded towards Georg's corner, confirming the truth of his words.

"How you amused me today, coming and asking me if you should tell your friend about your engagement. He knows it all already, you stupid boy, he knows it all! I've been writing to him, you see, because you forgot to take my writing things away from me. That's why he hasn't been here for such years now, he knows everything a hundred times better than you do yourself, he crumples up your letters unread in his left hand while he holds up my own letters to read in his right!''

He waved his arm over his head in his enthusiasm. "He knows everything a thousand times better!'' he cried.

"Ten thousand times!'' said Georg, to make fun of his father, but in his very mouth the words turned to deadly earnest.

"For years I've been waiting for you to come out with this

question! Do you suppose I concern myself with anything else? Do you suppose I read newspapers? There!" and he threw Georg a sheet of newspaper that had somehow found its way into bed with him. An old newspaper, with a name that was already quite unknown to Georg.

"How long you've delayed before coming to maturity! Your mother had to die, she was unable to witness the happy day, your friend is decaying in that Russia of his, three years ago he was already yellow enough for the scrap-heap, and as for me, you can see what condition I'm in. You've eyes enough for that!"

"So you've been lying in wait for me!" cried Georg.

In a pitying tone his father observed casually: "I expect you meant to say that earlier. It's not to the point any more."

And in a louder voice: "So now you know what else there's been in the world besides you, until now you've known of nothing but yourself. You were an innocent child, it's true, but it's even more true that you've been a devilish human being!— And so hearken to me: I sentence you now to death by drowning!"

Georg felt himself driven from the room, the crash with which his father collapsed on the bed behind him still sounded in his ears as he ran. On the stairs, down which he sped as if skimming down a slope, he collided with the charwoman who was on her way up to the flat to do the morning cleaning. "Jesus!" she cried and covered her face with her apron, but already he was gone. Out of the front door he sprang, across the roadway, towards the water he was driven. Already he was grasping at the railings as a starving man grasps at food. He swung himself over, like the outstanding gymnast who had once been his parents' pride. Still holding on, with a weakening grip, he spied through the railings a motor-bus that would easily cover the noise of his fall, called out softly: "Dear parents, I did always love you", and let himself drop.

At that moment the traffic was passing over the bridge in a positively unending stream.

Hartmut Binder

The Background ·

According to the September 23, 1912 entry in his diary, Kafka wrote this story "at one sitting during the night of the 22nd-23rd, from ten o'clock at night to six o'clock in the morning".[1]

From then on, the experience of that night became the yardstick by which to measure the true method of literary creation: "The fearful strain and joy, how the story developed before me...How everything can be said, how for everything, for the strangest fancies, there waits a great fire in which they perish and rise up again...Only *in this way* can writing be done, only with such coherence, with such a complete opening out of the body and soul".[2]

This unusual concept of being carried away by inspiration is found here in this magnitude for the first time, and Kafka, quite passively, felt at its mercy; it introduced a fairly long phase of increased productivity and generated an intensity of involvement which manifested itself among other things in the fact that Kafka, quite in contrast to his usual habits, would read his work aloud immediately after finishing it. He did this several times: first to his sisters;[3] next day, at Oskar Baum's, before several listeners: ("There were tears in my eyes. The indubitability of the story was confirmed.").[4] On October 6 he read it to

* Translated by Elke H. Gordon in collaboration with James L. Rolleston.

13

Max Brod (who had been away with Felix Weltsch, and whom Kafka greeted at the railroad station with the news that he had finished a short story for *Arkadia* [Brod's new Yearbook]. On December 4 Kafka read the story publicly during one of the "evenings of Prague authors" at the "Stephan"-Hotel—"I even enjoy reading it aloud", he wrote to Willy Haas,[5] and to Felice he said: "To appear in public with your story, and thus as it were with you, will be a strange feeling."[6] Finally he read it one more time on February 11, 1913, at the home of Felix Weltsch.[7]

The story deals, of course, with the conflict between father and son. Although Kafka considers it "somewhat wild and meaningless"[8] and fails to find in it "some straightforward, coherent meaning that one could follow,"[9] indeed is unable to "explain" it,[10] nevertheless during the proofreading process, on February 11, 1913, certain "relationships" did become clear to him which he in part records in his diary and later attempts to explain to Felice.[11]

On that occasion he presents the following overall interpretation: "The story may be a journey around father and son, and the friend's changing shape may be a change in perspective in the relationship between father and son. But I am not quite sure of this, either."[12] Two points of view can be distinguished here: first, that the elusive figure of the friend is an abstraction which combines the various aspects of the father-son relationship as they are deducible from a systematic elucidation of this web of relationships. This thesis is a further development of thoughts which Kafka, on February 11, 1913, entrusted to his diary: "The friend is the link between father and son, he is their strongest common bond. . . . In the course of the story the father, with the strengthened position that the other, lesser things they share in common give him—. . . the bride, who lives in the story only in relation to the friend, that is, to what father and son have in common, is easily driven away by the father since no marriage has yet taken place, and so she cannot penetrate the circle of blood relationship that is drawn around father and son. What they have in common is built up entirely around the father, Georg can feel it only as something foreign, something that has become independent, that he has never given enough protection, that is exposed to Russian revolutions, and only because he himself has lost everything except his awareness of the father does the judgment, which closes off his father from him completely, have so strong an effect on him."[13] This friend in Petersburg should not be regarded as being an independent figure, but rather as a function of that relationship. By improving his business and through his marriage, Georg hopes to overcome the possibility that is still alive within him, as becomes obvious from his hesitation to tell his friend about his engagement and from the reaction of his bride to this fact.

Secondly, Kafka's own interpretation of the course of the narrative makes clear that "The Judgment" has as its subject a father-son relationship, and this is supported by two additional factors. Firstly, Kafka intended to publish the story together with "The Stoker" and "Metamorphosis" in a collection entitled *Sons*. On the 11th of April, 1913, he wrote to his publisher, Kurt Wolff, that there existed "an obvious, and, more important, a secret bond" between those three texts, and he definitely wanted to present them together.[14] An analogy is especially apparent between "The Judgment" and "Metamorphosis", where one finds not only affinity of motif but also similarity of structure:

Three phases in the development of the families Samsa and Bendemann are juxtaposed. In the first phase, which in both stories is related by the narrative voice as past history, the father is an independent business man. Each time it is strikingly emphasized how this strong position of the father has its counterpart in the professional weakness of the son. This becomes immediately evident in "The Judgment" where Georg and his father work in the same business. In "Metamorphosis" the correlation is more indirect: After the collapse of the father's business, Gregor's present supervisor became one of his father's creditors. Thus the two businesses were commercially connected, and therefore the former power and position of the father must have had its implications for Gregor, who, at that time, was only a "little salesclerk".

One now arrives at a major turning point in both stories. In

"The Judgment" it is the death of the wife which makes the father become "less aggressive"[15] because it has "depressed" him and therefore accelerates the "course of nature" even more.[16] In "Metamorphosis" the business failure and the resulting financial misery put "everyone into complete desolation". This development, rather than sweeping along the sons, has them rise to be the heads of their families and put their fathers into a dependent situation which corresponds to their own former positions.

And now, once again, a major turning point is reached, both in "The Judgment" and in "Metamorphosis". Gregor turns into a cockroach and dies, and Georg Bendemann, after being confronted with his father in the image of a "bogey" man[17] executes himself in accordance with the death sentence of his father. This once again is a reversal of the conditions of power. Old Samsa, who up to that point was hardly able to stand up in the evenings and who had to stop on his walks when he wanted to speak, once more becomes professionally active, and he rules totally over his son, a fact which is already apparent in the external relationship of size: through his metamorphosis the son has fallen back into the state of an infant and has to be fed and taken care of like a child. And old Bendemann, lifting himself up from his bed, quite correctly regards himself as being "still much the stronger"[18] of the two, for during the dispute Georg falls into increasing inner dependence on his adversary, until at the end of the story he is completely dependent on him.

These correspondences clearly demonstrate in both texts a similarity of structure from which follows that any strengthening in the position of the father necessarily brings with it a weakening for the son, and vice versa. We are therefore in fact dealing with family conflicts.

Further proof for the idea that Kafka in "The Judgment" thematized the conflict of the generations can be deduced from the thoughts in Kafka's mind as he was writing: "thoughts about Freud, of course; in one passage, of *Arnold Beer* [a novel by Max Brod]; in another, of Wassermann; in another, *smash*, of Werfel's giantess; of course, also of my 'The Urban

World'."[19] The word *smash* appears in the manuscript and has now been inserted here.

The formulation shows that Kafka quite automatically connects the story as a whole with the teachings of Freud, familiar to him in various forms; the doctrine is centered totally on the Oedipus complex, that is, on the son's hatred, fear, respect, rebellion, and the will to power. To this corresponds an erotic fixation on his mother. The fact that Georg Bendemann can develop professionally and become engaged only after the death of his mother reflects this fundamental situation. By accepting his father's death sentence he acknowledges his relationship with Frieda Brandenfeld as desecrating the memory of his mother.[20] The mother is closely allied with the father and obviously also believes that the friend in Petersburg, unmarried and unsuccessful, would be a son after her own heart[21] (Compare "The Urban World," where Oskar is to withhold his new ideas from his mother, lest she be destroyed by the effort of coping with the sorrow they would cause her). In one instance old Bendemann says: "but your mother has given me so much of her strength". Similarly in "Metamorphosis" a close emotional bond is presupposed. Here the loving mother through her intervention at first saves the life of her devoted son from the threats of his father. The way in which Kafka analyzes the autobiographical background of the story brings to mind the mechanisms which Freud describes in *The Psychopathology of Everyday Life*. It would be wrong, however, to orient the interpretation of "The Judgment" solely towards the traditional psycho-analytical view of things, as is done on occasion.[22] For one thing, the previously mentioned interaction of Georg Bendemann's parents does not correspond to any grouping of the figures in Freudian theory but rather to the particular situation of Kafka's family. For another, the events seem to take place independently of the personal qualities, conditions and relationships of the people involved, and they go beyond the deterministic individualism of classical Freudian theory.

As to the literary origins of the subject matter in "The Judgment", one should focus not so much on the earlier expressionist works of, say, Sorge, Hasenclever, Bronnen, or the later Werfel, all of whom make the father-son conflict the focal point of their works;[23] rather, considering the thoughts Kafka describes as in his mind when writing, one is led towards literary works rooted in other traditions and literary movements. Only the dramatic fragment "The Giantess. A Moment of the Soul," which is mentioned by Kafka, can be called expressionistic, and even here the word applies primarily to the emphasis on pity for the humiliated and deformed human creature, so typical of Werfel's work. A scene on the fairground is presented. The impresario invites the audience to watch a magnificent giantess. J. Demmer believes that Kafka was thinking of the passage where the title figure, representing Pallas Athena, "shows us not so much that she is lofty and dignified as that we are as small as dwarfs".[24] The passage from the diary, however, in its complete form shows that *gigantism* was not the point of comparison for Kafka but rather the longing that Georg feels for his father's death: "What if he topples and *smashes* himself!"[25] Hence the echo of a passage like the following seems more plausible, where the generation-question is the subject, and where "Werfel" is addressing the giantess: "Sister, sister, is it possible? . . . you bear a monstrous fate on your shoulders, yet you smile, and are not groaning up to the clouds! . . . My own wickedness and that of my forefathers surely shares this guilt."[26]

The novel, *Arnold Beer*, which was held in great esteem by Kafka, had appeared shortly before he wrote "The Judgment". The following passage seems to have been influenced by it: "Perhaps during his mother's lifetime his father's insistence on having everything his own way in the business had hindered him from developing any real activity of his own."[27] In the novel its author says of Arnold: "He was not mistaken in his anticipation that the father, in his pedantic concern for the business, would not of his own will let slip from his own hands any important part of the business".[28]

Kafka of course knew many more literary works resembling "The Judgment". Toward the end of his life, he declared to Gustav Janouch: "The son's revolt against his father is an ancient theme in literature, and an even older problem of the world. Dramas and tragedies are written on this subject, but in reality it is the subject for a comedy."[29] Kafka was referring to Synge's *The Playboy of the Western World*. There the son boasts of having killed his father, and, while attempting to put his words into action he is prevented from doing so by the sudden appearance of the father, the very one he had hoped to murder.[30] Kafka's remark implies a rejection of expressionist modes and indirectly shows that the comical elements in "The Judgment" had been deliberately inserted there.

In September, 1912, Kafka was of course also involved with Grillparzer's autobiographical story "The Poor Fiddler" (Der arme Spielmann) which he read aloud, on August 9 of that year, with considerable emotion. The story deals with the weak son of a renowned and influential man who is incapable of standing up to his domineering, ambitious father. Failing in his profession, the son lives then unemployed and unnoticed in a tiny room, and psychologically broken, impoverished, he finally loses the girl he loves. He turns to art, only to end his life as an incompetent and ridiculed street-musician. The resemblance to "The Judgment" is obvious. In 1920 Kafka wrote to Milena that he was as much ashamed of "The Poor Fiddler" "as though I had written it myself".[31] Georg, who at first was dominated by his father in the business, also loses his bride and is, in the end, defeated by his father. Before the decisive turning point old Bendemann had been leading a life with a minimum of work, sharing the apartment with his son who hardly noticed him. In this family story Georg has the characteristics which Grillparzer assigned to the defeated fiddler.

In 1912 Kafka must also have been familiar with Dostoevsky. Max Brod mentions the Russian author in an essay published in October 1911.[32] Toward the end of the following year Kafka used in "Metamorphosis" certain narrative elements from *The Double*. However, a comparison will show that, more especially, details of the Epilogue from *Crime and Punishment* have entered into "The Judgment". Raskolnikov, in Siberia, is deeply burdened with guilt and is ashamed of himself for having been ruined "so utterly, so hopelessly, and so stupidly because of some blind decision of fate" and for having "to humble himself and submit to the *absurdity* of that sort of decision if he wished to get any peace of mind at all."[33] This statement does correspond in tone to a passage in "The Judgment".

Raskolnikov's correspondence with his friends in Petersburg and his relatives "was carried on through Sonia, who wrote to Petersburg every month ... At first her letters seemed rather dry and unsatisfactory" to the recipients, but later it becomes clear to them "that they could not be better, as they conveyed a complete picture of the life of their unhappy brother."[34] Raskolnikov took little interest in the news from home; the announcement of his mother's death "did not seem to make any great impression on him".[35] Finally, Raskolnikov turns "very pale" and becomes seriously ill. Sonia's visits annoy him at first, and he does not expect the situation to improve in the near future. In a moment of self-analysis he ponders why, after his deed, he had not committed suicide: "Why had he hesitated to throw himself into the river and preferred to go to the police and confess?"[36] A tremendous distance stood between him and his fellow-prisoners, "as if they belonged to quite a different species".[37] One bright and warm spring day Raskolnikov watched "the wide, deserted expanse of the river. From the steep bank a wide stretch of the countryside opened up before him ... He sat there, looking without moving and without taking his eyes off the vast landscape before him; his thoughts passed into daydreams into contemplation; he thought of nothing, but a feeling of great desolation came over him and troubled him."[38] Sonia suddenly appears at his side, and Raskolnikov realizes than how urgently he wishes to find his way back into human society, hoping for a bright new future, for a perfect resurrection into a new life. Kafka, true to his narrative intention, presented this course of action in reverse. Raskolnikov's hopeful, happy glance across the river becomes for Kafka the starting point for his story which also takes place on a beautiful spring day. Georg's thoughts resemble Raskolnikov's daydreaming. However, after this point of departure, Kafka's story takes a different course—

toward the suicide of the main character, which at least is hinted. The extreme isolation of the bachelor friend is linked by Kafka to Russia and Petersburg, no accident, to be sure, for in "Bachelor's Ill Luck" Kafka had called the extreme remoteness from family life an experience "so extreme...[in] solitude that one can only call it Russian".[39] One is reminded further of *Crime and Punishment* in that the pale face of the friend in Petersburg, who no longer has contact with his compatriots, is suggestive of an illness.[40] The news of Georg's mother's death reached his friend by mail, and the "dryness" of his response is attributed to his usual lack of interest.[41] (There exists, by the way, in this regard a subtle connection to young Bendemann who is reproached by his father for not having been "depressed" enough by his mother's death). Georg can thus limit himself to giving his friend "unimportant items of gossip",[42] for the friend at first, like Raskolnikov, does not expect major changes to occur in the future. Sonia's letters "are full of the most prosaic details...they contained no account of her own hopes, or her future expectations, or descriptions of her feelings.'"[43] Yet just as the friends in Petersburg are able to form their own picture of Raskolnikov—which is quite "distinct and clear"—, so Georg draws extremely self-assured conclusions from the correspondence of his friend. Thus it is clear that Kafka incorporated into his story the mood and atmosphere of *Crime and Punishment* rather than the direction of the narrative or the interaction between people, although in this respect he later probably found other models in Dostoyevsky, too. One diary entry from the end of the year 1914 proves that he was familiar with *The Brothers Karamasov*, and that he had analyzed it in connection with the father-son conflict.[44]

Furthermore, it can be assumed that a local legend of Prague, entitled *Die goldene Gasse* (The Golden Alley), may have played a role in the conception of "The Judgment". This legend starts out with scenes reminiscent of Kafka's story: "On the right banks of the River Moldau... where centuries ago the people of Israel were allowed to erect their huts, there also stood the small dwelling of the well-to-do Rabbi Kalman. One beautiful spring evening the rabbi's only daughter, Hanina, sat

pensively in front of her hut, her dark eyes directed toward the
setting sun whose last rays reddened the summit of the Laurenz
Mountain and turned into gold the domes of the high towers on
the Hradschin."[46] (It is interesting to point out here that the
Niklas Road where the Kafka family resided until November
1913, circled eastward around the Jewish ghetto, to which the
"long row of small, ramshackle houses... scarcely distinguishable from each other in height and coloring" seem to refer.)
Hanina is expecting her lover, who is not able to take with him
the resisting girl without "the paternal blessings". The father
appears, and he accuses his daughter of an "affair" and the
lover of having seduced the girl.[47] (Old Bendemann calls Georg
a playboy and his bride a whore.) The father takes Hanina back
into the house. The food, in great abundance, remains
untouched (Georg's father has hardly touched his breakfast),[48]
and even time is unable to cure his dejected heart. "From then
on he disregarded his enormous fortune, and neglected his
business."[49] In "The Judgment" old Bendemann's former love
for Georg is emphasized, and as the father in "The Golden
Alley," undergoes a similar change: "There's many a thing in
the business I'm not aware of... I'm not equal to things any
longer, my memory is failing, I haven't an eye for so many
things any longer." This state of mind will later be interpreted
as being the result of Georg's conduct.[50] Hanina, however, "as
swiftly as a frightened fawn runs from the house, down the
steep embankment into the raging waters... the waves
covering forever her delicate body" while the father "lies on the
floor, as if dead".[51] The parallel to Kafka's story is almost
perfect: Old Bendemann is collapsing on the bed while Georg
runs from the room and throws himself from the bridge into the
river;[52] he, too, does this—compare Kafka's self-interpretation
of the story—because the father drove from his side his chosen
marriage-partner.

These allusions to other sources do not, however, answer the
question why the writer was so attracted by the subject of
generation conflict that this articulation of it would then
introduce a new, major phase in his creativity. At first, the
obvious answer: it was Kafka's own lifelong problem. He

writes in the *Letter to his Father*: "There was no real fighting between us; I was soon defeated and the only thing left was flight, bitterness, grief, and inner struggle".[53] "One might have thought" we read elsewhere in the letter, "that you would simply stamp on me so that nothing of me would be left behind. That has not happened . . . but maybe something worse has happened."[54] Kafka elaborates further about what he meant in a letter to his sister Elli: if the children do not conform to the "very precise demands" of the parents, then they (the children) will be "cursed, or consumed, or both".[55] Kafka saw his relationship to his father as subject fundamentally to this curse. I and he always thought the curse to be at work when his relationship to Felice Bauer was stagnating or interrupted. Kafka's own attitude to his father was characterized by ambivalence. On the one hand, he emphasizes his dependence, then, on the other, his hatred for him ("my father and I . . . hate each other gallantly"),[56] which could easily be inverted into self-destruction because of the concomitant feelings of guilt. Only two weeks after finishing "The Judgment", but as a consequence of a process developing over a period of time, Kafka thought of jumping out of the window because the family wanted him to work in the afternoon in a factory where he and his father held a share.

Although Kafka had always considered his parents his "persecutors",[57] and although he had suffered deeply under his father even as a child, it would be incorrect to assume that the generation conflict, as just outlined, had existed all along. For until the autumn of 1911 Kafka had been, as a consequence of repressed fear, worry and sadness, terrifyingly "indifferent". Diary entries of July, 1919, and the story "The Urban World" of March 1911, make clear, however, how Kafka was starting his confrontations with his family, still rather tentatively and unconsciously, and under the protection of literary masks, for the subject matter of those fragments are problems of upbringing and generation-conflict. These diary entries can be regarded as poetic fragments because of their diction and because they exist in a total of six different versions. At the end of 1911 the open conflict broke out: in the course of only a few weeks Kafka had four major arguments with his father. For the first time he defended his own, idiosyncratic mode of living, and for the first time admitted his hatred to himself. His *Letter to his Father*, written in 1919, confirms this as the period of change through Kafka's contention that, until his attempts at marriage, he had lived like a business man from one day to the next "without keeping precise book".[58] Without doubt, the Yiddish theatre company whose performances Kafka often attended in the autumn of 1911 and the following winter played a major role in his change of attitude. At that time, when he discovered the world of Judaism—and not a year later as is often assumed—the change from the indifferent, passive and assimilated "child"[59] into the critic of society was taking place, and as a result, of course, his relationship to his own family had to be re-thought.

In view of these correlations it is not surprising to find that the Yiddish plays had a direct effect on the conception of "The Judgment". At the end of October 1911, Kafka attended Abraham Scharkansky's *Kol Nidre*. In this piece the father sentences his daughter to death; however, in order to forestall her father, she commits suicide.[60] Yet, above all, one should mention here Jakob Gordin's *God, Man, and the Devil*, a Job-Faust-Version, with which Kafka became acquainted a few days after *Kol Nidre*: The central figure of the play, Hershele, has become obsessed with wealth. He no longer respects his father and later throws him out of the house. He plunges into the madness of worldly pleasures, casts out his wife and starts a new affair. He forsakes his best friend who showers him with accusations; this results in Hershele's suicide. All of these traits reappear in "The Judgment": Georg "is strutting through the world" and "stalking away from his father".[61] In his father's opinion Georg, by wanting to marry Frieda Brandenfeld for physical reasons alone, disgraces the memory of his dead mother, who has the same function in the story as the first wife of Hershele. After his marriage Georg had intended to leave his father "living alone in the old house".[62] In addition, he "deceived" and "betrayed" his friend in Petersburg.[63] The father's guilty-verdict, then, is based on these factors.

The more grotesque elements in Kafka's story, such as the childish and comical traits of the father, also derive their impulse from Gordin's play. But especially a scene from Act II seems to have influenced directly that part in "The Judgment" where old Bendemann mockingly calls Georg's bride a stupid goose who had lifted her skirts in order to seduce the son. Hershele's father, in order to entertain his niece and show off some of his former glory, jumps on a chair and with a deadly serious expression recites one of the traditionally funny marriage speeches, where he calls marriage the end of care-free youth and warns of strangers who might kidnap daughters from their loving parents. Miss Beck writes of him and of old Bendemann: "His profession is considered so significant a part of his character that it is included in his name, Leyzer Badkhan, for Badkhan means 'jester' or 'fool'. In the play his stock-in-trade is whispering foolish secrets into people's ears ... It is difficult to separate his role as jester from the suggestion that he is slightly senile ... This fusion of Leyzer Bakhan's joking and hiding behind senility, while at the same time speaking the truth, may be reflected in old Bendemann, who has been variously judged insane, senile, or just playing games. In "The Judgment" it is extremely difficult to tell to what extent the father is playing some vast, diabolical joke, to what extent his image is distorted by Georg's perception of him ... Like Leyzer Badkhan, he acts the hero, but it is clear that he feels threatened by his son's success in business and is resentful of his engagement. Leyzer admits to feeling inadequate in Hershele's presence ... Old Bendemann also describes himself as feeling squashed by a son who prides himself on his importance. He plays on the word unterkriegen".[64]

Finally, it should not be overlooked how even structural peculiarities in "The Judgment" show the influence of the Yiddish Theater. For example, the abruptness with which the individual parts of the story are constructed and combined can be partly explained in terms of these Yiddish models. This also holds true for the manner in which persons are introduced and deployed according to their function—both features are without precedent in the early prose of Kafka. Kafka was struck,

in the theater program of Gordin's *Der Wilde Mensch* (The
Wild Person) by the fact that one could learn, beyond the mere
naming of dramatis personae, "only so much as the audience
has to know ... about a family exposed to their judgment".[65]
Schmul Leiblich is a "rich businessman", Simon "a student",
and Vladimir Vorobeitschik "Selde's lover", yet during the
course of action one would get much more differentiated
characterizations that would sometimes diverge considerably
from the given designations. There is a comparable discrepancy in "The Judgment" between the external naming of the
characters in terms of their social roles—"a young business
man", a "girl from a wealthy family", the friend in Petersburg,
the father—and their individual traits which compete with
these roles, as revealed in their speeches and actions.

Some essential structural elements in "The Judgment" were
derived from the theater: one finds a kind of exposition with
certain prerequisites like time and place settings (letter, Sunday
morning, spring time, private room) in which a "monologue"
(Georg's "erlebte Rede") familiarizes the reader with the
characters and their interrelationships, and articulates the
basic problem of Georg's bond with his friend. Set apart by
means of light effects (a major tool of the theater) the argument
between Georg and his father develops in explicit theatricality
where, aside from the spoken word, only the physical positions
of characters and details of mime and gesture are stressed—
elements which determine any action on stage. Georg's
soliloquies find their counterpart in the so-called practice of
speaking *a parte,* which in the Yiddish Theater—in contrast to
the stage practices in the German-speaking area—at that time
was still in wide use. The fact that the conversation of the two
opponents at first does not articulate the reason for Georg's
visit but rather superficially consists of everyday talk fits this
convention. However, below the surface the menacing aspect of
the situation is at once much in evidence. Such a technique is
the rule in stage dialogue; whereas the narrator of short
stories—such as Heinrich von Kleist—has to start talking at
once about the essential, and can often only put the highlights
of a dialogue into direct speech. That there is, in the end, a

secret in the very center of this dialogue which is gradually revealed to the reader and Georg is as much a dramatic technique as it is a method that is peculiar to the narrative. According to Janouch, Kafka was aware of this connection and once told him: "Dostoyevsky's *Crime and Punishment* is, after all, nothing but a detective story. And Shakespeare's *Hamlet*? That is a detective play. There is a secret in the middle of the action, and this secret is slowly uncovered. Yet is there a greater secret than truth?"[66] Mention should be made here of Heinrich von Kleist's "The Marquise of O—", held in great esteem by Kafka, for the technique of gradual revelations in this short story is modelled on *Amphitryon* (Kleist's adaptation of Molière's play) and ultimately on Sophocles's *Oedipus Rex*.

In the above discussion the form of the narrative has been described onesidedly, for it also contains elements that are typically epic. For one thing, the use of "erlebte Rede" is to be considered here, for in "The Judgment" Kafka mastered it completely for the first time. This speech supersedes the interior monologue, used particularly in "Wedding Preparations in the Country", where its close relationship to the monologue on stage is obvious. Specifically epic, also, is the peculiarity of the introductory scene which, starting with a fixed point of action that opens the text ("Georg Bendemann...with his elbow propped on the writing table was gazing out of the window")[67] recapitulates the story leading up to that moment. This is done here not as a flashback in the narration but rather as a reflection by the central character; this initial moment then has to be passed through again as the action proper begins to unfold. ("With this letter in his hand Georg had been sitting at the writing table, his face turned toward the window.")[68] Kafka might have adopted this method of representation from Kleist, the one author who realized this technique in its purest form in his "The Earthquake in Chile" where, however, the past history is presented as a review of events by the narrator:

In Santiago, the capital of the kingdom of Chile, at the very moment of the great earthquake of 1647 in which

many thousands of lives were lost, a young Spaniard by the
name of Jerónimo Rugera, who had been locked up on a
criminal charge, was standing against a prison pillar
about to hang himself.[69]

Thus the beginning of Kleist's short story, whose elements also
are reminiscent of the exposition of a drama. After picking up
the thread of the action again and after Jerónimo has decided to
commit suicide, Kleist continues: "Just as he was standing next
to a pillar, as we have said..."[70] As in "The Judgment", the
opening situation of the story is traversed a second time.

But above all, it should be emphasized that Kafka's aesthetic
ideas, which came to fruition in "The Judgment", underline
his demand for a gradual unfolding: from a simple point of
departure moving along continually, organically, avoiding
jumps, surprises, and turning points. From the drama of great
literature—Kafka at that time only had a loose relationship
with it—and from the Jewish folk-plays this method cannot be
deduced, for he reproaches the authors writing in Yiddish for
lacking "logical sequence" and "order".[71] And those plays that
he knew by Shakespeare, Goethe, Grillparzer, or Gerhart
Hauptmann he criticizes because they do not accord with his
own aesthetic perception in regard to rules of structure. In
accordance with this theoretical position Kafka now demon-
strates in "The Judgment" how little by little there occurs a
decomposition of Georg's consciousness, becoming finally so
evident that it no longer surprises the reader to see the son
execute on himself the death sentence that was pronounced on
him: even in his study he is in a state of absent-mindedness, and
when he enters his father's room he does not adjust to the
situation, is amazed at the darkness in there, and at the gigantic
size of his father. These are details which hint at his inner fear
and function as a foreshadowing of disaster. The father's
strange behavior then causes for Georg a certain difficulty in
concentrating and a certain embarrassment; these later grow
into a feeling of horror of which the father's image is the
externalization. In this phase the son is already quite distracted,
he forgets everything, the continuity of his consciousness is

suspended, and wishes for the death of his father, hitherto repressed, strike like a flash of lightning. The dissolution of the young business man's personality has by now been almost completed, and it manifests itself in the physical realm in the staring of his eyes, the grimacing and in sudden movements of his jaw which even injure him. At the culminating point of this development Georg's thoughts are merely connected outwardly and his answers are mindless repetitions of his opponent's arguments; his attempts at mastering the situation appear as senseless reflexes of the moment.

It might perhaps be argued that attempts to extract epic and dramatic elements are mistaken since Kafka himself pointed out in a letter to his publisher that "The Judgment" was "more of a poem than a story" and therefore needed "a lot of free space around it" if it were to "have its effect". Kafka argued in this way in order to obtain a separate printing in the series *Der jüngste Tag* which clearly mattered more to him than the aforementioned collection of short stories, *Sons*, which he was willing to give up for the sake of seeing "The Judgment" published separately. The advantage of this over a collection of stories would be "that each story could be regarded separately and could have its own effect".[72] Kafka's evaluation of the story obviously did not depend so much on formalistic elements *per se* as on the fact that, according to his opinion, "The Judgment" lacked clear-cut meaning. Also, that the free space Kafka says surrounds the story can be regarded as an image. As with a difficult poem with ambiguous images and an expressive content not reducible to external empirical conditions, the reader of "The Judgment" is in part directed towards this calculated artistic autonomy. In part also, the reader, like the author correcting proofs, must have the opportunity, undisturbed, to direct his thoughts in the most varied directions. With this in mind he wrote about "The Judgment" on the night of December 4-5, 1912 that "if it didn't express some *inner* truth (which can never be universally established, but has to be accepted or denied every time by each reader or listener in turn), it would be nothing".[73]

One question remains unresolved: how did it happen that it

was the 22nd of September, of all times, that the generation conflict, which had for a while been noticeable, became so severe that it burst forth in a key story which determined Kafka's life as a writer? It may be attributed to several events which occurred coincidentally: the encounter with Felice Bauer on August 13; the visit of Alfred Löwy, his charming uncle from Madrid; the birthday of his father on the 14th of the following month; the engagement of Max Brod, which became known at that time; the engagement of his sister Valli on the 15th of September, and Yom Kippur (Day of Atonement) of 1912, which occurred on the 20th and 21st of that month. E.R. Steinberg was the first to argue that "The Judgment" was a direct result of the preceding Yom Kippur, the holiest of Jewish holidays, when the faithful confess their sins and pray for forgiveness.[74] However, whether these events really influenced Kafka seems to be extremely problematic. Steinberg can only prove that Kafka attended the Synagogue for the Kol Nidre in 1911[75] (Kol Nidre is the prayer that opens the service on Yom Kippur). Supposedly on the same holiday of the following year Kafka had extreme feelings of guilt for having disavowed the Jewish religion, thereby sinning against God.[76] Thus Steinberg presents an allegorical interpretation of "The Judgment" which cannot be upheld scientifically. The room of the father is interpreted as being the Synagogue, Georg's intention of leaving his father behind after his marriage in the home of his parents is regarded as an expression of Kafka's refusal to grant God a place in his new home after his marriage to Felice Bauer.[77] Although it has been said that Kafka, had he married Felice, would have refused to take part in the usual festivities in the Temple for that holiday because he and his family had lost touch with the orthodox ritual, still the overall tone of the Letters to Felice—not yet available to Steinberg—clearly refutes the arguments.

However there are indications that the Yom Kippur of 1912 must have been quite significant to Kafka. Although till then he had been indifferent to religion, he could well have developed a deeper reverence for this holiday through Jacob Gordin's play Gott, Mensch, Teufel (God, Man, and the Devil).

On October 25, 1911 he had attended a reading of it by the Yiddish actor Yitzhak Löwy. In that play the main character (Hershele) emphasizes the inevitability of the Day of Judgment and already in the opening scene there is talk of a ritual bathing—so it is perhaps no accident that Georg is sentenced by his father to death by drowning.[78]

Furthermore, in a letter to Felice (January 8/9, 1913), Kafka tells her how—"two years ago"—on the occasion of his promotion, he had burst out in extremely inappropriate laughter before the president of the Workers' Accident Insurance Institute:[79] "Beating my breast with my right hand, partly in awareness of my sin (remembering the Day of Atonement)..."[80] This passage is of interest because it can only allude to Kafka's promotion to "Konzipist" on April 23, 1910. It is somewhat unlikely, though, that he wants to say that he remembered on that day, almost three years ago, the Yom Kippur of 1909, especially since, precisely at that period of his life he was endeavoring to forget his Jewishness as fast as possible. It seems more probable that in the beginning of 1913 this long-past occurrence was interpreted in the context of the experiences of 1912, especially since Kafka, in the introductory section of the letter, gives a problem-filled summary of his relationship to Felice during the first quarter year of their friendship.

The fact that Kafka wrote to Felice for the first time on September 28, 1912, (after having met her on August 13) also seems to increase the importance of the Day of Atonement of 1912. He wrote it while awaiting Yom Kippur, and although he had reflected on this letter in detail for many nights—"to avoid exaggeration I'll say 10"[81]—he was not too sure whether to write it at all. He had, moreover, immediately recognized after that 13th day of August how important Felice would be for him, and he had a feeling as if there were "an opening in my chest through which there was an unrestrained drawing-in and drawing-out until one evening in bed, when, by calling to mind a story from the Bible, the necessity of this sensation, as well as the truth of the Bible story, were simultaneously confirmed".[82] There is credible evidence to support the assertion that his knowledge of this religious text must have been at least indirectly related to Yom Kippur. That Kafka was able to evoke a written text as a means of articulating the concern of the day in question can be seen from a letter to his sister Ottla (February 5, 1919) where he tells her she should perhaps have chosen "students and teachers" as a topic for a speech: "This [topic] would represent your experiences as a student, a kind of reconciliation festival between students and teachers."[83] Significantly, Kafka later turns around the relationship in time between the origin of "The Judgment" and the first letter to Felice in what he later says to his beloved. His memory could not have failed him; the actual facts that would be so decisive and that were fairly recent could not have been forgotten, and were entered in his diary. Kafka writes, however, that on the evening of September 22nd the existence of Felice had made the world more precious to him than before, but that he had not written to her up to that date. In 1917 Kafka gave his opinion of his correspondence, and he said that in it there were several "disguises". We can include this statement among them. Obviously the reason for this behavior can be found in a statement by Kafka of November 1, 1912 (and later repeated) that "during a barren period I should never have had the courage to turn to you".[84] This obviously is intended to reinforce the idea that literary creativity is the essential element of Kafka's character. However, it is just around September 20 that Kafka finds himself in the "barren period", insofar as, on that day, he already had the contract which would settle the publication of *Betrachtung* (Meditation). He wrote to Felice about this publication exactly eight days later: "But it is not very good; better things will have to be written".[85] Kafka signed the contract only on the 25th, because he had hoped to improve a passage in "Der plötzliche Spaziergang" ("The Sudden Walk") which did not satisfy him. He was, however, unable to do so.

Why, then, does Kafka's first letter to Felice coincide with the Yom Kippur of 1912, if the reason is not to be found in a self-confidence which resulted from writing? One can argue that Kafka at that time was particularly sensitive about his

Jewishness, and that he was quite conscious of his guilt vis-a-vis the community before and on Yom Kippur. In *Letter to his Father*, Hermann Kafka emerges as the representative of that guilt, an almost divine law-maker. At the end of September 1912, and in the beginning of the following month, Kafka was supposed to devote his afternoons to the asbestos factory which belonged to the family, as he had also to do in January 1915, when he wrote concerning this demand: "The thought of the factory is my perpetual Day of Atonement".[86] This can only be interpreted in this way: the hateful inspection in the factory threatened to bring to a halt his literary productivity at that time and, because of Kafka's attempt to resist, created feelings of guilt comparable to feelings he had obviously had on the corresponding days of the year before. The fact that the Kafka family followed the rite of this holiday very carefully supports our argument. Although it would be wrong to consider, as some do, "The Judgment" as the thematization of the conflict between writing and married life, still, such a confrontation could have been one factor which helped trigger the writing of the story.

A short diary entry of September 28, 1917, is also extremely revealing: it obviously refers to the Day of Atonement that was celebrated two days before, and which, interestingly enough, summarizes the "five years" of his relationship with Felice. On the other hand, Kafka omits the date of August 13—in 1913 still able to generate some far-reaching meditations—and that of September 20. This could be an expression of the fact that in Kafka's memory the inception of this friendship with Felice had become linked with the Day of Atonement. This interpretation is supported by a postcard of Kafka, dated August 15, 1916, which starts as follows: "Dearest—about your anniversary letter; to tell the truth, I actually don't remember the date; in fact, without an effort, not even the year. Had I been asked to give it straight off without assistance, I would have said it was 5 years ago... On the other hand I certainly remember all other details far more accurately..."[87] The diary entry of September 28, 1917 reads: "I would put myself in death's hands, though. Remnant of a faith. Return to a father.

Great Day of Atonement."[88] Now that his tuberculosis had started Kafka felt finally defeated in his struggle for acceptance into society, and his guilt at having lived a life apart from society could only be redeemed through his own death—as in the story which was started in connection with the Day of Atonement.

The situation became still more acute in September 1912, when Kafka's uncle from Madrid, Alfred Löwy—according to Kafka the model for the friend in Petersburg—was in Prague at the beginning of the month. He shared with Kafka his experiences as a bachelor, and the dangers associated with such a life-style became quite apparent to him. Also, his father's birthday September 14—which, of course, every family member paid a great deal of attention to—might have had an effect on Kafka's thoughts on the future with its possibilities and problems. Hermann Kafka was, after all, the successful husband and father whom it seemed impossible to measure up to no matter how hard one tried. It is furthermore probable that Max Brod's situation must have intensified Kafka's reflections. The engagement between his friend and Elsa Taussig, which had begun to take shape, only became official on December 15. But it is no accident that Kafka was corresponding and in personal contact with Brod's future wife at the time when "The Judgment" was written, and Kafka had helped through sound advice to bring about the engagement. The introductory scene can even be read in the context of a biographical situation linked with this complex of relationships: On September 20, Kafka wrote a letter to Max Brod and Felix Weltsch during office hours—that is, during the period when the first letter to Felice was being phrased, a fact which is underlined by a kinship in the subject matter of the two letters—and this letter, significantly breaks off when he was about to tell his friends some news. Felice, whom Kafka, after all, had met at Brod's, is not mentioned at all although she must have been very much on his mind during those hours. Kafka instead mentions unimportant office trivia, just as in the narrative of "The Judgment". Here Georg does not give any "real news" to his bachelor friend who lives so far away, but rather is content with the enumeration of insignificant occurrences.[89] We should also bear in mind that Kafka at that time had entered into a shadowy fraternity of bachelorhood with Felix Weltsch, hence felt a kind of polar opposition between himself and the newly domestic Max Brod, which, in the story, corresponds to the basic antinomy between Georg and his friend.

Finally, we should mention Valli's engagement. This took place on the 15th of September, and Kafka was faced with the opposite pole of the conflicting tensions which were inwardly tearing him apart. This was of particular immediacy on the 22nd of that month: Kafka writes about the engagement that he is affected by every such occurrence in a peculiar way, as if a misfortune would come upon him "instantly and imminently". On the one hand he easily identified with others as a result of his extreme sensitivity and he therefore was able to imagine the unfavorable consequences that a marriage might have for those involved. On the other hand, in contrast to those feelings, he would lament his own seeming inability to commit himself to a woman's love and was therefore envious of the potential father-role in which his sister's fiancé must have appeared to him. Also, Kafka felt oppressed by the invasion of strange people, namely his new relatives, into his life, a process he elsewhere had called "the counterpart of the act of giving birth".[90] (It should be remembered that Kafka told Felice that "The Judgment" was a "giving birth".[91] That these feelings in Kafka had been especially active on September 22 can be proven. Whereas Kafka's mood on September 15 could be called "desperation", the following Sunday it had turned into a state of such misery that he "could have screamed". On that day he had "spent the entire afternoon silently circling around my brother-in-law's relatives, who were on their first visit to us".[92]

In the light of the opposing tendencies in Kafka's struggle in life which were apparent in the bachelorhood of his uncle from Madrid on the one hand and the engagement of Valli and Elsa Taussig on the other, his decision to mail the letter to Felice— which had been planned for days— must have provoked considerable inner turmoil (for he tipped the ambivalent inner balance in favor of the side which tended toward society). Kafka evidently mastered this emotional turmoil in "The Judgment". On August 14, 1913, still under the effect of the anniversary the day before of his first meeting with Felice, he writes: "Conclusion for my case from "The Judgment". I am indirectly in her debt for the story. But Georg goes to pieces because of his fiancée."[93] Besides the relationships which have already been pointed out one can relate the idea of "the indirect influence of Felice" to the fact that even while writing the story a major shift in the thematic area to be portrayed was taking place: "when I sat down to write . . . I meant to describe a war; from his window a young man was to see a vast crowd advancing across the bridge, but then the whole thing turned in my hands into something else".[94] One is probably justified also in seeing this initial imaginary confrontation as yet another version of Kafka's fundamental theme, for the metaphor of the struggle—which is also suggested by Dostoyevsky—for Kafka represents the central image of his inability to choose between isolation and the desire for marriage.

NOTES

1. D 1, 275.
2. D 1, 276.
3. D 1, 276.
4. D 1, 278.
5. Br, 112.
6. LFe, 78.
7. Tag, 297.
8. LFe, 86-87.
9. LFe, 265.
10. LFe, 267.
11. D 1, 278-279 and LFe, 265.
12. LFe, 267.
13. D 1, 278-279.
14. Br, 116.
15. CS, 78.
16. CS, 82.
17. CS, 85.
18. CS, 86.
19. D 1, 276. For Kafka's "The Urban World" see D 1, 47-54.
20. CS, 86.
21. CS, 85.
22. E.g., Falke: "Biographisch-literarische Hintergrunde".

23. Sokel: *F.K.T.I.*, 59.
24. Franz Werfel: *Erzählungen aus zwei Welten*, in his *Gesammelte Werke*. Frankfurt, 1948, 3 vols., Vol. I, 16.
25. CS, 86.
26. Werfel: *Op. cit.*, 17 f.
27. CS, 78.
28. Max Brod: *Arnold Beer. Das Schicksal eines Juden*. [Arnold Beer. The Fate of a Jew]. Berlin, 1912, 52.
29. Janouch: *Gespräche*, 101.
30. A German edition of the play had already appeared in 1912.
31. LM, 96.
32. Max Brod: "Kommentar zu Robert Walser." *Pan 2*, No. 2 (Oct 1911), 53 ff.
33. Fyodor Dostoyevsky: *Crime and Punishment*. Tr. by David Magarshack. Harmondsworth: Penguin Books, 1951, 551.
34. *Ibid.*, 549.
35. *Ibid.*
36. *Ibid.*, 552.
37. *Ibid.*, 553.
38. *Ibid.*, 557.
39. D 1, 214.
40. CS, 77.
41. CS, 78.
42. CS, 79.
43. Dostoyevsky: *Op. cit.*, 549.
44. D 2, 104.
45. "The Golden Alley" in *Sippurim, eine Sammlung jüdischer Volkssagen, Erzählungen, Mythen, Chroniken, Denkwürdigkeiten und Biographien berühmter Juden aller Jahrhunderte, insbesondere des Mittelalters*. [Sippurim: A Collection of Jewish Popular Legends, Stories, Myths, Chronicles, Reminiscences, and Biographies of Famous Jews of all Centuries, especially of the Middle Ages]. Ed. by W. Pascheles with the cooperation of Famous Writers. Prague, 1858 (3rd ed), I, 52.
46. "The Golden Alley," 53.
47. *Op. cit.*, 54.
48. CS, 81.
49. "The Golden Alley," 55.
50. CS, 86.
51. "The Golden Alley," 55.
52. CS, 88.
53. Hoch, 192.
54. Hoch, 165.
55. Br, 345.
56. LFe, 36.
57. LFe, 55.
58. Hoch, 220.
59. LFe, 86.
60. Cf. Beck: *Kafka & the Yiddish Theater*.
61. CS, 86.
62. CS, 84.
63. CS, 85.
64. Beck: *Op. cit.*, 80.
65. D 1, 113.
66. Janouch: *Gespräche*, 224.
67. CS, 80.
68. *Ibid.*

69. Heinrich von Kleist: "The Earthquake in Chile," in his *The Marquise of O—*. Tr. by Martin Greenberg. N.Y.: Criterion Books, 1960, 251.
70. *Op. cit.*, 253.
71. D 1, 112.
72. Br, 148.
73. LFe, 87.
74. Steinberg: "The Judgment in Kafka's 'The Judgment'."
75. D 1, 72.
76. Steinberg: *Op. cit.*, 24.
77. *Op. cit.*, 26.
78. D 1, 112.
79. LFe, 146.
80. LFe, 148.
81. LFe, 6.
82. LFe, 21.
83. BO, 64.
84. LFe, 24.
85. LFe, 7.
86. D 2, 107.
87. LFe, 487.
88. D 2, 187.
89. CS, 79.
90. Br, 252.
91. LF, 156.
92. LFe, 265.
93. D 1, 296.
94. LFe, 265.

Stanley Corngold

The Hermeneutic of "The Judgment"

For he and his property are not one, but two, and whoever destroys the connection destroys him at the same time.[1]

"The Judgment" is the only prose work of ten pages in world literature which does not belong to a sacred or classical canon and which in the West alone has inspired some 100 visible commentaries. The scandalous character of "The Judgment" invites reflection on its distinctive power to compel interpretation. This power unfolds as a paradoxical indifference and generosity. As the story draws readings to itself, it makes room in every instance for one more reading: its precincts are crowded, but no interpreter must ever turn away for lack of the gate which has been kept open uniquely for him.

To read "The Judgment" is to experience a force like that (for Adorno) of an onrushing locomotive. "Each sentence of Kafka's says 'interpret me...'"; and this is nowhere so much the case as in the story whose title "Das Urteil" means (in philosophical language) "The Sentence". "Through the power with which Kafka commands interpretation," Adorno writes, "he collapses aesthetic distance. He demands a desperate effort of the allegedly 'disinterested' observer of an earlier time, overwhelms him, suggesting that far more than

39

his intellectual equilibrium depends on whether he truly understands; life and death are at stake."[2]

These stakes are precisely thematized in "The Judgment". The force with which the story exacts interpretation is the force with which a sentence strikes Georg Bendemann. Powerless to interpret his sentence—to swerve—he accedes, and is "driven" out of his father's room, into the street, and to his death by drowning. This cautionary fable identifies the force it produces as the force which here destroys the overwhelmed subject. It warns, as it were, against a like accession: the assaulted reader must turn and judge what in himself is the willing accessory to the sentence. The reader who seizes his freedom to interpret executes the naive reader in himself and approximates the narrator of "The Judgment", who survives the execution he has arranged—survives specifically as the name of the joy and sheer force of the *"Verkehr"*, the erotic upsurge and infinite traffic of the concluding sentence.

The other side of this abundant power compelling interpretation is the curious meagerness that cries out for this supplement. Here the work displays its restless, unsettled character, its anxiety, as it takes its path through the "abyss" between its literal and signifying moments (Adorno). Its anxiety will not permit it—as Mörike wrote of a work of art—to shine and seem ecstatic in itself.[3] A work that invites so much interpretation can have inspired the production of meaning only as a function of its refusal of meaning.

If the story symbolizes the force with which it exacts interpretation, it cannot, however, directly thematize its refusal of meaning. It does approach an indication of this kind—as we shall see—through its allegory of character. There is a kind of refusal of meaning in the stubborn silence and withdrawal of the Russian friend. This refusal is implied clearly, though privatively, in Georg's bad faith and in the lies he unwittingly writes to his friend. The refusal of meaning in the strong sense is conceivable only as the intention of a literary text or as the act of a consciousness wholly transparent to itself, which knows that *as* a consciousness it cannot express itself. There can be no such consciousness dramatized in this work, since the leading perspective is that of Georg, who simply assumes the expressiveness of his meaning. He does not know the "feeling of falsity . . . while writing" which Kafka painfully registers some months before composing "The Judgment" and which prompts him to long, without hope, "to write all my anxiety entirely out of me, write it into the depths of the paper just as it comes out of the depths of me . . .".[4] Instead Georg speaks glibly of "communication". His concern is not the truth of what one could say but the shrewdness of what "one ought to say". For him the impossibility of "authentic communication" is a function of social tact. Yet it is precisely Georg who, in the course of writing down his meaning and then stating his meaning, unwittingly tells lies. He lies when he thinks that "there was indeed no obstacle" in the way of his friend's returning home and renewing all his old friendships. For Georg has registered his friend's own statement that "he no longer understood the way things were at home", and he has also noted the possibility that his friend would be oppressed at home "because of the facts"—the fact especially that he would no longer find himself in rapport with his old acquaintances. Georg lies once again when he writes his friend that he will acquire in Georg's fiancée a "sincere friend" and when he adds with conviction that "many things" would prevent his friend from visiting the couple even briefly. Indeed he even lies to his father when he says that he has "thought differently" about informing his friend of his engagement; in fact he has reacted directly to the importunities of his fiancée.

The father, meanwhile, is no more lucid than the son. He is presented in the convulsed perspective of Georg; his consciousness is inscrutable.

The work is thus obliged to withhold any direct presentation of the knowledge that it is "repudiating expression" (Adorno). It keeps inexplicit, maintains *as* the inexplicit, the non-coincidence of truth and fiction—the fact that truth uttered is fiction and hence no longer truth. The story allegorizes its own withholding of meaning mainly in the opaque figure of the lie. The lie, however, is central.

In its full sense, as the solicitation of falsity, it is another name for the "peculiar relation of correspondence" between Georg and his Russian friend. Theirs is a writing that never arrives at telling the truth; the point is dramatically illustrated in the father's image of the friend crumpling Georg's letters unopened. But their failure is otherwise apparent. For whether or not the friend reads these letters, he could not understand a writing that does not make sense, since Georg's text, a literature of self-justification, aims to conceal and suppress sense. Georg's meaning remains rigorously hidden from him. But if there is to be such a thing as a coherent interpretation of the story, one must assert that it is this meaning which is repeated in the scene that issues from its suppression, even if only privatively once more, as that sense which it is death to hide.

The conditions of the interpretation of "The Judgment" are the force with which it exacts interpretation and the abyss of the meaning it withholds. These terms have fallen counterparts within the story in Georg's inability to oppose his sentence and in his unwitting dissimulation. The latter terms are related as modes of interpretative activity. The meaning which Georg's letter masks, compels his intricate (if dishonest) reflection on his motives. His writing is again submitted to interpretation within the story. Georg tells his father that he has written to his friend with the aim of creating for him the very happiness which he has experienced in his engagement. His father sees in the statement a *fashion* of writing to his friend—that of deceit!—and arrives quite literally at his verdict. It is to declare, with violence, his son punishably guilty of treachery, of blindness, indeed of doing devil's work. Georg, his gaze open only to his father, cannot resist taking over this verdict as his own.[5]

Only because the story is explicitly conscious of such acts as reading and writing, telling the truth and lying, repression and deception—of the order of phenomena called hermeneutic— does it produce so forceful an interpretative activity in the reader. And indeed by its own depiction of hermeneutic force, it appropriates in advance the force with which it has compelled interpretation as a whole. In thus focusing on the power produced by acts of writing, justifying, and sentencing, the story assumes a distance toward its immediate life—the clash of desires, the craving for intimacy, the suspension of the will, the refusal of individuation, as they comprise the family romance. Here again the story is exemplary: it discourages the reader from taking direct access to the life which comes to light with ostensible self-evidence in his first reading. It encourages him to displace that reading as in fact a made and influenced and interested object (though one not made by him!). Its subtle shaping belongs to the play of force exerted by the *history of reading*, not negligibly, the way in which Kafka has been read during the sixty-year history of "The Judgment". "The Judgment" thus implicitly asks the reader to consider the history of its own commentaries, if he is to bring any measure of freedom into their domain.

II

Readings of "The Judgment", where they have not despaired of coherence, have traditionally pursued an idea of coherence which now seems restrictive. Interpretation has aimed to motivate the events that follow Georg's entering his father's room in terms of what has been revealed of Georg the writer; the final test of such theory is to motivate Georg's execution. To the elements of the dynamic field of son, friend, fiancée, father, and mother, values are assigned, the outcome of whose interaction is plausibly the rejection of the fiancée and the extinction of the son. This necessarily means ascribing to the father, for example, a value which will make his authority seem irresistible to Georg. Thus Walter Sokel describes the father as "the man who [unlike Georg] had enjoyed and been capable of true love".[5] He thus pre-forms his sense of the conclusion as Georg's gaining "the nourishment which fulfills him, ... unification with the will of the father".[7] For all such readings which define coherence as the consistency of mimetic reference, the value of each of the agonists has to be held constant, and the logic of the interaction maintained as one of progressive accumulation. For example, the (negative) value assigned early to Georg—viz. that Georg blindly conceals motives aiming at power and possession—is held to inform all his interactions. If his kisses in the first section aim to cover up awareness of how inconclusive his feelings for his fiancée are, then the fact that he does not bother to defend her against his father's abuse in the second section is taken as further evidence of his indifference—even though on its own terms his silence of course imports nothing of the kind.

Typically, the "repetition" of an original motive is held to strengthen the motive, so that the cumulative force of a number of such repetitions can begin plausibly to motivate the ultimate violence of his suicide. In fact, of course, there has been, not a number of repetitions, but only the repeated ascription of a posited value to a number of unknowns. The original value is allowed only the modification which it can accommodate without threat to its stability; and each modification (read, repetition) is made to reinforce permanently its initial identity.

Consider another case. If Georg is revealed early as a deluded writer (and there can be no doubt of this point), he is held in this fashion of reading to be a deluded speaker throughout the second part: what he states to his father as the expression of a motive can be only an unwitting dissimulation. The reproaches he makes to himself for having neglected his father, for example, are merely the workings of his intent to disenfranchise him. And thus (although commentators are inconsistent on this point), Georg cannot always have loved his parents, as he declares an instant before letting himself drop from the bridge.

But which of the propositions about Georg's or his father's psychological character is in fact decidable? Is Georg the devilish wastrel his father declares him to be? Surely not for having wanted to shroud from his friend's eyes his own brilliant fortunes. Can it be that Georg is the dissimulator of ultimately irreproachable motives? Doubts multiply. Can a single value be attributed in good conscience to *any* of these characters? Georg has lied to his friend. Is his friend therefore a sign of genuine existence, of a "pure self"?[8] How can jaundice, impassiveness, and the slide into bachelorhood suggest the attributes of authenticity? Whence has such a friend the authority through Georg's father, his "representative", to sentence Georg to drowning? The same doubts hover over even the less problematic figure of the fiancée. Why—as is often asserted—is Georg's fiancée accurate in saying that since Georg has such friends as the Russian bachelor, he ought never to have become engaged? It is not obvious that he admits the charge by responding, "Yes [this state of affairs], is the fault of both of us." He can be saying generously that it is only because he finds his fiancée so splendid that his embittered friend has become a problem. Nothing Georg has said or done before suggests that he has ever considered his friend a serious obstacle to his engagement. Indeed the outcome of the story implies that it is not his friend but the father who drives off the fiancée: Georg is crushed by his father's colluding with the friend. His fiancée should have said that it is because he has a father like Mr. Bendemann and not because he has a Russian friend that he should never have become engaged. Georg's father is therefore vicious but not entirely inaccurate in calling her a "repellent goose". Her "perception" may be stupid and indeed calculated to torment Georg. But of course we do not initially know enough about her to assign her any value, let alone insist that she abide her initial identity, especially within the play of perspectives which Kafka saw as constituting the piece.[9]

In no reading that I know has it been possible to assign to these characters values drawn from lived experience, to hold these values fast throughout their interaction, and to motivate Georg's execution. Walter Sokel's reading is among the strongest and most spacious, but his version reveals inconsistencies that jeopardize the whole. In general his reading seeks to make plausible the destruction of a specious ego masking libidinal and aggressive instincts by a strong if unconscious ego-ideal imaged in the alliance of friend (authentic self) and father (super-ego). It aims to counter the reading that sees the father as senile or insane, for then

Georg's execution of the death sentence would be either inexplicable or an example of the hypnotic effect of the irrational. But then the part of the story dealing with the father would in no way be related to those parts dealing with the fiancée and the friend, and we would have before us a completely incoherent story, one unworthy of an artist of the rank of Franz Kafka.[10]

The question is whether coherence must mean psychological plausibility.

Sokel operates with motives plausible for the psychic sub-agencies: super-ego, ego, and id. That the super-ego here operates with a murderous logic, a "barbaric law", will not seem strange to the reader of Freud's *The Ego and the Id*. But this reader must be ready thereafter to give up believing in the murderous *father*, for the father is no longer a character but instead a projection of conscience. If this is so, however, what does it mean when Sokel says that at the close Georg is aware that his life has gone astray and that it is guilty of having "cut itself off and detached itself from the roots from which it has emerged"?[11] These roots are perhaps in some physical metaphor the father, but in what sense are they in or part of conscience? "Georg sought to neglect and suppress the essential connection to the origin, to the parents and the friend."[12] What has happened here to the psychoanalytic drama? In what sense and for what psychic agency is the alliance of ego and super-ego the "origin"? In what way does the sick, celibate, floundering friend embody the ego as the integrity of the psychic field? If the price of innocence before the father's law is to "follow the call" of the friend to a wasting death in Russia, why does the friend desire an alliance with the father? Georg declares that he has at least twice before "denied" to the father the friend's presence in their house, since the father had no particular liking for him. The proposition makes sense, but what moment in the psychoanalytic drama does it illustrate? Evidently Sokel's reading makes the interesting sense it does only by his rapid (and inevitable) shifting from one metaphorical plane to another.

As a result of the shift in the plane of discourse, initially posited values are *not* held constant. The authority of the father cannot stem at once from his benevolence as a character and his cruelty as a super-ego. To the extent that Georg's execution gets explained, it is explained only figuratively as a sort of death in the service of psychic integration. But indeed these psychoanalytic correlations are purely contingent, since a Kleinian perspective, say, would suggest different correlations between textual terms and the various psychic sub-agencies generated from the Freudian triad by further schism and exchange.

There would seem to be no plausible motivation for Georg's death, where plausibility means the consistency of empirical reference. This is not because—as used to be maintained—Georg's suicide is not psychologically convincing. Neither psychological realism nor any other system taking the suicide as "a kind of death" can repeat in its own terms a work of such preponderant complexity of interrelation and poverty of firm signification, can correlate with empirical or theoretical chains held to be meaningful so intricate a play of elliptical and fugitive elements. The name Georg does not signify at the beginning what it signifies at the end; the name for the father does not designate at all times during their interview the same being. For intelligibility's sake the initial posit must in both cases be reversed, but that is the end of consistency.

In describing an impossible strategy of motivating "The Judgment", I aim to add my voice to a chorus of interpreters. The cry of the irreducible obscurity of dimensions of this story has been part of every faithful response. That obscurity has no sooner been asserted however than it is invaded. The horror of the implausible swiftly introduces a second strategy—that of radical intention. In despair of consistency, yet in pursuit of meaning, critics call the second half a *Wunschbild*, a dream-wish; here, in effect, Kafka's father joins forces with the "friend"—with the sickly, solitude-seeking, incomprehensible self of the son whom in life he has consistently derided—and condemns to death the self which in life he wished Franz Kafka to be. I have been alone among critics, I think, in writing of the second half not as a *Wunschtraum* but as an *Alptraum*, a nightmare, in which the surreptitious alliance of the father and the personality of the writer implies the death of Kafka's pursuit of autonomous language.[13] No one meanwhile has had the (entirely justifiable) audacity to say that the first half of the story is either a wish-dream or a nightmare, as if for a sensibility of Kafka's stringency the description of ordinary consciousness applied to the task of self-justification were not sufficiently horrible (although John Ellis has rightly perceived some of the bizarre and morbid fractures in this sensibility right from the outset).[14] But it is obvious that to motivate the second half of the text radically by the appeal to an extrinsic intention like wishing or abjuring, is to allow in principle the irregular application of extrinsic intention, which stamps at will individual elements as their pleasurable or nightmarish doubles. Thus drowning no longer means suffocation but "rebirth"; the collusion of father and friend is a joyous confirmation of true identity, etc. The pursuit of coherence among elliptical elements turns into the chaos of arbitrary revaluations applied from the outside—the unsettling freeplay of the psychoanalyst without a patient.

To declare at intervals, meanwhile, that the characters have changed, is only to replace the irregular extrinsic intention with an equally arbirary intrinsic fluctuation of perspective.

What is left for the critic to do? What else, after he has identified the disturbance—the story's punishing meagerness of determination and its inverse, the unsettling liberty it offers to interpretation—what else to do but double the critical consciousness—identify in the frankest way the types of substitution in which his criticism engages? The values we associate with the figures in this story may of course originate elsewhere—in the text of Freud, in the text of Kafka's confessional writings (thus there may be extrinsic reference). These values may indeed change (as a play of intrinsic intention), and the optic in which the reader views and feels them may change (as a play of extrinsic intention); nothing can restrict their number and combination. That we cannot and need not hold to a linear and progressive, end-oriented pattern in which the end has the power of organizing retrospectively everything that has preceded it, is evident for ever. It is Heinz Politzer's achievement to have seen the father's attack on the son—"an innocent child, yes, this you were truly, but still more truly have you been a devilish human being"—for the revolution in modes of order it imports. "Here," writes Politzer, "innocence and wickedness are no longer presented as consecutive stages in Georg's development from child to man. Rather the judgment, leaving psychology behind, speaks of the close interconnection in every human of good and evil, of promise and betrayal...."[15] Kafka asks us to take seriously the merely differential character, the implicit multivalence of his figures. But if undecidability is not to be degraded either to mystery or despondency, we must continue to read; and here we will not be wrong to re-introduce a notion of the writer's intention which enlarges the text of "The Judgment" toward the whole text of Kafka. The sense in the story which is death to hide—which occurs through Georg and all around Georg but not to Georg—is the punishment of the writer who would write to enthrall the world.

III

Kafka's own commentary on "The Judgment" focusses on the figure of the Russian friend—"the greatest bond" between father and son. Interpretation was helpless to identify this mysterious mask until Kate Flores' inspired suggestion that the friend's isolation, exile, and idealism reflect Kafka's identity as a writer. The idea has since been elaborated by Martin Greenberg, Eric Marson, and Jürgen Demmer.[16] It now seems most reasonable to say of the friend that if he is this kind of figure, he does not stand purely and simply for the writing destiny but for that destiny pursued under the condition of bachelorhood which in 1912 had been Kafka's sole experience of writing.

This way of stating the identification makes more evident the complexity and polyvalence of the friend. The friend can represent bachelorhood as a set of empirical circumstances under which writing might best be pursued. As a bachelor he can also stand for the intrinsic ideality of writing—its "purity", its longing for autonomy, its rigorous self-reflexiveness. Finally, as the condition in which Kafka has written hitherto, bachelorhood can represent all the (contradictory) values that belong to Kafka's writing until this point—briefly, its idealism and diabolism, its force and its sterility. Kafka hoped to write well and despaired of having written impurely, and he felt all the complex tones of this failure. He saw his writing as insufficiently wholehearted, insufficiently sustained, and—*as* the act of writing—inherently insufficient. The friend is thus a complex sign, but he is not therefore unbounded: he is a sign of writing in one form of its empirical existence, in its transcendental determination, and in its character as moral experience. The story modulates the meaning of the friend throughout the range of these significations and in their unfathomable depth of analogy and disjunction. My reading profiles the possibilities of analogy between the transcendental, moral, and empirical dimensions of Kafka's conception of writing. This is not to deny, however, the possibility of a reading of "The Judgment" which focuses on the disjunction of these planes.

The authority for assigning connections between the characters in "The Judgment" and aspects of Kafka's own life comes from Kafka's diary entry itself. Here Kafka associates Georg Bendemann with himself and Frieda Brandenfeld with Felice Bauer, the woman he had recently met and whom he was to detain as his fiancée for the next five years. Very little stress has been laid, however, on the fact that in this story Georg Bendemann is also a writer—of a letter to be sure; but to say this is only to specify the kind of writing he does. This writer is, as "Bendemann", inescapably a "Bindemann", the man who forms ties. According to Max Brod, Kafka knew a good deal of etymology; and the old Indo-Germanic root *bhendhe* yields the modern *"Binde-"* or "binding-".[17] Indeed the reflexive form *"sich binden"* yields the precise meaning of "to become engaged."

Georg's writing aims explicitly to bind his friend to himself and to affirm his engagement to his fiancée, to continue to enjoy their abundance of (contrary) properties. Indeed he describes his fiancée only as the daughter of a "well-to-do" family. In thus writing to another with an acquisitive design, he uses language *"vergleichsweise"*, that is, to make the comparisons which underlie acts of appropriation; it is the way, according to Kafka, in which language concerned with human inwardness, with something "outside the phenomenal world", must never be used. For "corresponding as it does to the phenomenal world, language is concerned with property and its relations", and to operate between the two parties *"vergleichsweise"* is to attempt to bring about between them a legal settlement.[18] To use language without respecting the difference between things invisible and things seen is forever only to speak of "property and its relations", is to confirm "writing's lack of independence of the world".[19] There remains, meanwhile, the more genuine mode of using language *"audeutungsweise"*, allusively, by which language conjures traces of an order not its own. Writing which aims at self-aggrandizement and self-justification does devil's work, in the sense that it sinks language ever more deeply into that species of blank captivation which Kafka terms "the world of the senses..., the evil in the spiritual world".[20] In writing's reflection on itself it would not be absurd for the crime of writing badly to merit capital punishment at the hands of its own endangered authority.

The Georg Bendemann we see is a writer, and as such he writes badly. The passage about "allusion" above hints at a truer use of language, yet no use of language escapes untruth, devotion to worldly interest. The virtual impossibility of another sort of writing makes *less* tolerable for Kafka the accession to the correspondence between language and the phenomenal world. Writing interestedly, however, is a writing that doubles its failure to make a difference by its defiance of the knowledge that not making a difference matters. Georg's manner of establishing connections is complacent and duplicitous and not tested against an aspiration which could diminish its fluency.

Georg's fluency is another name for his strong ego, his worldly success, and his playful consciousness of his own power. At the level of writing this competence suggests claims not unlike Kafka's early sentiments about the power of his writing. In the year before composing "The Judgment", for example, Kafka noted in his diaries: "When I arbitrarily write a single sentence, for instance, 'He looked out of the window,' it already has perfection."[21] There is none of the fastidious longing here that was later to restrict the "perfection" which all but allusive writing could achieve.

The exegetical value of seeing Georg as a writer is considerable; in this light "The Judgment" repeats and varies the dialogical structure of a number of Kafka's early works obviously centering on writing. In the diary entry for 1910 beginning "'You,' I said...", for example, an ostensible bourgeois and a bachelor embody contrary moments of *Schriftstellersein* (the writing existence). Here the bachelor focuses negative aspects of writing, suggesting the possibility that the anxiety constitutive of writing could freeze and come to a fatal standstill; the bourgeois speaker on the other hand is a more lucid and constructive figure whose voice merges with that of the narrator.[22]

In "The Judgment" of course the distribution of properties of the writing self is different. If we take Georg's friend as the projection of writing which arises from an avowed, non-manipulative, bachelorhood, then Georg represents writing as a manipulative process for which marriage is a comprehensive figure. Marriage conveys the seductive hope of a union between the law of writing and the world of the senses in which writing could also retain its "spiritual" privilege. (The fact meanwhile that in the story both Georg and his friend are "in business" authorizes the view that both are aspects of writing).

In "The Judgment", then, the essential opposition is not between a projection of Kafka's social personality on the one hand and his hopes as a writer on the other. This latter dichotomy, persistently repeated in criticism, is not telling if we recall that there never was any moment in Kafka's life when he could conceive of part of himself as separate from "literature". The distinction in this story is between a self (Georg) that writes in order to continue its connection with the world, by having the world serve it; and a self that pursues literature under the condition of a possibly propitious reclusiveness. The debate opposes marriage and bachelorhood and their subtle ramifications, not as either of these might second the world in its struggle with writing, but as conditions of the strongest writing. Indeed for Kafka being engaged to be married meant sheerly being engaged by the voluminous correspondence he carried on with Felice Bauer. Every thought of his fiancée belonged to the progress of their correspondence. That one mode of her absence/presence issued into letters; the mode of her absence/presence in which she was not figuring as a wife issued into fiction. But Kafka never conceived of a relation with his fiancée that implied the suspension of writing.

Georg, as a persona of Kafka's writing self, must resolve at the outset of "The Judgment" the claims of the fiancée and the friend, of a writing that takes the woman hostage and a writing that flows from solitude. When Georg decides that he will write his friend definitive news of his engagement, "The Judgment" comes into being: it will put on trial the mode of writing that issues from the alliance of the woman and the writer. Kafka's project is to test through Georg the unholy strategy of marrying in order to write well. This hypothesis is confirmed by Kafka's remark in the diaries that "the fiancée lives in the story only in relation to the friend";[23] the friend is the only mode in which Kafka has so far known the life of literature. This issue forecasts the K./Frieda nexus in *The Castle* and in its most general form the project of testing the very attitude of having a strategy toward writing.

The figure of Georg, however, is essentially in bad faith. He is at work suppressing consciousness of the scandal of an engagement that is bent on an increase in power, whether to the profit of the self or of the writer. Both terms are implicit in Kafka's phrase: "As I grow in strength [through marriage], I shall stand more."[24] Georg is the manipulator who manipulates even his own intent: he conceals it.

His anxiety emerges in the unwitting lies he tells himself— and in another significant detail. Georg dwells on the point that the friend has withheld sympathy upon learning of the death of Georg's mother. Georg does not know how to construe this lapse except to presume that grief on such an occasion is inconceivable to one who lives abroad. The "dryness" of the friend's response to the event is for Georg unintelligible, a response he cannot recognize or acknowledge. Whence this obstacle to understanding? It's plausible to think that Georg does not wish to know that he himself has not grieved for his mother's death, that he himself has suppressed consciousness of this death. The motive would be understandable. His mother's death liberates in him a mobile erotic energy; it is the precondition of his becoming engaged. This truth is troublesome to Georg for the opportunity of a vaunting triumph in the rivalry it implies with the father, but more so for the way in which it coerces him into this rivalry: he does not want to think of his act of becoming engaged as motivated but as free. (We must remember that *Kafka* is going through this experience with Georg: We know his horror of determination, of compulsion, of the broken will. But what Kafka sees and dreads is what in Georg is only the blind side of a lie. This is the structure of all of Kafka's novels).

In now writing to his friend, Georg makes his engagement a *fait accompli*. His hesitation in writing obviously stems from the possibility that this will prove the ultimate breakdown of his connection with his friend. As long as he has "this friend in Russia", he thinks he possesses the meaning of this figure; he has once before rejected the opportunity to share his life, but to stay in correspondence with him is to keep this possibility open.

When Georg finally sits down to write, this act is not his own but is compelled by his fiancée. In acting he will learn his determinateness, but this experience of constraint is masked at first in his elation, that ironically and privatively prefigures the narrator's elation at the close. Georg's delight in his letter is his first suggestion of the success of his new effort at enthralling others. At the same time he has not perceived that this delight issues from a blind play of coercions. He has induced his fiancée to place this compulsion on him. He at once forces it and distorts it by the violence with which he suppresses her argument for writing definitive news of the engagement to the friend. To send to the friend the first product of his alliance is doubtless to risk repudiation, for this product is no longer wholly Georg's but already the outcome of a play of forces, one of which belongs to the being he meant to control.

In this state of anxiety Georg enters his father's room. The turn to the father is as lucid and as expectable as if it were part of a logical demonstration. Now that Georg has embarked on family life, the decision to write under the condition of marriage has to be examined in the light of a more detached writing (the friend's existence) and in the light of marriage itself (the existence of the married man par excellence, the father). To manage this enterprise would assure Georg the surplus satisfaction of beating his father at his own game of flourishing from the power ceded to him by the woman.

A tonality of dread informs this interview. The language of the story turns into a different channel: the text has so far mirrored a text (the letter) and Georg's commentary on the text; its form is now a language of primary process, family conversation: that form of language for Kafka most liable to conjure chaos and self-dispersion. "Conversations", he wrote, "take away the importance, the seriousness, the truth from everything I think."[25] "Without human connections there are in myself no visible lies. The limited circle is pure."[26] Kafka's hatred of conversation is an expression of his hatred of the language wholly bent on an expansive totality of the self and the world.

Not surprisingly, Georg goes to pieces. The key thrust in this exchange is his sudden perception of his friend, the writing destiny, as something failed, estranged, and wholly vulnerable. Within the musical mixing of elements in the friend—the empirical and the pure—the major tone of the real writer emerges.[27] Writing is damaged, and Georg is guilty of the harm: he has not sufficiently protected it. Writing's revenge on an impure solicitation is its withdrawal, its inaccessibility.

Georg himself is now wounded: he will not defend his fiancée though she is abused. That the fiancée is only the name for a certain impure annexation of the world to writing has been confirmed: she is abandoned, leaving the field open for the struggle for remaining possession of the friend.

Georg cannot escape the falsehood of his original project. His dread finds its object in the horrible revelation of the intimacy between the friend and the father. The father asserts that the friend is a son after his own heart, his "ideal" offspring. The communication between the father and his correspondent is said to be one of perfect transparency: each flows into the other. Writing becomes the creature of the father—the father, the subject of writing, the representative of the writing destiny as it articulates itself. Writing is in the father and of the father— writing is his own reproduction. Writing strengthens the father, turns him against the son who would live in any fashion except solitude and self-denial. His ideal offspring is a fanatic of masochistic asceticism, an admirer of the mad priest who has carved a cross in his palm.

If the first stage of the alienation of writing is its lostness to Georg, the alliance of the father with writing conjures an even more abject image. In the poisonous atmosphere in which writing becomes the slut whom Georg has prostituted, the father's blessing is only a kiss of death. The friend is perishing of this alliance; the bond will prove as fatal to him as it will to Georg and his father. Georg's situation is impossible. He has lost the friend, he must grasp that the friend is corrupted and dying; but he has himself been defined from the start by his dependency on the friend, on the hope of a continuity with the being who is essentially writing.

The effort to keep the friend while annexing the power of the woman fails, quite as if to testify to the iron operation of a law of exclusion: the result of Georg's earlier unwillingness to make a choice between the loved mother and the friend who showed no grief for her death was to cede all her power to his father; now, too, Georg's unwillingness to make a choice between the friend and the fiancée has the perverse result of ceding the power of the friend to the father.

Georg is an impossible figure; writing, *this* act of writing, cannot proceed through his perspective. The narrator has in fact been steadily withdrawing from his persona in moving from identification to dialogue. He must now definitively withdraw, must assert his autonomy and find its narrative form. The autonomy of the narrative is the key issue for Kafka: is writing finally and forever only the babble of the family romance? Is there no chance in the writing destiny of a break-out from Murderer's Row? What sort of freedom can writing assert if it knows itself to originate with the father and like the friend take its essential direction from the father?[28]

The collusion is constituted in part by Georg's guilty perception of this state of affairs; his prespective must be surmounted. To acquiesce in the alliance of father and friend is to call down a death sentence. The experimental figure of the union of marriage and writing conjures a state which writing cannot survive: the alliance of friend and father corrupts writing with the father's alien will; the attempt to appropriate writing through marriage simply puts writing on a par with the acquiest of power the father has gained from marriage—the power to engender a devilish son. To marry in order to write would be only to reproduce the devilish offspring which the father has produced; Georg Bendemann, who seeks to bind himself out of his solipsism, would succeed only in reproducing himself.

The Georg of the outset who possessed writing through a sort of Faustian devil's bargain with himself is not the Georg of the close who can no longer "write", who cannot interpret the sentence laid on him. The father of the outset who in Georg's confident perspective was no obstacle to his double affirmation of sexual and literary power, is allowed, as the chief representative of family, to pose the question which touches the concealed doubt of Georg's whole enterprise. If Georg marries, he no longer keeps the connection with the Russian friend, the life of writing. To mingle marriage with writing is not to repair but only to repeat the fault which Kafka saw as writing's congenital fragility—the uncertainty that it could exist in definitive separation from the dying world of organic process, of family filiation. The voice which registers the "almost infinite" traffic over the bridge is not Georg's. It is a voice which aims to conjure a trace of the universal "family beast" at its source, at an order fundamental enough to justify the effort of writing to find access to it, there to litigate and contend.

IV

What relation does this reading have to the theory I asserted to govern all possible readings of "The Judgment"? Whatever consistency (intelligibility) it achieves is strictly speculative and is obtained by a deliberate process of substitution that reaches out beyond the text. I am attempting to recuperate unequivocal meaning from a work whose own terms resist it. If the identification of Georg as a dissimulator of texts is based on the text, certainly the link between the Russian friend and writing is not: it is based on an association of underdetermined signs (jaundice, solitude, Russia) with the sense they have in Kafka's confessional writings. If we allow this, we must also allow that the significances of these signs remain consistent through each repetition. The invocation of the St. Petersburg friend on the father's lips must also mean the writing destiny. In maintaining this continuity, however, we are merely exercising our will to coherence. The story neither allows nor does it disallow this assertion. But it is wholly evident how little the act which subjectively asserts meaning is equal to the act which originates the final impassiveness of the text.

The argument that the alliance between father and friend is intolerable to Kafka and must be construed as a nightmare, as a condition at all costs contrary to fact, is not given in the text but is extrinsically motivated by the intent of making meaningful the entire phenomenon *Kafka*. Without the existence of the confessional writings and the right to bring them into court, the motivation would be wholly arbitrary. The "nightmarish" text I read is only a moment in the autobiography of the writing consciousness in Kafka.

The irreducible reality of the work itself is its undecidability. We earlier identified this phenomenon as its "abyss of meaning", which has a fallen counterpart in the lie, the lie whose structure we are inclined to see repeated in the bad faith with which, and because of which, Georg accepts his death. We come closer to this phenomenon, however, by considering the father's sentencing of his son.

At the outset of this paper I envisioned Georg as a person of the status of the reader. It was then possible to declare the work cautionary, a negative example, because of Georg's simple accession to his death sentence. But in saying this I implied that Georg has good reasons, in the psychological sense, not to resist his sentence. This sort of implication is not encouraged by the text: the matter of his sentencing has to be put more appropriately.

Georg accedes to his sentence without even a velleity of resistance. The very utterance of the sentence brings about its effect. To sentence Georg to death is to set in motion a relentless process which brings about the state of affairs designated in the sentence.

The sentence is in effect a performative. It does not aim in its utterance to designate a state of affairs that is taking place and is extrinsically caused. It aims instead to bring into existence a state of affairs of which it is the sole cause. Merely as a set of signs the sentence "I sentence you to death" uttered at the appropriate moment by a judge in court brings about the fatal conclusion which the sentence also designates.

The sentence which Georg's father utters would constitute such a performative if Georg were under trial in a court of law. This perception encourages critics to construe Georg's accession as the act of the son who indeed places himself in a court of law upon entering his father's room. This theory needs the prior assumption that Georg considers himself guilty, and in effect turns himself in for sentencing. There is no good evidence in the text, however, for either of these assumptions.

Nothing requires us to grasp the sentence as a real performative. What is crucial is that in this text the sentence operates performatively contrary to the fact, and it does so by an act of will on the part of the narrator. One might recall a passage from Kafka's abortive novel *Wedding Preparations in the Country* written five years earlier, in which this sort of arbitrary authority over events in the world is explicitly named:

The carriages and people in the streets move and walk hesitantly on shining ground, for I am still dreaming. Coachmen and pedestrians are shy, and every step they want to advance they ask as a favor from me by looking at me. I encourage them and they encounter no obstacle.[29]

The dream of arbitrary omnipotence is fulfilled by a writing which is self-constitutive. Earlier I quoted the diary-passage in which Kafka speaks of "the special nature of my inspiration":

I can do everything, and not only what is directed to a single piece of work. When I arbitrarily write a single sentence, for instance, "He looked out of the window," it already has perfection.[30]

I said then that this bold claim lacked the fastidiousness of Kafka's later disclaimer of perfection in his writing. But it is clear now that this "perfection" is not to be construed empirically. It designates the eternally self-constitutive intent of fiction, its character of always meaning to speak in the performative mode. This is the power which the beleaguered narrator, who has earlier identified his perspective with the impossible optic of Georg, must assert in order to survive.

The assertion of the narrator's will aims to put his production into the order of the undecidable, since his intent is not to duplicate empirical consistency but to declare a break with consistency. The transgressive counterpart of this intent, meanwhile, is that of the interpreter, who in pursuing coherence opposes the arbitrary will of the narrator. This is the sense in which every interpretation undoes fiction: it undermines the will of the narrator, either privatively, by adducing a different and inappropriate standard of coherence or, more faithfully in Kafka's case, by conjuring the abyssal reality of the text. For over *this* reality, in which the performative figures as a mere tautology, the narrator's assertion of omnipotence is only one more metaphorical bridge.

The interpreter of Kafka must ask "as a favor" "every step" he "wants to advance"—but neither from the author nor the narrator, but from the text; here he has little ground beneath his feet and can finally pass over the abyss of meaning only by a construction of his own.

To be a writer of Kafka's order is to side neither with the narrator nor with that second narrator, the interpreter, but with the text. Kafka inhabits an order of the abyss which distinguishes him from every reader questing for a site somewhere in or over the work; Kafka exists not as the reader's pathos but as the large "impassiveness" of his text, somewhere off to one side of that bridge over which, in "The Judgment", there passes an almost infinite traffic.

This impassiveness is at the same time anxiety, in a way which may well point to the final undecidability of literature itself—that literature which Kafka declared, on good authority, to be wholly his case.

NOTES

1. D 1, 25.
2. "Notes on Kafka," in his *Prisms*. London: Spearman, 1967, 246.
3. Eduard Morike: "Auf eine Lampe," in his *Samtliche Werke*. Munich: Carl Hanser Verlag, 1964, 85.
4. D 1, 173.
5. *Ibid.*, 279.
6. Sokel: *F.K.T.I.*, 48.
7. *Ibid.*, 76.
8. *Ibid.*, 45.
9. BF, 397.
10. Sokel: *Op. cit.*, 53.
11. *Ibid.*, 58.
12. *Ibid.*
13. Stanley Corngold: "Introduction" to his ed. of *The Metamorphosis*. N.Y.: Bantam Books, 1972, xiv-xvi.
14. J.M. Ellis: "Kafka: 'Das Urteil'."
15. Politzer: *F.K.*, 59.
16. Greenberg: *Terror of Art* 47-68; Demmer: *F.K.*; Marson: "F.K.'s 'Das Urteil'."
17. Gerhard Wahrig: *Deutsches Worterbuch*. Gutersloh: Bertelsmann Lexikon-Verlag, 1970, 693.
18. Franz Kafka: "Reflections on Sin, Suffering, Hope, and the True Way," in his *DF*, 40.
19. D 2, 200-201.
20. DF, 41.
21. D 1, 45.
22. Cf. Stanley Corngold: "'You,' I said,...,: Kafka, Early and Late." *European Judaism* (London), VIII, No. 2 (Summer 1974), 16-21.
23. D 1, 278-279.

24. Brod: *F.K. A Biography*, 151. Cited by Kate Flores in *FKT*, 15, and elsewhere in the present volume.

25. D 1, 292.

26. D 1, 300.

27. Kafka wrote in a letter to Max Brod: "I have never been someone who carried something through at all costs... What I've written was written in a warm bath; I have not experienced the eternal hell of the real writer." Br, 100.

28. Cf. "Letter to his Father," in DF, 177. "[My writing] was...something, to be sure, which you were the cause of, but which took its course in a direction determined by me."

29. DF, 6.

30. D 1, 45.

Ronald Gray

Through Dream to Self-Awareness

Up till 1912, Kafka had written very little, and it was only under continual encouragement from Max Brod that he was able to put together the slim volume published under the title *Betrachtung* (Meditation). It was at Brod's flat while Kafka was arranging this for publication that he met Felice Bauer:

> I was putting the pieces in order last evening under the influence of this young lady; it is possible that as a result I have made some blunder, some juxtaposition that will be comic, though perhaps only confidentially.

Within a few weeks, during which he repeatedly wrote to Felice, they had begun a relationship which they were to continue, twice entering on an engagement to marry, and twice breaking it off, for several years. Kafka saw very little of her at this time (the autumn and winter of 1912), though he wrote her many letters. Throughout he was haunted by the thought that marriage, which he wished for and spoke of as the proper fulfilment of a man, was certain to make his writing impossible, the feeling "that if I had ever been happy apart from writing and all that went with it, it was precisely then that

I was incapable of writing". All the same, it is from the meeting with Felice that the flood of Kafka's writing really begins. He met her first on August 13, 1912. On the night of September 22-23 of that year he wrote, at one sitting, "The Judgment", the longest and most compelling story by far of any he had yet written, and though comparatively short, the most complete and most rounded, though also the first to end with the hero's death. How far Felice encouraged him, how far encouragement came from the publishers Ernst Rowohlt and Kurt Wolff, who now began to press him for publishable stories, is not determinable: all three, with Kafka's friends, acted simultaneously. The fact is that between September 1912 and early 1913 some six hundred sheets of *America* had been written, while the longest complete story Kafka ever wrote, "The Metamorphosis", was written in November and December 1912. In comparison with what he had written so far, this was a very great amount, and the indebtedness he felt was indicated by his dedication of "The Judgment" to Felice.

The story was Felice's in more than dedication. The initials of Frieda Brandenfeld, the fiancée of the central character, are hers, Kafka remarked, as are in a sense the initials of Fraülein Bürstner in *The Trial*. The autobiographical element in the story is clear enough, though Kafka's remark about the name of the young man Georg Bendemann is a further indication. ("Bende-", Kafka noted, has the same pattern of consonants and vowels as his own name; he was to allude to it again, later, in the name of Gregor Samsa, which is slightly closer to his own.) But more than a mere rewriting of his own experience was involved. He records in his diary his "terrible exertions and happiness" in writing the whole story of some three thousand words in eight hours, finishing at six in the morning. "More than once, this night", he writes, "I carried my weight on my own back. I realize that everything can be said, that there is a great fire prepared for even the strangest ideas, in which they vanish and rise again." And, contrasting the progress of his novel (presumably *America*) with this rapid outpouring, he goes on, "That is the *only* way to write, in a sequence like that, with body and soul completely open." The implications are those of another diary entry, in which Kafka counsels himself: "Open up. Let the man (*der Mensch*—implying also "the human being") come forth." It seems as though a total self-revelation were involved. The revelation was not purely conscious. Kafka thought of Freud, as he completed the story, and like a good deal of Kafka's writing it is what he called "a representation of my dreamlike inner life". That last phrase needs some definition. The story is clearly akin to dreams in its free associations, its strange logic, its acquiescence in fantastic happenings like the father's order to his son to kill himself, and its indirect relevance to Kafka's waking life. Yet it is also often lucid and precise in a way that dreams seldom are, and certainly much less dreamlike than "A Country Doctor". There is nothing magical, visionary, or exotic about most of Kafka's work—nothing like Nerval's, for instance. Presumably Kafka did not mean to say more than that his inner life proceeded as irrationally as dreams do, but the surveillance of his conscious mind is also apparent, at least some of the time.

As a story, "The Judgment" can be as telling as a nightmare. Only when the conscious, rational mind goes back over the experience of reading it does its obscurity come home. What passes at first sight as intelligible enough—though there may be hesitation from the start about this—is the significance of the mysterious friend in Petersburg to whom Georg has just finished writing as the story begins. This friend, who lives in almost total isolation, is the thread linking the whole together. Because Georg has been doubtful about telling the friend of his engagement, he goes into his father's bedroom to seek advice. The father's doubts whether the friend exists carry the story further forward, as does his sudden denunciation of Georg, not only admitting the friend's existence but claiming him as "a son after my own heart", with whom he has been in touch all along. And it is partly on account of Georg's supposed neglect of his friend that his father passes on him the sentence of death by drowning which, in the final moment, he executes on himself.

The story is clearly not dealing with any real world, unless the participants are supposed to be insane, which is in fact the interpretation made by Claude-Edmonde Magny. On the other hand, while still remaining ultimately obscure, it has more logical sequence than dreams ever have, and is rounded off, working to a climax, in a way that suggests a more conscious effort than the mere setting out of a dream. The story is a cryptic account of the gaining of self-knowledge by Kafka through a waking dream: its relevance outside his own situation is secondary to that, though genuine enough.

The dream-world is sometimes the most dominant aspect, as in the incident where Georg's father says he has a certain document in his pocket. The humor of the absurd is present here, as so often:

> "Pockets in his nightshirt too!" Georg said to himself, thinking with this one remark to ridicule him out of existence. He thought like that only for a moment, for he was forgetting everything all the time.

This compliance of the dreamer with any incongruities that chance to present themselves in his dream are less immediately apparent in the opening pages, when Georg reflects on the reasons why his friend in Russia cannot be told of his engagement. The description of the friend's circumstances, in fact the whole of the opening, could belong to any story of a perfectly realistic kind. Only gradually does the reader see that Georg's reasons for not writing any news of importance to the friend are not of the kind that anyone would rationally consider, though they seem to be reasonably set forth. They are rather the reasons that a person might use who was attempting to block some other thought from his mind, or the kind of pseudo-reasons that serve well enough in a dream: one has the impression that an argument is being given, and does not inquire too closely, resting content with the mere show. (There may of course be the same laxity in day-dreaming too.) So it is with Georg, who then goes on to reflect that, when only trivial matters are really fit to be communicated to the friend, he cannot tell him about the engagement. It is at this point that the strangeness of Georg himself begins to show, when it is

related that he preferred to write about trifles rather than
'admit' he is engaged to Frieda Brandenfeld, or when Georg
tells his fiancée that the friend would feel 'compelled, and hurt'
if he were invited to the wedding, and would then return home
alone, and everlastingly unsatisfied. These unlikely reasons for
not inviting him are, however, accepted unquestioningly by
the fiancée, who says—not very intelligibly by any realistic or
rationalistic standard, though very intelligibly, once one sees
the full inner meaning for Kafka—"If you have friends like
that, Georg, you ought never to have got engaged at all."

None of this is ever commented on in the story, which thus
remains mainly within the dream-world, despite the shaped
climax. Taking it at face-value, the story is so impenetrable that
one commentator finds in it "a discovery of the profound
significance of insanity as a paramount manifestation of the
fundamental irreducibility of all points of view". A better
suggestion is made by Kate Flores. It remains a suggestion, and
there can be no proof of so esoteric a point, but if it is acceptable
that Georg is to be identified with the outer Kafka, "a normal
enough young man, affable and debonair, suave, self-
contained, decisive, the favored son of a well-to-do merchant",
while the friend bears a striking resemblance to the inner
Kafka, "a reserved, silent, unsocial, dissatisfied person", as he
described himself, many otherwise obscure remarks become
clear. The explanation seems at first sight to run against
Kafka's remark in his diary that "the friend is the link between
father and son, he is their strongest common bond", but that
difficulty can be met later. If Kate Flores' view is accepted,
including the suggestion that the friend's business, now
stagnating, is Kafka's writing, which had not been going well
up to the time of writing "The Judgment", much of the
obscurity disappears:

> Georg Bendemann's soliloquy [on whether to write to
> his friend about his engagement] is Kafka's soliloquy, an
> objectification of his inner debate. It is an analogy, and a
> remarkably apt analogy: his inner self, his writing self, is a
> friend who for years has been in exile where, and only

where, he can pursue his business. However, his outer self, Georg, now wishes to marry...and Georg is concerned lest his marriage alienate his peculiar friend and cost him his friendship.

(It does not contradict this notion of "the writing self" when Max Brod observes that the friend has many traits of the Yiddish actor Löwy, a friend of Kafka's in real life to whom he did write of his engagement, and who was not only an artist, and thus close to Kafka as a writer, but also a man who lived in some desperation.) In such terms, the fiancée's remark that if he has such friends as this he ought not to get engaged makes perfect sense. So does his reply, which is otherwise, on the rational level, a *non sequitur*: "Yes, we are both to blame for that [being one and the same person]; but even now I wouldn't have it otherwise [I prefer to remain a writer, even if it means in the end not marrying you]." The friend's suggestion that Georg should join him in Russia becomes translatable as the idea that Kafka should devote himself entirely to writing. The father's doubts about the friend's existence become the father's disbelief in Kafka's talents as a writer.

The condemnation of Georg, however, gives a new twist to the relationship. The writing becomes particularly vivid here (with a characteristic exaggeration in the flying blanket, which gives an *élan* to the whole scene):

"Am I well covered up now?" asked his father, as though he could not see whether his feet were properly covered.

"There, you like it in bed already," said George, tucking the bedclothes more closely round him.

"Am I well covered up?" asked his father again, seeming to await the answer very expectantly.

"Never you worry, you're well covered up."

"No!" shouted his father, his answer almost clashing with his question, and flinging back the blanket with such strength that for a moment it straightened out in flight, he sprang erect on the bed. With one hand he held lightly to the ceiling. "You wanted to cover me up, I know that, you young lecher, but I'm not covered up yet, by a long chalk. And if it's the last strength I have, it's enough for you, too much for you."

It is with the condemnation of the intended marriage, however, that a new direction is taken. Though the writing remains vigorous, a new obscurity enters:

"Because she lifted up her skirts", his father began to twitter, "because she lifted up her skirts, the stupid slut", and to demonstrate the point he lifted his nightshirt so high that you could see the scar at the top of his thigh, from his war-wound, "because she lifted her skirts like this and this and this, you had a go at her, and so that you could get what you wanted from her undisturbed, you disgraced your mother's memory, betrayed your friend, and stuck your father in bed so that he wouldn't be able to move. But can he move, or can't he?"

And he stood up completely free of support, and kicked his legs out. He was beaming with joy at his own insight.

That this reflects not what Kafka's father would have said, but what Kafka "unconsciously" (though here, momentarily, consciously) would have liked him to say, is very likely. But the strange point about this story is that the sexual condemnation is not the most important, nor is the Oedipal relation with the father. Georg is accused of having "betrayed" his friend (a word which has no meaning in the given context, though it is quite intelligible in terms of Kafka's choice between marriage and writing), and shortly after, the father shouts that the friend is not betrayed: "I have been his representative in this place." It is this strange remark which suddenly reverses the role of the father, if the autobiographical suggestion is accepted. Kafka is realizing that the condemnation of marriage, though it comes from the hateful father of his unconscious mind, is nevertheless a condemnation he himself wants to accept, for marriage will prevent, so he believes, that relentless self-examination for which his writing affords the opportunity: it will destroy the conditions in which his dread exists and thereby destroy his only hope of salvation (however paradoxical that salvation may be). If the friend is not told of the engagement, that is, if Kafka cancels his own engagement and devotes himself to writing, he will be able to achieve that quasi-infinite awareness which the Kierkegaardian in him wants, even though it is an awareness of infinite guilt, for such awareness will give him a quasi-divine position. Naturally the father, the representative of the divine on earth, will associate himself with that part of Kafka that seeks such awareness, although, paradoxically, he will also condemn him for it. In this way the friend is indeed the link between father and son, in so far as the son, Kafka, realizes that devotion to the writer in himself is the only way to the Father, even that the Father and the writer in him are one. That Georg's father is the representative of the friend in this place means that Kafka's father's accusations are acceptable substitutes for the self-accusations which Kafka the writer was bound to make, the infinite trial which he was expecting to undergo. Or rather, not substitutes, but of the same substance, not ultimately different, the equivalent of the "Angst" which he was constantly recreating in himself.

The father's words of condemnation may thus have also a latent sense:

"So now you know what has been existing outside, till now you have only known about your own self! You were an innocent child, actually, but even more actually you were a diabolical man! And therefore, know that I condemn you to death by drowning."

Kafka knows, now, that his "Angst" is not merely private, that it is the very thing his father stands for, the thing he must accept, even though it means his extinction. He is diabolical because he is infinitely guilty, but there is nothing his conscious self can do about this, except give up marriage, give up all self-maintaining instincts, and, like Gregor Samsa in Kafka's next story "The Metamorphosis", calmly accept extinction. This Kafka, like Gregor, thinks of his parents with

affection in his last moment. But by dying he releases the writer
who has no human emotion (the friend was totally unmoved by
Georg's mother's death), the self who will be able to go on
recording his own infinite degradation. The hero is dead, but
the writer, the one part of himself which Kafka believed to be
indestructible, can continue.

An interpretation like this repeatedly makes sense when the
reactions of the characters, taken normally, would be nonsense.
This is true not only of the key expression "betraying the
friend", in connection with the intended marriage, which is the
most revealing of Kafka's devices. When the father says that the
friend "knows everything" (because the father has written to
tell him, though the phrase has overtones) the father adds "He
knows everything a thousand times better", whereupon:

> "Ten thousand times", said Georg, to laugh his father
> out of court, but in his very mouth the word acquired a
> deadly serious sound.

—which is to say that Kafka is aware (though he will not make
it quite plain) that the friend is in reality the fearful Inquisitor
of Kierkegaard's vision, the revealer of truth which the writer in
him can be, but one who is infinitely superior in knowledge to
the surface self represented by Georg. Similarly the father's
attack on Georg's sexual appetite corresponds to the words of
the priest in *The Trial*, when he accuses K. of seeking too much
help, especially from women. The thought is a constant one in
Kafka, continually dividing him between the spiritual struggle
represented for him by his writing, and the satisfaction he
looked for but feared from the other sex.

The interpretation works, and gives more satisfaction than
the mode of reading suggested by Mme Magny. Yet as Kate
Flores says, this is assuming that there is a "secret code which
Kafka evidently wished to remain a mystery", and the question
must arise, whether in that case the story has more than an
esoteric value. For Kafka it was important to realize that the
image of a condemning father which he had learned to fear was
also the representative, so far as he was concerned, of a mode of

being which he could respect: that is, that he wanted nothing better than to condemn himself infinitely, and could now find support for that in the father he had always held in dread. But the reader who is not so closely informed about Kafka's life is certain to be left with a sense of frustration if he inquires more deeply without referring to biographical details. And so it must be asked whether this story is more than a very surprising one, a means by which Kafka found himself able to write for another twelve years, because it made him aware of the only condition under which he could write at all, namely acceptance of his infinite guilt, or whether it is a masterpiece of controlled form. Has Kafka done more than cater for himself; is there anything here for the reader, in so far as he is a "common reader", someone who reads for pleasure and enlightenment rather than research? The quantity of biographical information needed for understanding the story suggests that it is essentially esoteric, that it has value for its position in Kafka's work, as a gateway, rather than as an accomplished achievement in itself. The achievement was to come with "The Metamorphosis". With that story Kafka became a writer of true distinction. But "The Judgment" had cleared the path.

John M. Ellis

The Bizarre Texture of
"The Judgment"

From a critical point of view, Kafka's strange but compelling style has been to some extent the victim of its own success: critics have become familiar with this bizarre and unfamiliar idiom, and what was outstanding for its unpredictability has now begun to be treated as if it were, predictably, "Kafkaesque". But such epithets leave unexplained the expressive power of what Kafka writes, nor do the commonly used words "nightmarish" or "dream-like" carry understanding further forward; still to be investigated is the characteristic quality and content of this, rather than any other kind of dream or nightmare.[1] Kafka's strange narrative convention is evidently an important part of his meaning, but it is all too easy to treat it in terms that are too general, or to discuss the characters and events in his work as if they were given to us not by Kafka's narrator, but by the more familiar realistic narrator. Consider, for example, this characterization of Georg: "Georg is not capable of any real relationship; his bride is for him an object of pleasure and a means of guaranteeing his material existence."[2] Or the following summary of the story: "Georg Bendemann is condemned by his old, widowed father to a death by drowning because of his plan to marry and his success in his father's

73

business, and he carries out the sentence on himself."[3] This seems reasonable enough; but is this really the kind of story in which one can say that the father has two perfectly ordinary reasons—Georg's intent to marry and his business success—for his judgment? Any summary falsifies what is summarized to a degree, but that is not the issue here; the point is that what is characteristic of a Kafka story may vanish when the motivation of the characters is spoken of in this way.

Part of the trouble lies in a misdirected response to the mysterious quality of Kafka's texture. Instead of treating this as a means of expression, and instead of examining the meaning and function of this enigmatic quality, critics have tended to want a kind of translation into a more normal mode. This would imply that Kafka's meaning is not radically different from anyone else's but that it is expressed in a kind of private code;[4] one goes to the diaries and letters to get the code, uses it to decode the works, and is then left with a meaning which is now independent of Kafka's style of writing and freed of its former bizarre trappings. Throughout Kafka criticism there occurs the telling phrase: "for Kafka, x means..." According to von Wiese,[5] for example, one must know that the notion of "nourishment" has "for Kafka a coded meaning". Edel gives another entry for the Kafka lexicon: "child and childlikeness are not unambiguously positive tokens for Kafka".[6] The critic mediates between reader and work by supplying the key to the code, and the story has been made less challenging; no longer is it the strange thing it was before. Kafka did not say all that he meant, and the critic supplies what is necessary. But this is a most paradoxical position. Can the source of Kafka's powerful and original effects be even in part a failure of expression? This is inherently most unlikely. The biographical information often supplies what is already available; for example, both English and German allow negative and positive values to the concept of a child (*childish* and *childlike, kindisch* and *kindlich*). Only an illusion of deciphering the enigma has been given. But in the process an important assumption has been made: it is that Kafka has a standard use of "the child" (or "Russia", and so on) which is constant throughout his work.

And this must involve the further assumption that one can state the meaning and value of such a notion in "The Judgment" without examining its use in the story. But that use must always be regarded as the primary source of its meaning; the possibility must always exist that in any given context a motif may be used by Kafka in a way which is different from any of his previous uses of that motif, and for a different purpose. And once that is conceded, it follows that looking at his uses elsewhere of motifs which occur in "The Judgment" produces only the knowledge they are or are not used differently in this text, not any determination of their meaning here.[7]

It is evidently the temptation to simplify Kafka that leads to criticism which proceeds in this way. The simplification may seem to provide a way of dealing with the baffling quality of Kafka which substitutes for the pursuit of more appropriately complex answers. To produce an equation of a concept in the story with a phrase from a diary is a tempting escape for a reader in that floundering condition that Kafka obviously *wants* him to be in, but to offer that escape is to do the reader a disservice. Kafka obviously saw some purpose in his bizarre narrative convention, and his readers have responded with a fascination which confirms that its purpose is indeed achieved, though they know nothing of his possible private code. It is surely with this public effect, not Kafka's private world, that the critic should concern himself.

The main weight of "The Judgment" lies in the interview between Georg and his father, to which there is a prelude (Georg's thoughts about his friend in Russia) and an epilogue (the judgment and its fulfillment). The central episode, unlike the first part of the story, is highly unrealistic and "absurd"; and yet, as we shall see, much of that effect is derived from its being slowly prepared in the earlier part of the story. The story's opening is worth close attention:

It was a Sunday morning in the very height of spring. Georg Bendemann, a young merchant, was sitting in his own room on the first floor of one of a long row of small, ramshackle houses stretching beside the river which were

scarcely distinguishable from each other except in height
and coloring. He had just finished a letter to an old friend
of his who was now living abroad, had put it into its
envelope in a playfully slow fashion, and with his elbows
propped on the writing table was gazing out of the
window at the river, the bridge and the hills on the farther
bank with their weak green.

This is apparently a realistic description, demanding to be
evaluated as such, and yet it is in many ways a strange one.[9] The
reference to the row of houses, for example, seems oddly
phrased. The emphasis of "scarcely distinguishable from each
other except in height and coloring" suggests that there is a
general effect of sameness, only slightly relieved. And yet if the
houses are all of different size and color, only their design can
be similar, and this would create an overall impression of
difference, not of sameness; design would be the least striking
of the three factors, for the design of adjacent houses is very
commonly similar. The descriptive phrase at first seems
reasonable, until we see its internal contradiction; the houses
could only seem that way to an onlooker who was concentrating on the one factor (design) to the exclusion of the others.
Now in so doing he would, though in one sense seeing what is
there, nevertheless be viewing it in such a selective way that it
became distorted and unreal. The quality of Georg's vision is
already apparent here: he seems in touch with reality, and yet
he focuses on things around him in such a way that they
become, through his emphases, quite unreal. Throughout the
following train of thought concerning his friend in Russia he
focuses sharply on some issues and ignores everything else, in
the process distorting even what he sees by getting the
proportions of the whole scene quite wrong. Another peculiar
detail here is the color of the "hills on the farther bank with
their weak (*schwach*) green". "*Schwach*" is unusual as a
qualifier of green; more normally German uses lightness rather
than weakness to indicate relative intensity of color. The
reference to weakness, then, seems out of place. Again, this is a
prefiguration of something characteristic of Georg, namely his

obsession with strength and weakness. The adverb "playfully",
too, adds to the unreality of the scene, as if suggesting that
Georg is in fact remote from what he is doing.

All of this cannot fail to put the reader on his guard; the
introduction is mainly realistic, and yet there is something
wrong with it, a suggestion that the whole scene is slightly out
of focus. This raises the question of the perspective of the
narrator. It may not be quite precise to say that we experience
the story through Georg's eyes,[9] for Georg is not the first person
narrator. But it is true to say, more precisely, that almost all of
the story is narrated through the medium of Georg's thoughts,
and a series of comments on them. During the interview
between father and son, for example, we have only impressions
of the exterior of the former (i.e., what he says and does), but
with the latter we also have what he is thinking. Thus the
strangeness of the narration throws doubt on the adequacy of
Georg's relation to what is going on outside himself. As yet,
however, this doubt is no more than a subdued hint, and it is
counterbalanced by a contrary development: the reader is
gradually drawn into Georg's version of what is going on
around him by a lengthy, very explicit and at first sight
reasonable train of thought concerning his friend in Russia.
Yet even this sequence of thoughts has its disturbing side. It
appears at first to be sensible and well-intentioned, but it can
also seem obsessive, over-subtle and fundamentally self-
congratulatory too. We can think of it in the first of these two
ways if we accept Georg's own point of reference; he is
concerned for his friend, and would like to help him or at least
to spare him the unhappiness which might result from his
becoming too aware of the discrepancy between his current
pitiable state and Georg's good fortune. And yet the obsessive
length of this train of thought makes it questionable; Georg
seems to be using his friend's life to dwell on his own successes,
so that his thoughts seem to be more concerned with his own
feelings of self-satisfaction than with his friend's welfare.
Georg's reflections are in fact very largely concerned with the
contrast between his own successes and his friend's failures.
The friend's business in Russia "had long been going

downhill" while Georg's family business in the last two years had doubled its personnel and quintupled its turnover, with even better prospects. While his friend had seemed to be preparing himself for becoming a permanent bachelor, Georg was about to make a marriage with a girl from a well-to-do family. While his friend was isolated and in exile in Russia, Georg still enjoyed an existence at home and among his family. The reader may well get the impression that Georg is rehearsing his own successes with some satisfaction. And the superficial impression of the breadth of his human sympathy for his friend is overshadowed by a contrary impression of narrowness in Georg's judgments of value, for judgments of his friend's life are made rigidly on the basis of Georg's values. To be a bachelor may well be a *choice* for his friend,[10] but Georg insists that only a failure to achieve marriage can be involved, which then must lead him to envy Georg. This narrowness of judgment corresponds to a narrow view of marriage which emerges when Georg persistently calls Frieda a "girl from a well-to-do family"; in thinking of a successful marriage Georg evidently thinks more of the success than the marriage.

Georg's geographical views are similarly narrow; home is an ultimate value and any other place is automatically undesirable, so that leaving home can only be taking flight and not a positive choice. No value is allowed by Georg to leaving home in a spirit of enterprise and adventure, for example: the only associations which he allows for such a journey are those of danger, loneliness, and so on. In this connection, there are interesting discrepancies between Georg's judgment of his friend's wretchedness and what he reports as fact. His friend had tried to persuade him, too, to leave home, which is not consistent with his unhappiness abroad, but Georg quickly dismisses the possibility:

In earlier years, perhaps for the last time in that letter of condolence, he had tried to persuade Georg to emigrate to Russia and had enlarged upon the prospects of success for precisely Georg's branch of trade. The figures quoted were microscopic by comparison with the range of Georg's present operations.

In like manner, Georg refuses to take seriously his friend's excuses for not returning home in the last three years:

> It was more than three years since his last visit, and for this he offered the lame excuse that the political situation in Russia was too uncertain, which apparently would not permit even the briefest absence of a small business man while it allowed hundreds of thousands of Russians to travel peacefully abroad.

His friend, then, insists that he stays away because his business is demanding, and argues that Georg should follow him; Georg interprets this as a flight from home, and a fear of feeling small if he returns. We know little if anything about Georg's friend and his real personal or commercial position;[11] but it seems distinctly possible that Georg converts all that he hears from his friend to his own version of life, in which his own values are paramount, and his success by those standards unquestioned. Now this is the same selective vision that occurs in the story's first paragraph, and the same ability to project emphases onto a situation which are Georg's, but not those of the situation itself. In the light of this, we cannot avoid suspecting that Georg's pity for his friend is possibly misplaced, and that it may be primarily a defensive stratagem on his part. It could well be that for Georg constantly to tell himself that his friend is unhappy is essential to his own well-being. There is, after all, something destructive in Georg's "considerateness" towards his friend; it seems to provide the opportunity for an orgy of denigration of him, a very full series of imaginings of his helplessness, wretchedness and even disgrace which are very congenial and flattering to Georg, as though he were savoring the thought that he had completely defeated someone who was his main competitor:

What could one write to such a man, who had obviously run off the rails, a man one could be sorry for but could not help. Should one advise him to come home, to transplant himself and take up his old friendships again—there was nothing to hinder him—and in general to rely on the help of his friends? But that was as good as telling him, and the more kindly the more offensively, that all his efforts hitherto had miscarried, that he should finally give up, come back home, and be gaped at by everyone as a returned prodigal, that only his friends knew what was what and that he himself was just a big child who should do what his successful and home-keeping friends prescribed.

Scarcely beneath the surface of the "considerateness", Georg is mentally destroying his friend. It is unnecessary to conjure up this vision of his friend's disgrace, of his being a public spectacle, of his being abjectly forced to listen to the denunciation of his errors and his childishness; all this is for Georg's own delight, a confirmation that of his contemporaries he has achieved most and proved wisest. Georg even reflects, with twisted logic, that all this must be mercilessly explicit in order not to be even more injurious! Does Georg really want his friend to return at all? For having said that there is "nothing to hinder" this return, he then goes on to make it impossible by the shameful vision of his friend's fate. The real hindrance must be Georg himself, if this is the welcome he has in mind.

The parable of the prodigal son is implicit in the situation of Georg's having stayed at home while his friend, a kind of sibling rival ("He would have been a son after my own heart," says Georg's father) has ventured afield. Georg interprets that venture negatively: it is for him a running away from home, to loneliness and failure. But the parable interprets it more positively, stressing the adventurous spirit of those who brave new country, and insists that they are worthy of a splendid welcome—not a disgrace. And so we can neither rule out the positive side of going abroad[12] (e.g., enterprise, adventure, and standing on one's own feet) nor ignore the negative side of staying at home (opting for safety and the comfort which has been the result of the work of one's father). In the parable the stay-at-home sons are angered by their more adventurous brother's reception, and betray their own insecure feeling that he did what they dared not do; Georg's hostility to his friend is less overt, but his "considerateness" seems to be a defensive reaction to one who has chosen a harder course than owing everything to his father. The friend's return might well provoke the welcome envisaged in the parable, not the abject position which Georg imagines (and wishes) for him, and this once more arouses the suspicion that Georg would not himself welcome this return.

At the beginning, Georg's negative attitude towards his friend appears only in certain implications of the text, but it slowly becomes more explicit. For example, Georg's initial intent is to prevent his friend's learning of his engagement. But he afterwards admits that "I can't prevent (*verhindern*) that, of course", which reminds us of his earlier protestation that there was no hindrance to his friend's return. And meanwhile Georg does everything he can to get the news to his friend without seeming to do so. Thus he tells his friend obsessively "three times in three fairly widely separated letters...about the engagement of an unimportant man to an equally unimportant girl". Having thus caused his friend to become interested in this repeated information "quite contrary to Georg's intentions", (!) and having raised with his friend the issue of engagements, he then takes up the matter with Frieda and allows himself very quickly to be convinced that he should in fact tell all. There is a very strange sequence of statements which introduces this conviction:

"Since your friends are like that, Georg, you shouldn't ever have got engaged at all." "Well, we're both to blame for that; but I wouldn't have it any other way now." And when, breathing quickly under his kisses, she still brought out: "All the same, I do feel upset," he thought it could not really involve him in trouble were he to send the news to his friend.

This is a sudden conversion indeed. It is much shorter than his initial series of thoughts which led in the opposite direction; his scruples are brushed aside in an exchange that is less convincing than anything in the story up to this point. But the final demonstration of Georg's underlying motives comes in the letter which he writes; after all his thoughts of sparing his friend's feelings, the letter could scarcely be more injurious:

> I have got engaged to a Fraulein Frieda Brandenfeld, a girl from a well-to-do family, who only came to live here a long time after you went away, so that you're hardly likely to know her. There will be time to tell you more about her later, for today let me just say that I am very happy and as between you and me the only difference in our relationship is that instead of a quite ordinary kind of friend you will now have in me a happy friend. Besides that, you will acquire in my fiancée, who sends her warm greetings and will soon write you herself, a genuine friend of the opposite sex, which is not without importance to a bachelor.

Georg is at pains to identify Frieda as being "from a well-to-do family", he alludes to his friend's still being a bachelor in a way which is condescending (as usual, under the guise of talking about what is good for his friend) and stresses his own improved status as someone no longer "ordinary", again under the guise of talking of his friend's gain from the changed situation. It is now no longer a suspicion, but clearly a fact that the point of Georg's earlier train of thought was to gloat over his successes; for the letter makes it clear that Georg has no real concern for his friend's feelings. Having said that he wanted to do one thing, Georg does precisely the reverse. His exhortation to his friend to attend the wedding, giving all hindrances the go-by, is undermined by the final sentence "still, however that may be, do just as seems good to you without regarding any interests but your own". Even if it were not becoming more and more clear that hindrance is Georg's favorite word for masking his self-deception, these final words of the letter would still indicate that Georg is very ready to contemplate his friend's non-arrival.

After six pages the story turns to Georg's interview with his father, which, though increasingly grotesque and unreal in character, is basically a continuation of the same themes in a different context. As the disturbing factors below the surface of the prelude are progressively revealed, the story slides more and more into a fantastic mode. The central feature of the whole interview is his father's questioning Georg's version of reality. When Georg tells his father what he proposes to do—to tell his friend of his marriage—he begins to sound even more obsessive as he repeats his former words: "'I said to myself that someone else might tell him about my engagement, although he's such a solitary creature that that was hardly likely—I couldn't prevent that—but I wasn't ever going to tell him myself.'" By now, these protestations have a rehearsed and fixed quality. But the whole house of cards[13] which Georg has built in his mind is attacked when Georg's father says quite directly: "'Do you really have this friend in St. Petersburg?'" This thrust is the beginning of the end for Georg; his response to it consists of a retreat into a way of speaking and thinking which matches exactly that of his earlier reflections on his friend, but the context of this response in the conversation with his father sheds more light on the first pages of the story. Georg's earlier train of thought was given no context, for his friend never appeared. But now we see much more clearly that Georg's long and elaborate considerations concerning his father's need for help and sympathy are a retreat following an attack by his father; Georg retires into a cocoon of words and logical arguments which he spins out to provide a protective convering for the private version of the world which he must defend against a threat to question it. Here is surely the key to the air of unreality of Georg's thoughts on his friend. The content of his speech is similar to the earlier thoughts too.

There is the same concern for the other's welfare which puts Georg into a superior position in the relationship, and allows him to avoid the issues raised by his father, since the implication is that everything he says can be attributed to infirmity or sickness; and there is the same shutting out of communication in order to expand a version of what is happening that is obsessively reasonable in tone:[14]

"Never mind my friends. A thousand friends wouldn't make up to me for my father. Do you know what I think? You're not taking enough care of yourself. But old age must be taken care of. I can't do without you in the business, you know that very well, but if the business is going to undermine your health, I'm ready to close it down tomorrow forever. And that won't do. We'll have to make a change in your way of living. But a radical change. You sit here in the dark, and in the sitting room you would have plenty of light. You just take a bite of breakfast instead of properly keeping up your strength. You sit by a closed window, and the air would be so good for you. No, Father! I'll get the doctor to come, and we'll follow his orders. We'll change your room, you can move into the front room and I'll move in here. You won't notice the change, all your things will be moved with you. But there's time for all that later, I'll put you to bed now for a little, I'm sure you need to rest. Come, I'll help you to take off your things, you'll see I can do it. Or if you would rather go into the front room at once, you can lie down in my bed for the present. That would be the most sensible thing."

All of this evidently aims to reduce the stature of Georg's father until he is no longer a threat; and we can infer that Georg's pitying his friend has the same purpose of preserving his self-centered and self-satisfied view of his life against a possible challenge. In spite of Georg's benevolent tone, he is on both occasions making a counter-attack of a deeply aggressive nature, its aim being the subtle destruction of the opponent. It is because we see this defense mechanism spring into action against an attack by his father that we can assume that it was a response to a need to defend against his friend, and it is easy to see where the need arises; his friend has acted on a set of values very different to Georg's, and Georg may well feel this alternative to his own actions as a pressure on him needing to be relieved by preserving the belief that his friend is in error, wretched and childish. But Georg is in even more danger from his father, who as a father is the ever-present censor of what Georg is doing, the original critic of Georg's life, and the one man above all before whom Georg feels he must always justify himself.[15] For one so concerned with justifying himself to himself, practicing much self-deception in the process, his father is a constant threat to Georg's precarious mental world. Georg had felt himself compelled to present his action in relation to his friend for his father's scrutiny, and the story is much concerned with Georg's experience of his father as a powerful force. As Georg enters his father's room his instinctive reaction is: " 'My father is still a giant of a man,' " and his father's later emergence from his state of being nearly "covered up" is conspicuous as above all a display of power:

> "Don't worry, you're well covered up." "No!" cried his father, cutting short the answer, threw the blankets off with a strength that sent them all flying in a moment and sprang erect in bed. Only one hand lightly touched the ceiling to steady him. "You wanted to cover me up I know, my young sprig, but I'm far from being covered up yet. And even if this is the last strength I have, it's enough for you, too much for you."

Within the convention of the story, the judgment of his father is so strong as to compel Georg's death.

Throughout the conversation with his father, it is evident that Georg is attempting to refuse communication and to avoid answering what his father says. But the issue of communication has been present from the beginning of the story; Georg raises it as he thinks over his friend's reports: "By his own account he had no regular connection with the colony of his fellow countrymen out there and almost no social intercourse with Russian families, so that he was resigning himself to becoming a permanent bachelor." After these thoughts on his friend's lack of communication with other people, Georg then goes on to reflect that he too finds it impossible to communicate with him: "For such reasons, supposing one wanted to keep up correspondence with him, one could not send him any real news such as could frankly be told to the most distant acquaintance."

Yet another impression of separateness and lack of communication emerges from Georg's thoughts as he enters his father's room. He reflects that he has not entered the room for months: "There was in fact no need for him to enter it, since he saw his father daily at business." In any case, he thinks, they often sat together "each with his newspaper, in their common sitting-room". In protesting to himself that he really does have contact with his father, Georg gives us an odd picture of both sitting physically near each other but mentally separate, their newspapers providing a convenient barrier between their mental worlds. Georg had complained that his friend made separateness inevitable, but here it seems to be Georg who does it—another hint at a reinterpretation of Georg and his friend— while his father may be seeking to avoid the barrier by peering round the edge of his newspaper: "His father was sitting by the window in a corner hung with various mementoes of Georg's dead mother, reading a newspaper which he held to one side before his eyes in an attempt to overcome a defect of vision." Does he really want to read it at all? But by the middle of the interview it has become clear why communication is such an issue. His father speaks very directly, and Georg avoids what he says, because communication is the great danger to Georg's mental world; it can only stay intact if everyone else is kept out of it. Real communication would subject it to the test of a different view of the world, which might sweep away all Georg's defenses, and with them his delusion of being both a great success and a kind, considerate person. For this reason Georg is extremely busy in his avoidance of communication, trying one means after another. The first, as we have noted, is his normal flight into an elaborate monologue, kind and considerate to his father, yet with the unspoken implication that the old man's mind is wandering too much for him to be taken seriously. His father counters the long monologue with a single syllable: "'Georg,'" said his father in a low voice, without moving."[16] The rejection of all that Goerg has said is subtle; it is achieved by the formal contrast of the monosyllable with Georg's copious speech, the former simple, direct and with much unspoken force, the latter weak and evasive in its fullness. Faced with this accurate answer to and rejection of his first line of defense, Georg immediately makes another attack on his father, this time a wordless one; he kneels beside him, "lifting his father from the chair and slipping off his dressing gown as he stood feebly enough". Now he treats him as a child, undresses him, and puts him to bed, resolving to take care of his father in future in terms which are as condescending as they are hopeful of failure: "But now he made a quick, firm decision to take him into his own future establishment. It almost looked, on closer inspection, as if the care he meant to lavish there on his father might come too late."

As Georg's attitude to his father emerges more clearly, a fresh assessment of what has happened in the family business is called for. Georg's view was that he had produced a great expansion since his mother's death and his father's subsequently taking less part in the business; but his father's complaint is that Georg has attempted to exclude him from knowledge of what is happening while profiting from his father's preparation of the direction to be taken by the business. The outline of the situation is by now familiar; Georg's success and someone else's failure, with the suggestion that both are brought about by Georg's subtle undermining of the other.

Georg's putting his father to bed is an attempt to pretend that he is senile, weak and bedridden, and thus no longer one whose power must be feared; but his father emerges stronger than ever, throwing off the bedclothes and the position which Georg has assigned to him. Now he is a giant again, and Georg's second attack on him has failed, as has his second line of defense against his father's understanding of him. Increas-

ingly desperate attempts now follow; he cannot reduce his
father's stature by pity or condescension, and so tries to avoid
the awareness of his own plight by pitying his friend once
more, a move which by now seems a pathetically inadequate
attempt to shore up his crumbling position: "Georg stared at
the bogey conjured up by his father. His friend in St.
Petersburg, whom his father suddenly knew too well, touched
his imagination as never before." Georg's formerly well-
polished defensive system has here degenerated to a feeble and
automatic response, a despairing attempt to divert his attention
from his own plight to that imagined for another. The
retrospective reinterpretation of the early pages of the story
continues; Georg's dwelling on his friend's inadequacy is there
too to be regarded as an avoidance of his own problems. But
this defense now becomes useless as his father assures him: "But
your friend hasn't been betrayed after all!" and reveals that
"I've been representing him here on the spot." At this Georg's
very last instinctive defense appears: "You comedian!" Georg
could not resist the retort, realized at once the harm done and,
his eyes starting in his head, bit his tongue back, only too late,
till the pain made his knees give. Though he regrets it, it is all
he has left, and so he now deliberately tries to make fun of his
father. His father tells him that his friend in Russia already
knows the circumstances of Georg's present life "a thousand
times better", and his response is: "'Ten thousand times!' said
Georg, to make fun of his father, but in his very mouth the
words turned into deadly earnest." These two instances link
with his father's calling Georg a "joker", and the story's
opening with Georg sealing his letter "playfully"; joking and
playing are also part of Georg's defensive armory of devices for
keeping reality at arm's length, by not taking things seriously
which would damage his version of it.[17]

That the narration has been from Georg's point of view has
allowed us to be drawn into his world and to get a sense of its
inner logic and persuasiveness, though to be sure we also get an
uneasy feeling of its unreality.[18] We therefore experience the
challenge to that world by Georg's father from within it.
Georg's father brings reality into Georg's unreal world, but

from our vantage point and that of Georg it appears as a sudden eruption of irrationality, terror and unreality; sanity appears as insanity, and fantasy has become so ordered that what interrupts it seems the thing that is fantastic. Yet at the same time, we also begin to see floating to the surface of Georg's mind reactions which begin to acknowledge that his father's version of events is the real one, an acknowledgment eventually to be made openly to his father. The first of these is his "'My father is still a giant of a man,'" an instinctive reaction not consistent with the fantasy about his infirmity. But the first really explicit crack in Georg's view of his life comes after his father has refused to co-operate in Georg's attempts to ignore what he is saying by treating him as a senile person in need of care; at last, the truth begins to emerge:

> A long time ago he had firmly made up his mind to watch closely every least movement so that he should not be surprised by any indirect attack, a pounce from behind or above. At this moment he recalled this long-forgotten resolve and forgot it again, like a man drawing a short thread through the eye of a needle.

This feeling becomes more and more explicit, after a curious projection of the kinds of connections and inferences that are made in Georg's mind: "'He has pockets even in his shirt!' said Georg to himself, and believed that with this remark he could make him an impossible figure for all the world. Only for a moment did he think so, since he kept on forgetting everything." Thoughts float around Georg's mind without any secure point of reference, once that provided by his well-ordered mental world has been shaken; other visions of safety then need to be seized on, and much needs to be forgotten. His attempts to create reality by his own language and reasoning are stripped to their essentials here in a fantasy wish that is a kind of reduction to absurdity of his tactics so far; he now suffers openly from the delusion that his thought about his father's shirt-pockets can achieve the reduction of his father that has escaped him until now. The absurdity of the inference highlights the need for the conclusion, and is a comment on all previous sequences of thoughts leading to a similar conclusion; their logic was just as spurious, under a much better covering. Full awareness of the danger from his father, and an explicit wish for his destruction, emerge at last in Georg's "what if he topples and smashes himself," and "So you've been lying in wait for me!" His real feelings of being threatened by his father's presence break through into the open at last, as does the awful fact of the conspiracy against him, when his father announces that he has been writing to the friend in St. Petersburg. It was fear of others uniting against him that led him to attempt to destroy the relationships between them, to insist that his father really did not like his friend: "I could quite well understand your dislike of him, my friend has his peculiarities. But then, later, you got on with him very well. I was proud because you listened to him and nodded and asked him questions." Here Georg was trying to lead his father into his own negative attitude towards the friend, and then a condescending one in which nothing which his friend says is taken seriously.

The final judgment pronounced by Georg's father ties together many of the threads of the story: "So now you know what else there was in the world besides yourself, till now you've known only about yourself! An innocent child, yes, that you were, truly, but still more truly have you been a devilish human being!—And therefore take note: I sentence you now to death by drowning!" Georg's father is not drawing a distinction between Georg's knowledge of himself as against his ignorance of the alliance against him,[19] but between his living in his own mental world as opposed to the world in which people exist outside himself. Georg allows others no independence of his values, and they are forced to exist as satellites in a system of which he is the center. If by nature they tend to threaten this system, they are subtly undermined and destroyed. This self-centeredness is in one way the innocence of the child—it contains no explicit malice—but it is devilish in its destructiveness. Thus it is not inconsistent that Georg cries, as he falls into the river to his death, "'Dear parents, I have always loved you, all the same;'" this childish love existed but was never outgrown. Yet his father, since Georg behaved as if everything were a potential danger to him unless crippled or destroyed, can also cry, without inconsistency: "'Do you think I didn't love you, I, from whom you are sprung?'" For Georg has behaved as if all the world were hostile to him, and he could trust nobody. He has said that his friend is "a big child", but this seems rather to refer to Georg, whose childish egocentricity has survived after his childhood is over.

The last words of the story are a comment on what has gone wrong with Georg: "At this moment an unending stream of traffic was just going over the bridge." The end of Georg's lonely, isolated and unreal world is accompanied by a vision of the enormous activity around him that was separate from but ignored by him. Its ceaselessness and diversity are its health while Georg's sickness lay in the uniformity and isolation of his outlook; and in the taking up once more of the motif of "traffic",[20] there is a suggestion of the movement to and fro, the communication, which was absent from Georg's shut-off private world. In these final words the narrative perspective changes abruptly. No longer are we looking at the world with Georg; he has dropped to the river below, and is gone, while the narrator describes the scene above. At last, Georg is part of the scene rather than its centre. And as part of the scene, he is now no longer noticeable, as the noise made by everything outside of him makes the noise of his fall inaudible. Georg's father has sentenced him to death to pay for his egocentricity,[21] but the narrator sentences him to be removed from occupying the center of the narrative; in death he will no longer be central to what happens in the real world, and we are suddenly made to see the scene in its true perspective, rather than in Georg's.

An element of the meaning of the story often overlooked is its network of biblical and Christian imagery, which on the surface appears to be contradictory. The sequence of such images includes the maid's cry of "Jesus" as Georg rushes out to his death, and her covering her face as if the sight were one arousing dread; Georg's father announcing that he is the "representative" of the friend in Russia (the fact that the friend lives in the city of St. Petersburg is another echo of the word "representative"); the implicit situation of the parable of the prodigal son; Georg's denial "at least twice" of his friend in his father's presence; the story of the priest in Russia who cuts a cross of blood in his hand; and finally Georg's own hanging from the bridge as if crucified.

Even without these explicitly Christian motifs, it is clear that "The Judgment" is concerned with ideals that play an important part in the ethos of Christianity, e.g., loyalty and betrayal, meekness and childish innocence, and the sacrifice of one who was (apparently) meek and childlike. But the explicitly Christian motifs underline the fact that in "The Judgment" the values of Christianity are thrown up in the air, and come down in an unfamiliar shape. For one thing, the positions occupied by Georg, father and friend within the Christian scheme seem to change all the time. At one point, Georg seems to the maid to be Jesus, and fulfills that role with his being condemned to death for his "meekness" and hanging as if crucified from the bridge.[22] But at another time, his friend is the Christ-figure, denied by Georg, and with Georg's father as his "representative". It may seem puzzling that both Georg and his father play Peter to the friend's Christ, albeit different stages of Peter, but the confusion is increased by the friend himself being Peter of St. Petersburg, and telling stories of how the gospel is preached with blood in Russia. But this uncertainty as to who occupies the center of the system of values here is a mirror of the uncertainty of the system itself, for the story explores the ambiguous and dark side of the Christian ethic. Christ was crucified because his humility was felt to be arrogance, his meekness to be aggressive and his advocacy of childlike innocence to be devious and insidious. But in Kafka's story, the ethic of peace and good-will towards men really *is* an expression of arrogance and aggression, Georg's innocence is devilish, his sympathetic concern for others is aggressive and destructive, his lack of self-assertion is at a deeper level highly assertive and selfish, and his self-criticism is a means of maintaining a high degree of self-satisfaction. Kafka can thus make Georg analogous to Christ to bring out this darker side of the Christian ethic, can make him seem dreadful to the servant-girl, and deserving of his crucifixion. The assignment to Georg of the "wrong" place in the Christian scheme has something profoundly right about it; and the rest of Kafka's jumbling the roles likewise has much point. For the same kind of turning the Christian ethic upside down is visible in Georg's denial of his friend; Peter's loyalty to Christ wavers at the moment of his denial because of his wish to save himself, while Georg's very "loyalty" to his friend is the means of his preserving himself, so that his denial is only a final emergence of his more fundamental disloyalty. The priest's spreading the gospel with blood on his hands is in the same vein; it brings to the surface the violent basis of the ethic of love, just as Georg's father links the ideal of childish innocence with devilishness.

Kafka's story is evidently a tightly-knit piece of narration, small in compass, but dense in texture. Its bizarre surface must not be removed and discarded by a process of decoding,[23] but considered seriously as part of its meaning. It draws us slowly into the world of Georg, at first comfortable enough apart from an odd hint of its artificiality, and from this position we experience the nightmare, fantastic quality of his father's challenge to it, and its final disintegration into utter disjointedness. And by this technical achievement Kafka can then do what is the point of the story; he can turn upside down the values we start with, and which are apparently Georg's— loyalty, concern for and protection of others, unselfishness, sympathy and love—and allow the final emergence of their selfish, aggressive, destructive, self-aggrandising basis. The familiarity and unquestioned nature of these values adds to the comfortable quality of Georg's world in which we enter the story, and the increasingly fantastic character of the narrative as they become reversed is consistent with the fact that seeing their other side is indeed strange. Kafka's narrative is very much part of his theme; the aggressive nature of love is a paradoxical idea, and a paradoxical narrative is the result.

NOTES

1. E.g., Beissner; "Kafka the Artist," in Gray: *K*, 25, who finds in "The Judgment" the portrayal of a 'dream-like inner life' "—a conception so general that it could be applied equally to works by other writers as well as any of Kafka's other works.

2. Edel: "F.K.: 'Das Urteil.'" 217.

3. Sokel: *F.K.*, 44. Or Politzer: *F.K.*, 63: " 'The Judgment' does not convey any clearly discernible message beyond the warning against the loss of bachelorhood."

4. Nobody has put this attitude more clearly than Politzer: "Being hypersensitive to his own weaknesses, Kafka produced a veritable wealth of clues from his own life to decipher the undecipherable" (64). Though the German title of his book announces a concern with Kafka the artist, then, Politzer relies heavily on biographical material. Beissner, too, indicates in his title a concern with the artist Kafka rather than the man, but still makes much use of letters and diary entries in a critical approach that is still biographical to an important degree; e.g., we should read Kafka "with a delicate and exact regard for his ability to portray his dream-like inner life" (26).

5. B. von Wiese: "Franz Kafka: *Die Verwandlung*," in *Die deutsche Novelle von Goethe bis Kafka*. Dusseldorf: Bagel, 1962, Vol. II, 327.

6. Edel: *Op. cit.*, 219.

7. Critical arguments of this kind can always be settled by a dilemma: *either* the element of meaning diagnosed by means of a diary entry is already provided by common linguistic usage and associations, the context of the word or idea in the story, or a combination of both, *or* there is no evidence that the meaning so diagnosed is relevant to the story at all, in which case an intent which was incompletely executed has to be assumed without any evidence for that assumption.

8. Zimmermann: "F.K.: 'Das Urteil,' " 191 (1966 ed.), comments appropriately: "We recognize the characteristic stamp of Kafka's narrative in the increasing alienation of reality, which is achieved by the author's using realistic means to integrate the absurd into everyday happenings." I am not entirely in agreement with his view (192), however, that until Georg's entry into his father's room the story presents only a "world in which there is nothing unusual," and which follows "the familiar laws of causality and psychology," or that Georg's early train of thought is the product of "compelling logic as well as human considerateness." The early part of the story does have its disturbing signs.

9. Sokel: *Op. cit.*, 45.

10. The text does not allow the opposite assumption, that bachelorhood and asceticism are positive values for the story. Cf. Politzer: *Op. cit.*, 57-58. "But in the same measure in which Georg has abandoned his bachelorhood, the friend has grown in old Bendemann's mind to personify all the virtues of the bachelorhood Georg has forfeited." This deviates from the text in that Georg's father was apparently happily married, in that we know almost nothing of the friend's life, and in that the story in general contrasts egocentricity unfavorably with communication and relationships; the self-sufficiency of asceticism and bachelorhood would clash with this value system. The text by itself would provide no occasion for the perception of these values, which are evidently derived from biographical concerns (Kafka the ascetic and bachelor). The widowed father can scarcely be seen as being in and valuing a second bachelorhood without *his* expressing a sense of having betrayed the first; to the contrary, he expresses a positive attitude to his late wife.

11. Georg's view of his friend is often taken to be completely reliable; e.g., Sokel: *Op. cit.*, 64-65: "The difference between Georg and his friend is fundamental . . . because Georg has known true innocence and lost it, while his friend never had it. . . . He was

too cowardly to stick it out in his life at home. Not only that, he is also too much of a coward to return."

12. Thus "Russia" in "The Judgment" is primarily a symbol of openness, as opposed to the closedness of an existence at home. Home and Russia are contrasted as places of safety and unenterprisingness on the one hand, as opposed to danger and opportunity on the other. Both sides of the opposition have positive and negative aspects. Kafka's diary entries cannot therefore be allowed to limit the meaning of "Russia"—and those entries in any case are not consistent with each other.

13. Sokel thinks of the father's question in narrower terms: "With his question, Georg's father seems to doubt the existence of his friend in St. Petersburg.... But if the stress falls on the word *friend*, then the question refers to the nature, the character of its object. Then the question is: has Georg a *friend* in St. Petersburg, or perhaps an enemy" (53). But, alas, the stress does not fall on that word; Kafka did *not* italicize it, so that Sokel's proposal amounts to changing Kafka's text. It seems preferable to take the thrust of the question in the broadest way; Georg's father is questioning not just the existence or the friendliness of the friend, but the whole edifice of Georg's version of his own life in relation to his friend's.

14. Politzer views this as Georg's attempt to "change the subject" (55) missing the thematically more important aspects of his returning to the mode of thought with which the story began.

15. The meaning of the figure of Georg's father in the story is of course an abstraction from what he does and says as well as his effect on others, and is neither to be derived from Kafka's other works nor from Freud.

16. Ruhleder: "F.K.'s 'Das Urteil' " 15, says that this single word "seems to express neither support not reproach," and thus misses the point of the contrast of Georg's length with his father's monosyllable.

17. Sokel views the word "playfully" (*spielerisch*) differently: "A lack of seriousness is noticeable in the word 'playfully'. When Georg seals the letter playfully, he expresses in this gesture the fact that his attitude to the engagement—and with that to growing up—is neither serious nor firm" (73). But it is surely not seriousness of purpose that Georg lacks, for on the contrary he is quite ruthless in his pursuit of what he wants. There is no evidence to support the view that Georg is not serious about the marriage to Frieda; once more, the biographical parallel with Kafka and his fiancee is achieved only at the cost of changing the text.

18. Beissner's view is that for the sake of "unity of meaning" the narrator has "completely transformed himself into the lonely Georg" (25). This statement of the purpose of the narrative scheme appears to me too vague and general to catch its specific purpose, and the description of the scheme blurs the distinction between narration by Georg and narration from his point of view.

19. Contrast Sokel: "What is the knowledge which Georg achieves? Until now he knew only himself, now he knows 'what else there was in the world besides [him].' But what existed 'besides him?' The alliance between friend and parents, which originated as revenge for Georg's betrayal, and which reveals his sad isolation and seals his doom" (54). But the point on which the meaning of the whole story depends, is that Georg's father is attacking Georg's egocentric refusal to allow for the existence of people separately from himself. Thus his increased awareness at the end must not be narrowed down to the awareness of the conspiracy against him.

20. No English translation can deal adequately with the word *Verkehr* here, the final word of the story. The literal meaning at this point is "traffic"; but on the first page of the story where Georg is thinking of the poverty of his friend's existence, the phrase *gesellschaftlicher Verkehr* is best translated "social intercourse" or "social contact" and the verbal phrase *verkehren mit* (referring to Georg and his father) means "to have contact with". The dominant idea in all the uses of the root in this text, then, is

communication. The word is capable of a specifically sexual meaning in German, though not one of its contexts in the story suggests that meaning. Only Kafka's own well-known comment on the last line ("Ich habe dabei an eine starke Ejakulation gedacht") could have caused critics to narrow down the meaning in this way; e.g., Ruhleder (13) cites this as the "true meaning" of the last sentence simply because Kafka said it. Cf. Politzer: *F.K.*, 60. But there is of course no reason to allow an offhand comment by the author to take precedence over the factors in the text (mainly the other uses of the word in the text, and its various contexts) which control the meaning of a word. Ruhleder concedes that the narrower meaning would be "far-fetched" if not suggested by Kafka. It *is* far-fetched, and remains so.

21. By contrast, Politzer finds the judgment unjustified, and this lack of justification a "technical" flaw: "On closer scrutiny we cannot establish a poetic truth that would justify this judgment on the evidence provided by Georg's life. Part of the enigma presented to us by the story is due to this artistic imperfection" (63).

22. Cf. Ruhleder: *Op. cit.*, 16.

23. The most elaborate decoding attempt is that of Ruhleder, who assigns various elements of the story to a mythological system including Chronos, Uranos, Aphrodite, and so on. The translation is systematic, but no less distorting for that.

John J. White

Georg Bendemann's Friend in Russia: Symbolic Correspondences

At the beginning of Kafka's "The Judgment", the central character, Georg Bendemann, has just finished writing a letter to his friend in Russia, containing the belated information that he has recently become engaged. The story's dramatic turning-point comes later when Georg, who has told his father of the letter's contents, is asked by him point-blank: "Do you really have this friend in St. Petersburg?"[1] Instead of simply replying in the affirmative, as the reader might expect on the basis of all that he has so far heard about the friend, Georg "rose in embarrassment", and in the subsequent exchange with his father he energetically seeks to divert attention from the fundamental question with which he has been confronted.

Much in the story seems to depend on the issue of Georg's friend in Russia, indeed the whole judgment itself is directly related to it. Yet the exact implications of old Bendemann's question—and the wider subject of the friend's importance within the story—have tended to divide critical opinion substantially. The problem here is partly one of narrative perspective. The story is related by a narrator whose viewpoint largely coincides with Georg's version of reality, so the reader has the choice of either sharing this perspective or reading

97

"against the grain". And this situation is further complicated by the conflicting views offered at different stages by the various characters who speak.

Because the skepticism implicit in the question "Do you really have this friend in St. Petersburg?" would appear to be irreconcilable with much of the information that the reader has so far been given in the tale, there has been an understandable reluctance on the part of many to take it at its face value. It has been seen as evidence of old Bendemann's insanity,[2] and as less a matter of the friend's sheer existence than of whether this man in St. Petersburg is really a true friend to Georg (and vice versa).[3] In asking about him, old Bendemann has been seen to undermine "the whole edifice of Georg's version of his own life in relation to his friend's."[4] And yet the manner in which the question is formulated casts doubt specifically on whether the man himself actually even exists. Whatever other implications there are to this question, it invites consideration at the literal level on which it is put. The reader is encouraged to ask whether there really is such a man.

This enigma has been recognized as crucial to the interpretation and evaluation of "The Judgment" as a whole. Critical reactions to the handling of Georg's friend range from the suggestion that he is "the one strange element in "The Judgment", the one aspect which transforms it from a simple naturalistic story into a truly Kafkan riddle"[5] to the charge that he is "the one failure in a story of vivid, succinct art," that the friend is "unable to come alive [...] with the meaning that Kafka wished him to have,"[6] which assumes that there is a single, unequivocal meaning intended, if not achieved. But is there? And how relevant is such an inference?

In his discussion of the friend in Russia, Politzer has suggested that "whatever we learn about him is negative: he is absent, nameless, unmarried, unsuccessful and ailing".[7] But there is at least one detail about Georg's friend which is not merely negative, as the aspects cited by Politzer appear to be: the narrator informs us that Georg and his friend "correspond." In the German they are said to stand in a "Korrespondenzverhaltnis," a compound literally meaning "a relationship of correspondence." The obvious and immediate implication of this detail is that Georg and his friend exchange letters; but there is a secondary meaning (of corresponding *to* one another) which proves to be of even greater relevance to the story as a whole. It is not so much that all we know about the friend in Russia could be deemed negative information, but that what we learn concerning him always stands in some form of correspondence to what we know about Georg. The tokens of Georg's success, for example, are almost mathematically counterbalanced by the misfortunes suffered by his friend in Russia. During the past two years Georg's "business had developed in a most unexpected way, the staff had had to be doubled, the turnover was five times as great, no doubt about it, further progress lay just ahead." The friend, by contrast, "was wearing himself out to no purpose in a foreign country," he had "obviously run off the rails" and "all his efforts hitherto had miscarried." While Georg spent every evening "out with friends or, more recently, visited his fiancée," the friend in Russia "had no regular connection with the colony of his fellow-countrymen out there and almost no social intercourse with Russian families". (As Kate Flores observes, "it is a little hard to conceive of a business abroad which calls for no association with one's compatriots and practically none with the natives,"[8]—which indicates that the details' importance lies more in their contrastive relationship to Georg's business success *and* socializing, than in their own right.) The man about to enter on a good match is contrasted with the "permanent bachelor," the ostensibly contented self-made man with the friend who was given to complaining about his lot on his increasingly rare visits home. Georg's predominantly materialistic attitude is emphasized not only in his preoccupation with success in business, but also in the very physical way in which his relationship to his fiancée Frieda Brandenfeld is described: both by the narrator (who refers to her "breathing quickly under his kisses") and by Georg's father (especially in his charge that "because she lifted her skirts like this and this you made up to her, and in order to make free with her undisturbed [. . .]"). These two aspects of materialism are combined in Georg's repeated stress on the fact that he will be finding sexual satisfaction with "a girl from a well-to-do family." In contrast to all this, the friend's way of life seems markedly ascetic and spiritual, he is associated with an anecdote concerning a Russian priest (which will be considered later) and it has even been suggested that the beard he now wears signifies "his desire to look like a Russian monk."[9]

The chronology of "The Judgment" makes all these details seem more than a simple matter of character-antithesis. We learn that it is three years since the friend's last visit and only during the past two years has Georg's business apparently "developed in the most unexpected way." It is almost as if Georg's good fortune is in some sense dependent on his friend's absence, just as his wedding is something that he does not want his friend to attend.[10] Frieda's reaction to this attitude is highly significant: "Since you have such friends, Georg, you shouldn't ever have got engaged at all". She not only points to the marked contrast between Georg's present way of life and his friend's, but does so in a peculiarly generic way: her retort is not "since you have this friend in Russia," but "such friends." Similarly, the choice is not presented as being between Frieda and this man in St. Petersburg, but between engagement *(as a state)* and having *such* friends. The friend and Frieda are being treated as representatives or symbols of diametrically opposed ways of life.

Most interpreters of "The Judgment" have enumerated the various contrasts between the friend in Russia and Georg (and also with Frieda), but in seeking to relate these details to the question put by old Bendemann they have tended to disagree, often radically. There are those who conclude, with Politzer, that "undoubtedly the friend exists"[11] and hence see the father's question as a rhetorical move. His existence is tacitly assumed by some, with the real interest lying in the extent to which the friend in Russia, as presented in the story, is more a fiction superimposed on the real man by Georg for largely self-congratulatory reasons.[12] Others, seeing in old Bendemann's question a clue to the fact that the work is more symbolic than realistic, have interpreted the friend in Russia as a metaphorical alter ego: as a personification of the spiritual side that

Georg has betrayed in himself, [13] as a projection of his former "pure self"[14] and, in one case, even as "another side of the narrator's self."[15] Clearly, some of these readings do not exclude others, for the friend in Russia could well combine the fiction of "existing" according to the conventions of realism with a symbolic function. Yet most interpreters have decided to opt *exclusively* for just one of these possibilities. What needs to be brought out more than has been hitherto is the way in which Kafka's story plays with the issue of whether or not the friend actually exists, offering various images and parallel episodes relevant to old Bendemann's question.

Frieda's declaration that with such friends Georg should not have become engaged is countered by him with a very bold metaphor, and one that is most pertinent to the issue of his friend's existence: "I cannot cut out of myself a person who would perhaps be more suited than I am for friendship with him."[16] Assuming that friendships are based (as is implied here) on similarities of personality, we can see how Georg's image clearly concretizes the differences between him and his friend. Georg cannot cut out from his self the kind of character that would please his friend because he knows he has betrayed that side of himself—though the fact that they were friends in their youth implies that Georg once possessed such qualities. The thought that he should seek to split himself in this way is in fact typical of his self-deception and the way in which he betrays his friend. By extension, Georg's metaphor could be taken to show that the friend in Russia symbolizes that side that cannot be cut out of Georg any more: because it has already been excised or at least suppressed. However, this figurative confession is hardly satisfactory evidence in itself that the friend in Russia is a symbolic "alter ego," something complementary, cut out of Georg and therefore not existing as an independent person. It only raises this interpretive possibility, whereas elsewhere in "The Judgment" other kinds of esthetic roles are suggested for the friend in Russia.

When faced with the difficult task of breaking to his friend the news that he has become engaged to Frieda, Georg ostensibly shirks his responsibility: not by telling his friend *nothing*, but by offering him the information in a displaced form.

> And so it happened to Georg that three times in three fairly widely separated letters he had told his friend about the engagement of an unimportant man to an equally unimportant girl, until indeed, quite contrary to his intentions, his friend began to show some interest in this notable event.

As John Ellis points out, "Georg does everything he can to get the news to his friend without seeming to do so."[17] And not surprisingly, Georg's friend "began to show some interest" after it had been repeatedly relayed to him. But what also needs to be recognized here is that Georg's method of indirectly communicating with his friend closely resembles the friend's method of elsewhere transmitting information to him.

At the point where old Bendemann has put in question all his claims about the friend in Russia, Georg seeks to remind his father of the man by recalling certain earlier incidents:

> "...He used to tell us the most incredible stories of the Russian Revolution. For instance, when he was on a business trip to Kiev and ran into a riot and saw a priest on a balcony who cut a broad cross in blood on the palm of his hand and held the hand up and appealed to the mob. You've told that story yourself once or twice since."

On the surface, it might seem as though Georg is simply using this particularly memorable anecdote to prove to his father that his disputed friend in Russia really does exist: "'If you think back you're bound to remember. He used to tell us the most incredible stories [...]'". However, in citing this episode, Georg in fact merely succeeds in showing just how completely he has misunderstood its significance, and he thereby practically condemns himself out of his own mouth. For this Russian anecdote is central to the whole misunderstanding between Georg and his father, and the way in which it is told (whilst misconstrued by Georg) opens up for the reader further interpretive possibilities to the story as a whole.

The episode with the cross of blood involves motifs of self-imposed suffering, linked, by the crucifixion overtone, with martyrdom,[18] and publicly displayed self-sacrifice. One possible reading of this anecdote is that Georg's friend in Russia is trying to tell him how he should behave, and in fact prophesying how he will behave at the end of the story, after the father's judgment. (This would help to explain why old Bendemann has repeated the story once or twice since.) Self-inflicted punishment, the crucifixion motif, and suffering in public are common to both the friend's anecdote and the end of "The Judgment". Having duly received his father's sentence to "death by drowning", Georg rushes down towards the river to perform the task. And while still on the stairs, we are told, "he ran into the charwoman on her way up to do the morning cleaning of the room. 'Jesus!' she cried and covered her face with her apron, but he was already gone." Perhaps too heavy-handedly for some, with what others may find an appropriately theatrical sense of irony, the story here indicates that Bendemann's end has the same quality of self-sacrifice that the anecdote about the priest sought to convey. That "an unending stream of traffic was just going over the bridge," as Georg let himself drop from it, gives his death the same public setting that the priest's gesture has.

On the other hand, the friend's story could also be an indirect way of telling Georg about his own self-imposed suffering out there in Russia (the act of bearing witness to suffering in the one case being to hold up the stigmatized hand and show it to the mob, and in the other to communicate an image of it in letter-form). Either way, whether the friend is trying to suggest what Georg really ought to be doing or seeking to convey his own 'martyrdom', the method of statement is indirect. In talking about the priest, he is either alluding to Georg or to himself (or both of them). Politzer refers to the friend's "interest in the scenes of upheaval he has witnessed, perhaps even his sympathy with them;"[19] but one can go further than this and see the scenes of upheaval that he chooses to mention as an indirect indication that there is need for similar upheavals in the Bendemann household. The fact that Georg merely finds such tales "incredible" only serves to suggest that the method has completely failed, that the friend is preaching to the unconverted. He sees no covert message in such anecdotes; and, ironically, in seeking to demonstrate to his father that the friend really does exist, all Georg offers is proof of his own radical misunderstanding of what the man represents.

Vicarious confessions and the displacement of information are features of certain parts of "The Judgment"—in the case of Georg's references to an apparently inconsequential engagement and in the episode with the cross of blood—and the obvious extension of this pattern is to the relationship between Georg, his friend in Russia and old Bendemann.

On the particular day on which the story is set, Georg has finally put pen to paper to tell his friend of his engagement. But the surprising turn that then follows in the early part of the story lies in the importance that Georg seems to attach to going to tell his father of what he has done and in the subsequent concentration on Georg's relations with his father—to the point where the friend in Russia merely becomes a pawn in both of their games.

There is an element of displacement in all of this. Writing about his engagement seems to give Georg an opportunity to raise the matter with his father, too (indeed, this may be his main aim): "he put the letter in his pocket and went out of his room across a small lobby into his father's room, which he had not entered for months [. . .] 'I really only wanted to tell you [. . .] that I am now sending the news of my engagement to St. Petersburg.'" Georg is grudgingly praised for what he has done ("'You've come to me about this business, to talk it over with me. No doubt that does you honor'"), but the center of interest soon shifts from the issue of confessing the truth to his friend in Russia to telling "the whole truth" to his father. It is as if the friend is more a pretext than the real focus of Georg's endeavors. This does not necessarily mean, either, that the friend's existence is thus denied but his role is largely subordinate to the Georg-father relationship.

One of the most dramatic twists in the story comes at the point where old Bendemann, having repeatedly interrogated Georg about his friend, suddenly reveals his own close connections with the man:

"[...] Of course I know your friend. He would have been a son after my own heart. That's why you've been playing him false all these years. Why else? Do you think I haven't been sorry for him? And that's why you had to lock yourself up in your office—the Chief is busy, mustn't be disturbed—just so that you could write your lying little letters to Russia. But thank goodness a father doesn't need to be taught how to see through his son. And now that you thought you'd got him down, so far down that you could set your bottom on him and sit on him and he wouldn't move, then my fine son makes up his mind to get married!"

"How you amused me today, coming to ask me if you should tell your friend about your engagement. He knows it all already, you stupid boy, he knows it all! I've been writing to him [...]."

The significance of this second secret correspondence (again in both senses) between Georg's father and the friend in Russia is summed up by old Bendemann in the following terms: "'... your friend hasn't been betrayed after all! [...] I've been his representative here on the spot.'" Strictly speaking what he means is that the friend in Russia has not been *totally* betrayed, for he has had a second source of information; yet this cannot detract from the fact that he has in a way still been betrayed by Georg—something for which Georg has to be punished.

Old Bendemann's claim to have been representing the friend in Russia involves more than simply having kept him in the picture by also writing to him. Even physically and in the conditions he has to suffer, he can be seen to *represent* Georg's exiled friend. Since his wife's death the old widower is not so different from the "permanent bachelor" in St. Petersburg. Both are generally isolated, not successful at business and not enjoying the best of health. The friend's yellow skin seems to be symptomatic of "some latent disease," in Georg's eyes, and in his father's case there is the suspicion that "the business is going to undermine [his] health." Much of the following contrast between Bendemann and his son is reminiscent of the antithesis, earlier in the story, between Georg's successes and his friend's failure:

> "[...] what else was left to me, in my back room, plagued by a disloyal staff, old to the marrow of my bones? And my son strutting through the world, finishing off deals that I had prepared for him, bursting with triumphant glee and stalking away from his father with the closed face of a respectable businessman."

The parallels between Bendemann senior and the friend in Russia are most forcefully brought out in the exchange between Georg and his father about whether the latter is well covered up. Having had his whole version of reality challenged, Georg seems anxious to reduce his father to the status of a childish imbecile (whilst doing so in the guise of filial concern). In Bendemann's repeated question "Am I well covered up?" there is clearly a play on words with the father not just asking whether his son is satisfied with the way he is tucked up in bed, but whether he has succeeded (by swapping roles, exchanging rooms and generally ratifying the position of supremacy he has already begun to assume in the business) in covering up his true significance, perhaps even metaphorically burying him. In denying that he has been effectively smothered in this way, the father refers to Georg's behavior towards his friend in terms which emphasize the correspondences between them:

> "And now that you thought you'd got him down, so far down that you could set your bottom on him and sit on him and he wouldn't move, then my fine son makes up his mind to get married!"

This image of Georg sitting on his friend, whilst a vivid metaphor for suppression, might seem to be an exaggeratedly crude version of the way in which Georg was described as treating his friend in the first part of "The Judgment". There, Georg gives the impression of showing great concern for the friend:

> What could one write to such a man [. . .] a man one could be sorry for but could not help [. . .] he shrank from letting his friend know about his business success [. . .] so Georg confined himself to giving his friend unimportant items of gossip [. . .]. All he desired was to leave undisturbed the idea of the home-town which his friend must have built up to his own content during the long interval.

And yet, as Ellis' interpretation of this part of the story has demonstrated, "the obsessive length of this train of thought makes it questionable; Georg seems to be using his friend's life to dwell on his own successes, so that his thoughts seem to be more concerned with his own feelings of self-satisfaction than with his friend's welfare."[20]

A key image which reveals this—and one which is later to be dramatized in Georg's handling of his father—is that of the friend in Russia as "just a big child who should do what his successful and home-keeping friends prescribed". After he has been asked by his father whether he really has this friend in St. Petersburg, Georg begins to treat his father in exactly the same way in which he feels the friend should be treated: "'I'll put you to bed now for a little, I'm sure you need to rest. Come, I'll help you to take off your things, you'll see I can do it.'" Subsequent images of Georg carrying his father to bed "in his arms", of the father "playing with his watch-chain" like a child and then being tucked up in bed and repeatedly (like an anxious infant) asking whether he is adequately covered up, all reinforce the idea that Georg is trying to reduce his father to the role of child that he has patronizingly applied to his friend in Russia; and for a while old Bendemann plays along with Georg.

Georg's apparent concern for his father—reproaching himself for not having taken care of him, when confronted with the dingy room, the dirtiness of his father's underclothes and the generally pitiful state of his living conditions—thus becomes double-edged. Filial concern in fact turns out to be a way of seeking to gain control over the father and eliminate him with a clear conscience; and the symbolic correspondences between old Bendemann and the friend in Russia emphasize what a betrayal this will be.

However, there are not only correspondences between the friend in Russia and old Bendemann in the way in which Georg maltreats them; after the metamorphosis of Georg's father into an omniscient all-powerful figure, he and the friend are linked by a judgment motif. Bendemann tells his son that the friend "knows everything a hundred times better than you do yourself [...]"; and the image which he chooses to dramatize this fact is an Old Testament image of judgment: "[...] in his left hand he crumples your letters unopened while in his right hand he holds up my letters to read through!" Georg's father, "still a giant of a man," at one point able to threaten "I'll sweep her from your very side, you don't know how!" and exercising absolute power over the life and death of his son, is an equally patriarchal judge-figure. Just as the way in which the friend "judges" Georg via his letters is described with a Biblical image, so the sentence ordered by Georg's father is accompanied by a series of religious overtones. Both father and friend are described as omniscient figures in the latter part of Kafka's story: "He knows everything a hundred times better than you do yourself" Georg is told; "Ten thousand times!" Georg said, to make fun of his father, but in his very mouth the words turned into deadly earnest. Of the father we learn: "His insight made him radiant".

A complete *volte-face* takes place in "The Judgment" concerning the presentation of the friend in Russia: the figure who during the first half appeared to be the friend, albeit the betrayed friend, of Georg Bendemann now emerges standing in alliance with his father. The contrasts between Georg's success and his friend's failure are mirrored by a whole series of parallels between the friend and the father. Both in his actions and in the way he was obliged to live by Georg's neglect, old Bendemann had become the friend's "representative here on the spot." Georg's father, sitting in an ill-lit room with only an old newspaper and surrounded by breakfast remains corresponds to the friend in Russia, cut off from the truth by Georg (contrast the later image of the father's being "radiant" with knowledge), with only out-of-date news and "lost in the vastness of Russia [. . .]. Among the wreckage of his show-cases, the slashed remnants of his wares, the falling gas-brackets [. . .]" (another image suggesting lack of light). And ironically, because all of Georg's proud signs of outward success so confidently rehearsed in the first part of the story turn out to be deceptive, there is in fact a parallel between the early Georg's condescending view of his friend and what he himself turns out to be. Like the friend's (as Georg sees him), "all his efforts hitherto had miscarried;" just as he tends to think of the friend as "just a big child," so Georg in turn becomes a "stupid boy," a "child," in his father's eyes. The tables have been turned and the symbolic correspondences have become uncrossed.

This reversal of the situation is, however, not as completely unprepared for as it might at first appear to be. That Georg must in some way sense the fact that his father is his friend's "representative here on the spot" is indicated by the fact that he is more concerned with talking to him about the contents of his letter than in going off to post it. Having practically forced his father's hand, Georg does suffer something of a relapse, though: having told part of the truth to his friend in Russia and his father and yet still trying to minimize the implications of marriage for his friendship, Georg is encouraged by his father to draw the ultimate conclusions from his position and decide one way or the other. But instead of facing up to this choice, Georg puts up a smoke-screen ("A thousand friends wouldn't make up to me for my father") and then proceeds to entertain a course of action which will betray both friend and father. And yet despite this final aberration, which is largely a token of panic, Georg's behavior is not absolutely reprehensible. He has obvious difficulty in deciding between the world represented by

Frieda and that symbolized by his friend in Russia. He still remains in contact with his friend, even if the relationship is one of betrayal and deceit. The religious motif of denial—the friend's living in *St. Peter*sburg, Kafka's use of the same verb for 'denying' as Luther's Bible uses for Peter's betrayal of Christ, and the various plays on the notion of triple denials (telling about an unimportant engagement three times) or refusing to answer leading questions "at least twice"—all relate to the notion of denying with a guilty conscience. The alacrity with which Georg seizes on Frieda's suggestion that he ought to tell his friend of their engagement, the way he goes to tell his father and the readiness with which he accepts his father's judgment all bear out the idea that the betrayal has been far from absolute. It is almost as if there were still two sides to Georg: the Georg who locks himself in his office at work to write deceitful letters to his friend, and the Georg who, appropriately, decides on this particular Sunday to write and tell him the news that he has become engaged.

Having seen the way in which the relationship between Georg, his friend and his father are re-aligned in the latter half of "The Judgment", so that Georg's view of the world is stood on its head, one is still left with the fundamental question of what father and friend themselves represent. Two possibly contradictory solutions would seem to suggest themselves here.

The father's pronouncements, just before passing sentence, would seem to imply that Georg's main guilt is one of egocentricity. "So now you know what else there is in the world besides yourself, till now you've known only about yourself! An innocent child, yes, that you were, truly, but still more truly have you been a devilish human being!" This penetrating accusation appears to support a realistic reading of the story, with both the friend in Russia and old Bendemann as independent human beings (rather than projections of suppressed parts of his own personality), as people betrayed by him. All the mawkish details of old Bendemann's badly lit room, his dirty underwear and neglect at the hands of his son, could all be taken to corroborate such an interpretation of where Georg's guilt lies.

If this is his principal offense, then there is a great deal of irony to the way Georg behaves when under pressure in the middle of the story.

He had not yet explicitly discussed with his bride-to-be what arrangements should be made for his father in the future, for they had both of them silently taken it for granted that the old man would go on living alone in the old house. But now he made a quick, firm decision to take him into his own future establishment.

Yet Georg's father seems as irreconcilably opposed to this marriage as Frieda is to Georg's remaining on friendly terms with the man in Russia. Any move to have old Bendemann living under the same roof as Frieda and himself would be the very opposite of the kind of care Georg is pretending to show! There is a double irony to his protestations of concern and the "quick, firm decision" he takes. The form his solution takes shows no appreciation of his father's position, and thus substantiates the charge that he has "known only about himself." Added to which is the irony that such a display of humanity, even if it were in the right terms, has come too late to be anything but an evasive ploy: "It almost looked, on closer inspection, as if the care he meant to lavish there on his father might come too late". Just as he had earlier tried to keep his friend and marry Frieda, so here Georg wishes to marry against his father's wishes and even move his father into "his own future establishment." It is clear that the only action which would satisfy his father would be for Georg to remain a bachelor—which in a sense his father makes him do, for as well as punishing him for his behavior, the ultimate death sentence also ensures that he does not marry Frieda.

Other details in "The Judgment" suggest a different kind of guilt on Georg's part than that of ignoring the world outside himself. The man in St. Petersburg is specifically a friend from Georg's youth, there is a reference to "the face Georg had known so well since childhood" and the father, the friend's representative here on the spot, is condemning Georg in the

name of his friend in particular—not just on behalf of the
world outside this young man, whose claims he has chosen to
ignore. What unites Georg and his Russian correspondent is
not so much "their common bachelorhood"[21] (which is merely
part of the catalyst) but the fact that they once understood one
another and have now grown estranged. The distance between
them is a symbol of this; Georg's exclamation "Why did he
have to go so far away!" could in fact, if he were honest enough,
be reversed and expressed as self-accusation: "Why have I
moved so far away from him?" It is significant that when Georg
is in the process of obeying his father's judgment and enacting
the self-sacrifice which his friend's anecdote about the blood-
cross sought to encourage, he is referred to as swinging himself
over the railings of the bridge "like the distinguished gymnast
he had once been in his youth." It is as if the gulf between
Georg and his pristine state, in which he enjoyed the friendship
of the young man in Russia, has been bridged by this act of self-
sacrifice. That Georg, in his growing materialism, has betrayed
a largely spiritual, ascetic friend from his youth (who bears no
individuating name, unlike all other characters in the story),
who is known to his father and has not returned since Georg's
mother died, would all seem to invite interpretation as a picture
of a man betraying some of his own potential—seeking, and yet
unable, to suppress it completely.

These two kinds of guilt—the guilt of ego-centricity and that
of trying to betray part of oneself—are interwoven in the story.
The fact that in denying part of himself Georg betrays
responsibilities to others and even fails to understand the world
outside himself is presented in a story where it is impossible to
distinguish categorically between a realistic depiction of one
man's relationship to those around him and a kind of
externalized[22] psycho-drama, where father, friend and Georg
all represent aspects of the same person. And the symbolic
correspondences between the main figures in "The Judgment"
also both serve to highlight Georg's ego-centricity and at the
same time make more vivid his betrayal of himself.

NOTES

1. This, and all following quotations from "The Judgment", are based on the Muirs' translation. In places a more literal rendering has been found necessary in order to bring out certain of the implications inherent in the German.

2. See Magny's "The Objective Depiction of Absurdity". *KP*, 75-96.

3. This reading has been suggested by Politzer: *F.K.*, 57, and Sokel: *F.K.T.I.*, 56. The main argument for such an interpretation is offered by the following sentence in "The Judgment": "Oh yes. To your friend, said the father, with peculiar emphasis."

4. Ellis: "Kafka: 'Das Urteil'." 199.

5. Flores, K.: "The Judgment". *FKT*, 10.

6. Greenberg: *Terror of Art*, 59 f.

7. Greenberg: *Op. cit.*, 55.

8. Flores, K.: *Op. cit.*, 13.

9. Politzer: *Op. cit.*, 56.

10. Since old Bendemann's view of the friend substantiates largely the picture given by Georg, it seems likely that the details of his predicament, although stylized to emphasize the contrast with Georg's successes (Cf. Ellis: *Op. cit.*, 192 ff.), are fundamentally correct.

11. Politzer: *Op. cit.*, 57.

12. This aspect is explored in great detail by Ellis.

13. See H.S. Reiss: *F.K. Eine Betrachtung seines Werkes*. Heidelberg: L. Schneider. 1952, 43.

14. Sokel: *Op. cit.*, 45.

15. Greenberg: *Op. cit.*, 53.

16. The Muirs' translation of this ["I can't cut myself to another pattern that might make a more suitable friend for him"] obscures the point that it is not simply a matter of Georg changing his outline to some degree, but of being unable to find within his present self the makings of a friend for the man in Russia.

17. Ellis: *Op. cit.*, 197.

18. The priest is not "spreading the gospel with blood on his hands" (Ellis: *Op. cit.*, 210); such a description suggests the blood of others, whereas this is the blood of self-sacrifice.

19. Politzer: *Op. cit.*, 56.

20. Ellis: *Op. cit.*, 193.

21. Politzer: *Op. cit.*, 54.

22. Sokel stresses the latter possibility, seeing the story as an example of a "classically Expressionist" narrative structure (*Op. cit.*, 49).

J. P. Stern

Guilt and the Feeling of Guilt

1.

"The Judgment" is one of the few stories Kafka was proud of having written and continued to find satisfactory; with it begins the work of his maturity. It was composed in the night from September 22 to 23, 1912, and published later that year. It is dedicated to "F", Felice Bauer, whom Kafka had met for the first time that summer; the peculiar irony of the dedication is patent to any reader.

I have chosen it for interpretation for three closely connected reasons. First, as an outstanding and outstandingly clear example of the way Kafka draws autobiographical material into his fictions.[1] An interpretation of the story should therefore illuminate one side of his literary undertaking, the other side of which is the fictionalizing of his autobiographical and private writings. Secondly, the story is characteristic of a preoccupation central to the overwhelming majority of his writings and patent in their titles—his preoccupation with guilt, punishment, and the law according to which these are connected and assessed. It is, clearly, a moral preoccupation. Thirdly, the story is an early but accomplished example of a certain rather puzzling but if anything even more characteristic narrative manner of conveying that preoccupation: a way of

114

writing which seems to be especially designed to insinuate and establish the connection between a certain kind of action or state of being and its punishment in the face of the reader's expectations to the contrary. For all its apparent simplicity, this narrative manner amounts to one of the most astonishing inventions in twentieth century German and European fiction.

2.

The fact that all Kafka's important works are marked by strong autobiographical elements is one among several reasons why any interpretation of them should proceed with particular caution. They remain of course fictions. There is, however, an especial temptation to read into them attitudes, ideas, and evaluations not found there but in his diaries, letters, or other documents. The autobiographical pendant to "The Judgment" is Kafka's "Letter to his Father", written seven years later. I shall quote from it here because it provides several pointers to an understanding of a story that is difficult, not in order to impose on the story an evaluation and a meaning derived from the "Letter" but missing from the story itself (which is what many critics have done). The story is as complete as any Kafka ever wrote. How complete *that* is, we shall see.

Kafka's letter to his father, which was never sent,[2] is intended to describe and account for the unhappy relationship between father and son, and it does this mainly by analyzing specific episodes ("Vorfalle") from the son's childhood and adolescence. Here is one of these episodes:

One night I kept on whimpering for water, not, I am certain, because I was thirsty, but probably partly to be annoying, partly to amuse myself. After several vigorous threats had failed to have any effect you took me out of bed, carried me on to the balcony and left me there alone for a little while in my nightshirt, outside the shut door. I am not going to say that this was wrong, perhaps at that time there was really no other way of getting peace and quiet that night, but I mention it as typical of your methods of bringing up a child and to characterize the effect of those methods on me. I dare say after that I was obedient all right, but I was left inwardly damaged. That senseless request for water—for me the most natural thing in the world—and the extraordinary terror of being carried outside were two things which I, my nature being what it was, could never properly connect with each other.

There is no need to expatiate on the nature of this traumatic experience (which reads like a textbook case from *Imago*, Freud's contemporary psycho-analytical journal[4]), but two aspects of the letter-writer's description of it need emphasizing. First, his scrupulous, perhaps over-scrupulous attempt to see the event from the father's point of view. There was in all probability no good reason for the child's complaining (which, moreover, is referred to quite coldly as "ich winsele": "I kept on whimpering"); the horrendous action (which, for the father, lasted only "a little while": "ein Weilchen") is not called wrong or unjust; and, in any event, ("all right": "wohl schon" again impersonates the father's attitude), the action had its intended result. We shall see that this concern to say all that is to be said on the other (here it is the father's) side is not a piece of empty rhetoric, but a substantial part of the narrative manner. The second remarkable thing about the passage is its brief and simple yet circumspect statement of that dominant preoccupation which I have mentioned at the outset. No objective law or conception of justice is invoked: "I, my nature being what it was, could never properly *connect*" the supposed crime with its terrible punishment.... In story after story this attempt to connect will be made, but we shall see that in the course of the attempt the narrator will muster all conceivable evidence against its being successful.

What makes the "Letter" the remarkable thing it is (rather than a tedious and embarrassingly explicit exercise in family recriminations is its literary quality. The following passage is built round a metaphor, in itself rather unpromising, of the almighty father in his easy chair. However, it is not the metaphor itself but the way it is explored that matters. For here is the place where a merely private and autobiographically meaningful observation is transformed into a literary and thus commonly valid image—the very place where a private grievance becomes art:

> You had worked your way up alone, by your own energies, so you had unbounded confidence in your opinion. As a matter of fact, for me as a child that was not as dazzling as later for the growing young man. From your armchair you ruled the world. Your opinion was right, every other opinion was crazy, wild, meschugge,[5] not normal. With all this, your self-confidence was so great that you had no need to be consistent at all and yet never ceased to be in the right. It might even happen that you had no opinion at all about something, therefore all possible opinions on that matter were bound to be wrong, without exception. You were capable, for instance, of berating the Czechs, and then the Germans, and then the Jews, not only selectively but wholesale, until in the end nobody was left but yourself. You took on for me that enigmatic quality which belongs to all tyrants whose right is founded not in reason, but in their persons. At least that is the way it seemed to me.[6]

The scene is not without its grim humor, which derives from the consequential way in which the numerous implications—indeed all possible implications—of "the tyrant in the armchair" are examined.

Almost any letter-writer with sufficient animus could enumerate such a list of pet hatreds ("the Czechs, the Germans, the Jews..."). But to give that list the stamp of exhaustiveness, to frame it as an image of absolute solipsism, with its inescapable premise of "no opinion = all opinions are false" and its equally compelling conclusion, "so that finally nobody was left but you," is to go beyond the autobiographical occasion and to be engaged on a literary enterprise.

It is an enterprise that involves descriptive powers of a very high order:

> Your mere physical presence was enough to depress me. I remember for instance how we often used to undress together in the same cabin. There was I, skinny, frail, slight, you strong, tall, broad. Even inside the cabin I felt a miserable specimen, not only in your eyes, but in the eyes of the whole world, for you were for me the measure of all things. But then, when we came out of the cabin to face everybody, with me holding your hand, a little skeleton, unsteady, barefoot on the boards, afraid of the water, unable to copy your swimming-strokes which you, with the best of intentions but actually to my profound humiliation, kept on showing me—then I was frantic with desperation, and at such moments all my bad experiences in all spheres fitted magnificently together.[7]

The vivid, poignant elaboration of this contrast is obvious. But what are we to make of that "all my bad experiences in all spheres fitted magnificently together," with which the passage closes? Kafka's writing, like the writing of most major German authors of his time, is informed by a powerful literary self-consciousness—a consciousness of the kind of thing he is doing and of the literary ends he is pursuing.[8] The insight that is here ascribed to the little boy is sophisticated. We are told that he saw how all these awful episodes of suppression and deprivation *fitted together* into one picture, and that there was something magnificent in that harmony of horrors. Was the boy really capable of that vision? We do not know. What is clear is that this is what the mature writer hoped to achieve in his fictions. This is the strange "congruence" and harmony he aimed at—again, at the greatest odds against achieving it that his powerful imagination could devise.

3.

Our story has for its theme the father-son conflict. There is nothing remarkable about that, especially in view of its date of composition. 1912 is commonly held to be the first year of the Expressionist revolution in German literature[9] and, from Friedrich Sorge's *Der Bettler* onwards, the father-son conflict is a favorite theme of Expressionist writers; what Kafka shares with them and with Frank Wedekind, their immediate literary ancestor, is the conveyed conviction that this is a conflict of life and death. With this goes a remarkable heightening of the figure of the father—something quite like a physical exaggeration—so that in the penultimate scene of the story he stands before us more like a giant than a human being. Numerous Expressionists were concerned to underline their meanings by ascribing to their literary characters some real or apparent physical abnormality. Such devices, too, were common to Prague German writers like Gustav Meyrink and Paul Leppin, with whose works Kafka was familiar. (It is not often realized how close he came to being stuck in that literature of provincial sensationalism; nor is the fact that throughout his life he never met a single important writer outside this circle.) In Kafka's story the sensational is avoided because the transition from the realistic to the surrealistic or fantastic is gradual. The father appears as a giant, but only to the extent that we see him through the eyes of the son.

These two things, then—the theme of conflict and the heightening of the hostile father, implying a diminution of the threatened son—are the sum total of Kafka's involvement in contemporary German literature.[10] Everything else about the story is, as far as I can see, wholly novel and original.

4.

The story ends with the son's suicide by drowning:
He was still clinging on with ever weakening grasp, and then, glimpsing between the railings a bus which would easily drown the sound of his fall, he called softly: "But I always did love you, dear parents", and he let himself fall. At that moment an almost endless stream of traffic was passing over the bridge.

The son, Georg Bendemann, kills himself in strict and immediate compliance with his father's verdict:

And therefore know this: I sentence you now to death by drowning!

This verdict in turn comes at the climax of a violent quarrel, or rather a lethal attack which the father has been conducting against his son. The discussion between the two of them, held in the dark, airless bedroom at the rear of the Bendemanns' house in which the father has been living since his wife's death, begins peaceably enough; it is occasioned by the son's visit to his father. Georg Bendemann has come to show his father a letter which he had written, a little while before, to his— Georg's friend, who has been living for several years in distant Russia. The letter itself, which Georg is writing in the first scene of the story, appears to be intended partly to renew contact with the distant friend whom Georg Bendemann is conscious of having neglected, and partly to inform his friend that he, Georg, has now become engaged and is about to marry a girl called Frieda Brandenfeld. And here, in the briefest outline, we have the whole story.

I have retold it backwards in order to enable us to concentrate straight away on the central issue that is bound to occupy us as readers of the story. I mean the question how reasonable, how acceptable we find the verdict of death at the end; what narrative connection we may discern between the bulk of the tale and its catastrophic conclusion; what Georg Bendemann has done to deserve such a verdict; or more generally, what is the manner of Kafka's motivation. We are asking about the nature of that "congruence" of which Kafka speaks in the "Letter to his Father".

The model is the situation of the child standing on the dark balcony. In Kafka's account of that situation there was, as we have seen, a measure of guilt in the child's conduct. His transgressions, however, were not enough to explain the monstrous punishment, to "connect" it, as Kafka put it, with the crime. What was added, in the "Letter", was the element of might, of sheer physical power which overrode all considerations of justice.

This is not the situation in "The Judgment". Certainly not in the physical sense of the word. The father never physically coerces the son at all. What takes the place of brutal physical force cannot be anything other than the authority behind the father's command. The question then arises, what that authority is based on. The possibility of an external sanction or appeal is not broached at all. In the situation that Kafka presents to us (and this is the measure of his convincingness) it never occurs to us to ask what the father could do if the son chose to disobey his order. The structure of this authoritative situation—indeed of any authoritative situation—is based on the acknowledgment of authority by one side, by him who obeys. This acknowledgment in turn can only occur where he who obeys is in some sense, and it must here be a psychic, mental sense—weaker than the authority. And this weakness, finally, in the situation of "The Judgment", springs from a feeling of guilt.

5.

It is here that critics of Kafka's work usually interpolate the word "ambiguity". They argue or imply that the ambiguity (or "ambivalence") of the subject's situation is identical with, or tantamount to, his feeling of guilt. The argument certainly looks plausible, but that does not make it valid. Ambiguity— here or in any wider context—is not the same either as guilt or a feeling of guilt. This much is obvious. But since Georg Bendemann's guilt is unclear, and may well turn out to be inadequate or incommensurate with the punishment that is meted out to him and that he accepts, it is then argued that it is this inadequate guilt which is ambiguous. This too, however, is a misconception. And in calling it that we have respectable linguistic usage on our side. When we read in a newspaper that an old woman has been sentenced to two years in jail for lifting a bag of sugar from a grocery store we do not commonly say that the judge has been ambiguous, but we do say that he has been unjust.

The point to insist on[11] is that this whole notion of ambiguity has been badly overworked in Kafka criticism (and in literary criticism generally; but that is another story). It may well be that some of his stories *end* ambiguously, leaving two or more options open for a development that never comes. (Whether or not he wrote fictions of this kind, "The Judgment" is not one of them.) But stories, that is connnected narratives of an action however peculiar, cannot *contain* ambiguities, they are composed of elements which cease to be ambiguous the moment they are connected in a story-line. Every situation A inside a story is followed by "and then B happened." Whether or not B was adequately connected with A, B could only happen *as part of that story* if the choices available at A were either explicitly reduced to one, or can be seen to have been so reduced.

6.

And this is the case in our story. We have spoken of Georg Bendemann's feeling of guilt—not his guilt but his feeling of guilt. This is adumbrated in various ways throughout the first two-thirds of the text. A powerful example of it occurs in the third paragraph, when he considers whether he ought not to have written to his friend more fully and more candidly. Rather than quote the passage in full I shall paraphrase its main narrative line without following its exact wording and syntax, emphasizing merely its logical connections:

What should "one" write to such a man? One feels sorry for him but cannot help him. One may offer advice: come back, take up your old friendships again, rely on your friends. *No reason* why she should not do this. *But:* is this not an insult? Would it not be an intimation of his failure, of the shamefulness of his return, his friend's superiority? Anyway: *in that [wholly hypothetical] case*, is there any point in bringing him back home? Would one's advice not go unheeded? *In that case* he would remain in Russia after all, more estranged and embittered by the well-meant advice than before. But *if he did follow the advice?* Assuming that on his return he did fail in business and found himself pushed to the wall? Now he would be floundering with his friends' help *and without* it—find himself deprived of his home country and friends alike. Would it not be better, *in that [equally hypothetical] case*, if he remained abroad after all? Is there, *in those [hypothetical] circumstances*, any chance of his really succeeding at home? *These are the reasons* why, if "one" wished to maintain this correspondence at all, one could not send him any real news, etc. etc....

I take this passage to be exemplary of Kafka's mode of writing, of what is frequently singled out as his "ambiguity"; there are at least two other similar passages in our story. The process of deliberation is taking place in Georg Bendemann's mind. It is nothing if not eminently reasonable. Bendemann is putting himself in his friend's position, and yet he is addressing not his friend but his conception of that friend. It is a fictive dialogue in which the one stable thing is his assumption that every suggestion (every "advice") will be taken in the wrong way; a chess party *en solitaire*, in which he assumes that his friend is his opponent and that the opponent's every new move will be false. This is the condition—apparently the only condition—under which Georg Bendemann is capable of forming his conception of his friend.

When we have come to the end of this passage we have a feeling of exhaustion. It seems to us that not just every relevant but every possible point of view has been considered, every assertion once made has been taken back again. But this is not so. For we realize that at the end of it a definite platform has been reached, that we have descended one step lower than the level on which Georg Bendemann's story began. The upshot of the exhaustive argument is quite clear: the relationship appears in a very peculiar light. We ask whether in fact this is a real friend at all, whether the ties that bind Georg to him are really those of friendship. The answer we are bound to give is again clear: they are less than the ties of genuine friendship. Two pages later Kafka will again take back a part of this argument. He will show that there is enough of a bond for Georg to feel the need to tell his friend about his engagement to "a young girl from a well-to-do family." But this again is a move which is not only a sign of a positive feeling for his friend. More than that, it is partly dictated to his fear that the friend might find out about the engagement, partly it is the sign of an anxious obligation Georg feels—friendships, we note are not normally hedged in by anxious obligations—to tell his friend about his own more fortunate prospects, and in this sense to free himself from this friendship, to repudiate it by moving away, into married life. And so the invitation to his own wedding which Georg pens at the end of his letter *seems* ambiguous: and when, finally, he leaves the decision of whether or not his friend should attend the wedding to him, he more or less clearly expresses the hope that the friend will not come. I dwell on this detail in order to point to the extraordinary narrative triumph that is achieved here, where the words on the page are assembled ostensibly to assert proposition A but in reality—and I do not mean any obscure, hidden reality, but the narrative reality conveyed through the text—but in reality assert *nonA*. To assert a weak *nonA* is not an ambiguity.

But what is the purpose of this peculiar narrative feat? What is the point of asserting *nonA* through an ostensible A? In this complicated and yet astonishingly sparse and economical way Kafka is conveying a psychological situation of the utmost weakness, the psychic dimensions of a feeling of guilt. Such a situation, you will remember was necessary to the structure of the story, it was necessary if the father's authority was to be effective, if the author was to show at least a foothold for that authority in the mind of the subject.

The objective facts in which this feeling of guilt is founded are few and, coming to them with our own normal way of measuring guilt, we are likely to find them trivial, inadequate. Let me briefly enumerate them. It is a fact that Georg has been neglecting his friend. He has also been neglecting his father. The dark back room is a sign of that, and so is his initially condescending tone towards the father. While making plans for his forthcoming marriage, he has toyed with the idea of letting his father live alone. Now we come to further facts: his getting ready to marry; his getting on in the world and doing well in the family business from which the father has now retired; has retired, and this is important again, at the moment when his wife—Georg's mother—died. But these latter facts cannot be counted as accruing to an objectively valid guilt as we calculate guilt, in the same way that the first set of facts I mentioned—the neglect of the friend and of the father—are objective facts of guilt. Is he guilty because he intends to get married? Most critics say he is. But the fact is that we know too little about his relationship with his fiancée (other than the father's condemnation of it) to answer the question. The critics tell us that in ceasing to be a bachelor Georg is betraying an important ideal. We do not know. If (as we shall see) the ultimate accusation is one of heedless egocentricity, then getting married might be at least as good a way of curing that as remaining a bachelor.

In order to make Georg Bendemann an obedient subject to the father's authority—in order to make the subject into a victim—Kafka employs endless variations on that strange and complex narrative method we have examined. He establishes a kind of spider's web of insinuations by uniting the objective and subjective strands of guilt, so that we seem unable to distinguish between them; and at the very point where we are prepared to accept them as one—as objective guilt deserving of the punishment the hero receives—he shows us that they are not one, that the subjective strand, without which the guilt would be inadequate, is indeed subjective and arbitrary. To put it another way: the author endows a partly arbitrary ("subjective") law with the validity and power of a wholly objective law, *and shows that this is what he is doing*. Or, finally: he shows us the working of an oxymoron called "subjective law".

7.

I have spoken of the originality of Kafka's undertaking, and it is clear that this strange disposition of mind, in which guilt and feeling of guilt are conjoined without being coextensive, is apt to strike us as a thoroughly modern, twentieth century phenomenon. In a fuller account of Kafka's work it could be shown that here lies its prophetic aspect, that in showing this psychic disposition at work he is intimating the darkest parts of the psychology of terror as it was practiced in the German and Russian concentration camps years after his own death. What does not seem to have been noted, however, is the fact that this state of mind was familiar to the least "Kafkaesque" of German poets—I mean to Goethe. I know no closer parallel in all literature to what is being conveyed here than the maledictory lines that "Sorge" addresses to the aged Faust—"Soll er gehen, soll er kommen/Der Entschlub ist ihm genommen/...."—all the way to his "being prepared for Hell."[12] But of course this is only part of the picture Goethe presents, whereas it dominates Kafka's entire vision of man.

8.

So far we have looked at the situation from the subject's point of view. But this is only one half of the story. For just as Georg descends step by step ever deeper into the abyss of his deprivation, so the father rises higher and higher in his position of authority. And indeed, the two movements are connected: the more passively and weakly authority is acknowledged, the more firmly it is enacted. When the father first appears, it is he who is weak, senile, he seems not quite right in the head. The images of neglect—the toothless mouth, the slightly soiled underwear, the unread old newspaper, the dark room—all these work both ways. They show the end of a situation in which Georg has wielded power, that has now become the situation from which spring the objective elements in his guilt, but at the same time they show the first and lowest step from which the father begins his climb to power. The father begins his ascent by doubting the reality of his son's friend. He does this in the course of a long rigmarole full of suspicions he has about transactions in the business:

"In the business quite a few things escape my notice, perhaps nobody is concealing them from me—I'm not now going to assume that they *are* concealed from me— I'm not strong enough any more, my memory is going, I no longer have an eye for all these things. In the first place it is nature taking its course, and in the second place the death of your dear mother depressed me much more than it did you. But because we are just on the subject, this letter I mean, I beg you, Georg, don't deceive me. It is such a small matter, it's not worth the breath, so don't deceive me. What about this friend of yours in Petersburg?"

The function of this argument is twofold: first, and quite obviously, it does, as I suggested, show the nadir of the father's position, where he himself acknowledges that his senility causes him to forget things (an objective fact). At the same time this suspicion is the first more or less clear indication of the hostility between the two of them and to this we must add *the accusation* that since the mother's death the son has been intent on overpowering the father. This again, you will have noticed, is slightly taken away again—"in the first place it is nature taking its course"—but the accusation remains.

But there is another reason for the father's denial of the friend's reality at this stage. It is the father's implied suggestion that as a consequence of Georg's gradual betrayal, the friend is not a genuine friend any more, that he has ceased to exist as a friend for Georg, and this fact will therefore make it particularly consistent for the father, in his ascent on the ladder of power, to appropriate the friend, to show that he has been in secret communication with him all along, that he has been conspiring against Georg in order to bring about, in concert with the distant friend, Georg's destruction.

Again, the formulations are vertiginous: the emphasis is presumably on "Do you really have this *friend in Petersburg?*"[13] But the subjective evaluation "he is no *friend* of yours!" is made as nearly in the form of the objective statement "there is no such person, it's all your invention and joke"—as it is possible to make it:

> You haven't got a friend in Petersburg. You always were a joker and you couldn't leave off, even with me. How could you have a friend there, of all places!

All these details, then, are assembled in defiance of any ordinary notion of verisimilitude. Kafka quite deliberately stacks the cards against himself, making the father's gradual rise to power as difficult, as ostensibly improbable as he possibly can. And what follows now could be called "Description of a Struggle" (the title of one of Kafka's earliest stories) if it were a real fight. But the point is precisely the diminution of a fight, the ebbing away of it. As the father rises in his bed, growing as it were into a giant statue so that his hands touch the ceiling and his nightshirt barely covers his thighs (like all incipiently funny situations in Kafka's work, the joke of it is likely to die upon our lips as we follow the story), so he launches his full invective against the son's proposal to marry, which in the consistency of the accusation, but only in that consistency, comes to figure as a betrayal:

> "Because she lifted her skirts," his father began to trill, "because she lifted her skirts like this, the revolting creature," and by way of illustration he lifted his nightshirt so high that his war scar could be seen on his thigh, "because she lifted her skirts like this, and this, and this, you tried to get off with her..."

We recall a passage from "Letter to his Father" seven years later: "She probably put on some special blouse or other, the way those Prague Jewesses know how to, and on the strength of that you naturally decided to marry her..."

9.

Here now, in some detail, we have the double movement at work in the story: the descent into deprivation on the son's part, the ascent to the seat of authority on the father's. The result is that we can no longer distinguish—the whole force of the narrative urges us to abandon the distinction—between objective guilt and neurosis, between objective guilt and neurosis, between guilt and feeling of guilt. And the final moment of the verdict sums up both the content of the story and the form in which the content was achieved:

> And louder: 'So now you know what else existed outside yourself, until now you've known only about yourself. You were an innocent child, that's indeed true, but what's even truer is that you were a devilish human being. And so know this: I sentence you now to death by drowning!'

The verdict indicates the overall content of the story. For we can now see the entire finely-spun argument in which guilt and feeling of guilt were combined leads to this accusation; that all Georg's acts and thoughts have in common his exclusive preoccupation with himself; that he measures everything around him in terms of his own hopes and fears. It is more than egocentricity, it is a kind of moral solipsism. And the sentence *Until now you've known only about yourself* accurately sums up his life as we know it from the story. We may think that this kind of preoccupation with the self does not merit the verdict it receives. We could hardly think otherwise and yet continue to live. Kafka on the other hand is conducting in his writings (and also incidentally, in his life) experiments in absolute morality. If Georg's life has been informed by such a solipsism, he tells us, then once that solipsism has been destroyed, that life has nothing to support it and the verdict of death is the consequential and appropriate verdict on that life. And in this way Kafka does what some of the greatest writers of all times have done: he illuminates and challenges our habitual moral judgments. But that absolute morality is tarnished—is itself liable to be challenged—since it is being administered by agents whose authority is partial and subjective only. This may not invalidate the summary *Until now you've known only about yourself,* but it certainly throws doubt on the justice of the verdict. It is as if the Christian moral doctrine (e.g. St. Matthew 8:28, "whosoever looketh on a woman to lust after her hath committed adultery with her already in his heart") were presented to us as the ideology of a power-corrupted demiurge.

The verdict indicates also the form of our story, in the sentence:

> You were an innocent child, that's indeed true, but what's even truer is that you were a devilish human being.

It serves as a kind of summary of Kafka's narrative method. The sentence *looks* as though it were an example of the ambiguity his prose is said to affect—an assertion taken back by a counter-assertion. Yet the two statements do not cancel each other out, just as the meaning of the invitation that was not an invitation was not cancelled out. For the second statement is introduced by *what is even truer* and thus remains unchallenged: indeed, it is not the truth, but the truth as the father in his wrath sees it. And these—the apparent cancellation that is not a real one; the partial withdrawal that yet results in a further degradation— these are the patterns that dominate both the texture and the situational logic of Kafka's fiction.

Time and again critics have identified the father-figure of "The Judgment" with some Christian or Judaic or secular notion of absolute justice. Yet in the lines immediately following the verdict we read:

> Georg felt hounded from the room, the crash with which his father hit the bed behind him was still sounding in his ears as he left.

Not only does the son descend into the pit of his degradation as the father rises to the height of his authority, but at the same time the son rises up into a sphere beyond his solipsism ("But I always did love you, dear parents" are Georg's last words before he jumps to his death). Accepting the punishment he less than fully deserved, the son rises into the sphere of righteousness which the father had usurped, while the father descends towards and is sullied with the son's guilt in the act of meting out that punishment from a position of authority less than fully warranted.

Only now the pattern and the rhythm are complete—as complete as, in Kafka, they ever will be: this is the choreography of the lethal dance, the "magnificent congruence". The movements in this strange dance belong partly to a moral scheme—to the extent that the son's guilt is involved; and partly to a psychological scheme—to the extent that his feeling of guilt is involved. The two flow into each other. The resources of Kafka's art are employed to make it as hard as possible for us to prize open the connection. Yet when we do so we are left with a father whose authority is in the last resort arbitrary—psychic force without full moral sanction. And here the story ends. In an important, not accidental way Kafka's work is fragmentary. That last gap between crime and punishment is never quite closed, an incommensurability remains and is shown to remain. To fill that gap he would have to write out the objective law (there is no other) according to which sentence is passed; to validate it by a positive covenant, by an image of a righteous authority. Who says the father is just? There is no image of the just father. Kafka does not give us such an image. He gives us the dark side of the moon. He does little to strengthen our hope that this is only one half. His unique prose is designed to persuade us that he who reports from those parts has "nothing but [his] experiences"[14] to go by, and that these experiences are limited. This is the measure of his truthfulness.

NOTES

1. See Erich Heller's introduction to *LFe*.
2. For details, see Wagenbach: *F.K.*, 8 and 339, and his *Franz Kafka*. Hamburg: rororo. 1968, pp. 120-122.
3. F.K.: "Letter to his Father," in *DF*.
4. "Thoughts about Freud" are mentioned in the entry for Sept. 23, 1923, in D 2.
5. "Meschugge" is Yiddish for crazy.
6. F.K.: "Letter to his Father." The passage could serve as a motto to one of the most remarkable books of our time—H. Picker's *Hitlers Tischgesprache*, ed. Schramm, Hillgruber, Vogt. Stuttgart: 1965. See e.g., the passage on lawyers (pp. 224 ff.), the English (p. 279), and the Jews (*passim*).
7. F.K.: "Letter to his Father."
8. See Heller & Beug: *F.K.*
9. See the chapter on "1912" in Michael Hamburger's *Reason and Energy*. N.Y., 1957; also Politzer: *F.K.*
10. I leave to one side Sokel's plea for Kafka's "classical expressionism"—see his *F.K.T.I.*
11. I am here indebted to Ludwig Wittgenstein's argument in *The Blue Book*. Oxford, 1958, pp. 33-34.
12. Goethe's *Faust*, Part II, Act 5, lines 11471-11486 [Ed. Note: in Philip Wayne's translation (Penguin Books, 1975, 266)—"Come or go? Or in, or out/His resolve is lost in doubt."].
13. See Sokel: *Op. cit.*, 56.
14. Franz Kafka: *The Trial*, last scene.

James Rolleston

Strategy and Language: Georg Bendemann's Theater of the Self

That Georg Bendemann is a character divided against himself is obvious enough: the problem for the critic is to locate the source of this division. In postulating a source at the "deepest" level possible, Walter Sokel dissolves the "figure" of Georg as he presents himself to the reader into a hierarchy of compartmentalized urges. The results are contradictory; while the observing, rational self is a "facade" and the instinctual substratum expresses the "true self" repressed by the facade, it also appears that the true self is "regressive" and the facade embodies the "responsible human being." The only way out of this maze of conflicting value judgments is to assert that oneness is superior to duality. This Sokel does in finding the conclusion of "The Judgment", with its total negation of Georg's individuality, to be a resurrection".[1] As Lawrence Ryan points out, his view runs counter to the whole atmosphere of the story and rests heavily on an a-priori definition of the river's symbolic function:

It is by no means the case that Kafka affirms the guilt-ridden submergence in the "stream of life" and, as it were, glorifies the extinction of the individual life in those blood-ties which hold together the family in the most primitive sense. Rather, precisely the opposite occurs in this work, namely Kafka's liberation into an artist's state, to which he remains loyal throughout his life.[2]

Ryan's view is that the ascetic friend in Russia has found the correct way of life. In a modernized form, Sokel and Ryan represent the two traditional approaches to Kafka's characters. For Sokel, the archetypal forces at work in the story are so strong that it hardly makes sense to talk of Georg as an individual; the reader is merely witnessing a fate so inevitable that it can scarcely be termed tragic, the dissolution of a life that has never functionally existed. Ryan, on the other hand, sees Georg as all too much the individual, a man who could have chosen otherwise, whose way of life is presented to the reader for implicit condemnation.

The figure of Georg Bendemann encompasses both of these readings without being limited by them: he is closer to "everyman" than Ryan allows, yet more firmly delineated as an individual than Sokel's approach suggests. Kafka has certainly utilized the archetypal conflict between father and son as the motor force of his story. But his focus is on the mechanism of Georg's responses, the sequence of actions and through processes that the reader transmutes into a human identity. The first part of the story shows that Georg is a man who, to an exceptional extent, stands outside his own life, ceaselessly arranging and defining it in terms of the commonsense norms embedded in language. He has so ordered his role by means of "rational" categories of behavior that he can no longer perceive the instinctual, self-serving purposes that have produced those categories. "The Judgment" is a precarious, unrepeatable structure combining an undisguised portrayal of life's most basic power conflict with a protagonist so self-absorbed that he has come to deny the existence of any conflict whatever. In order to synthesize these extremes Kafka has combined ordered thinking with its antithesis in such a manner that the reader can no longer distinguish one from the other. On initial reading the first half of the story seems sane, real, and undramatic, while the second half is a dramatic concentration of two whole lives, surreal to the point of insanity. Subsequent readings, while not invalidating this impression, set another one beside it: at the outset Georg is consciously transforming all "reality" into a mental drama centered on himself, while at the end the destruction of these mental categories forces Georg to a self-annihilation void of dramatic purpose, a helpless acknowledgment that his entire consciousness is now, quite literally, lifeless.

Georg interprets a dynamic, fluid situation in static terms; the life he sees is like a chessboard, on which every shift is reasoned out and takes place according to rules of his own making. But as he does not acknowledge his own motivation towards accretion of power, so he is always taken by surprise by the independent action of others, for example the friend's interest in the indifferent matters of which Georg had been writing. On Georg's mental chessboard the friend has been pushed ever farther away as he represents a life of integrity on which Georg has turned his back; into his orbit he is now drawing his "queen", the "girl from a well-to-do family (Mädchen aus wohlhabender Familie)"—and as for the father, Kafka himself sums it up: "he believes he has his father within him (er glaubt den Vater in sich zu haben)."[3]

The intensely visual quality of Georg's thoughts is emphasized in Kafka's commentary. The dangerous move Georg is contemplating is the recall of the friend into the group close to him on the chessboard. If he could have the friend "within him" as well as his father, then the shape of his life would be complete, containing both the authenticity of the past and the moral validity given by the friend's integrity. The danger lies in the autonomous, as it were, magnetic, force possessed by the friend. By bringing the one unabsorbed element back into the almost closed circle of his life, Georg opens the way for the father to escape, turn over the chessboard, and, instead of scattering the pieces, absorb them into himself. Kafka says of the fiancée that she lives in the story "only in relation to the friend (nur durch die Beziehung zum Freund)"; in a deeper sense, this is also true of the father. He gains his power from "the common bond" (*die Gemeinsamkeit*), from the fact that Georg has chosen to open up what had seemed to be closed; as Kafka puts it, Georg "rummages voluptuously in this consciousness of what they have in common (wühlt in diesem Gemeinsamen mit Wollust)." The ultimate "voluptuousness" lies for Georg in the entry into his father's room to display the letter, the seal of his final triumph, as if to say, "Soon you will be joined in this prison by the person through whose integrity alone, because the memory of it persists in me, you have any remaining hold over my life." The result of this premature celebration of power is conveyed visually by Kafka as, drawn out by the friend's magnetism, "the father rises up out of what they have in common, out of the friend (aus dem Gemeinsamen, dem Freund, der Vater hervorsteigt)." Then, in the most striking image of all, "what they had in common is now all piled up around the father (Das Gemeinsame ist alles um den Vater aufgetürmt)": the constructed world of Georg's mind, in which every element has its own compartment, has suddenly been replaced by the unmediated world of direct confrontation. Georg's elaborate tactics, however, are geared exclusively to the indirect conflict of his mental theater, and are ineffective on any other stage. The father is not really powerful; his strength is only "enough for you (genug für dich)," in effect handed to him by Georg's false move in connection with the friend.

It is wrong to lend undue weight to the archetypal nature of the father-son conflict; as with Gregor's parasitism, this is to attach oneself to the obvious elements of the story and neglect the specific role of the hero in bringing about his own end. Georg's defeat has nothing to do with fate or retribution; true, he has behaved without any regard for morality, but moral issues do not decide questions of power. What happens is that Georg, as he savors the coming triumph, neglects the formality, the indirectness, that underlies his image of order, entering almost sensually into his own world of "play". The word "playful" (*spielerisch*),[4] which in the first paragraph alerts the reader to the significance of Georg's letter, can be understood on several levels. Georg is being consciously "casual", concealing from himself, as he usually does, the import of his own action; he is making a gambler's "play", staking his past winnings to achieve what he thinks is a virtually certain final victory; and he is staging an internal drama in which all the pieces move according to his own predetermined vision.

Sokel points to the "dramatic" sequence of imagery in "The Judgment": "When, at the beginning of the story, he had looked out upon the bridge, a quiet emptiness, a kind of frozen suspension of life, prevailed. His dying re-animates life."[5] But whereas he regards the story as a "dionysiac" tragedy, even inflating the laconic final sentence into a "resurrection", I see it rather as an inversion of the Promethean story, an attempt at displacing established order not through "excess" of life but through its degradation by means of psychic ingestion. The letter to the friend is the act of hubris, the assertion that Georg can incorporate into his wholly egocentric existence the element most alien to it: human integrity. What the reader witnesses in the first part of the story, in the guise of rational thought processes, is the mental drama leading up to the act of hubris. A vital point is that these rationalizations are not "thoughts" in the sense that Georg is experiencing the actual process of self-deception and imparting it to the reader directly. On the contrary, Georg has *already* sealed the letter whose contents are the outcome of this sequence of reasoning. Georg is reenacting, in the long-established terminology of his own script, the sequence of events which has culminated in this final gamble.

The story's second paragraph, which presents facts only slightly colored by Georg's viewpoint, can be legitimately read as Georg's "thoughts", moving from the just-completed letter to the ascetic enigma who is its object. But the third paragraph reveals immediately the level to which Georg has moved. "What could one write to such a man, who had obviously run off the rails...(Was sollte man einem solchen Manne schreiben, der sich offenbar verrannt hatte...)": these words show in three respects how Georg has shifted from the actual friend to the reconstruction of the friend necessary to his own subjective drama. First, the rhetorical question itself, given that the letter is already sealed, shows Georg moving from the present moment to the reconstruction of events that have led up to this moment; second, the generalizing phrase "such a man" is an attempt to deny the friend's uncomfortable uniqueness, to dismantle him, as it were, into components that Georg can assimilate into his own world view; and finally, the imagery of "who had obviously run off the rails" just does not follow from the decisive words, "adjusted himself to being permanently a bachelor (richtete sich so für ein endgültiges Junggesellentum ein),"[6] which conclude the preceding paragraph. The friend has been allowed to describe himself just enough for the reader to be aware that Georg is here presenting an outsider's caricature, a caricature essential to the picture of his own sympathetic superiority which he then develops. The friend is not the vacillating failure Georg would have him appear to be, and as Georg's reasoning moves ever further from the minimal facts of the second paragraph, it becomes clear that the friend is simply "the other", both a persisting obligation from Georg's earlier way of life and a symbol of moral independence that Georg cannot reconcile with his own unacknowledged surrender to a wholly selfish mode of living.

What is troubling Georg and causing him to review once more all the moves he has made thus far is that the writing of the letter goes against all that the ruthless caution of his instincts had told him. Originally he had decided, quite rightly from his point of view, not to invite the friend to his wedding. After marriage, Georg's way of life would be finally legitimized, because his ambitions would be officially justified by the firm grounding and perpetuation of the family (as Kafka points out in his commentary, the reason the fiancee is "easily driven away" is that she is not yet part of Georg's "circle of blood relationship"). As a married man Georg would be in a stronger position to build protective rationalizations against the friend's integrity. Until then he is in the typically exposed position of the Kafka hero, suspended between two worlds. A bachelor, he has turned his back on the insights of bachelordom, with their concomitant insecurities; but the persisting need to justify to himself his behavior toward the friend shows that he has not finally entered the "swamp world" (*Schlamm-welt*)[7] of unreflecting egocentricity. And so Georg has been pushing the friend ever further from him, weaving explanations for the friend's behavior that are exquisitely compounded of fiction and cliché. "Two years ago [Georg's] mother had died ... his friend had of course been informed of that and had expressed his sympathy in a letter phrased so dryly that the grief caused by such an event, one had to conclude, could not be realized in a distant country."[8] The simple explanation for the friend's "dryness", of course, is that he is annoyed at not hearing the news directly from Georg; Georg conceals this from himself first with the ambivalent *wohl*,[9] a word used with increasing frequency as the rationale for his own behavior becomes shakier, then with the resounding cliché about "grief", a phrase all the more grotesque because of Georg's own calculating, unemotional tone.

This process culminates in Georg's "putting the friend to bed" with his letters on indifferent matters. "All he desired was to leave undisturbed the idea of the home town which his friend must have built up to his own content during the long interval."[10] Once again the indicative mood is modified by *wohl* (contained here in "must have"), but this time Georg presumes to penetrate the friend's actual state of mind with his speculations, having previously confined himself to reorganizing the facts. He cannot of course know that the friend prefers a nostalgic image of his home town; nevertheless, this is presented in the indicative, his reconstruction of the friend having finally supplanted the original in Georg's inner drama.

The essential turning point of the story, as the language indicates, is not Georg's entry into his father's room but the scene with the fiancée. To take an analogy from a "real" play, this resembles Macbeth's scene with Lady Macbeth before the murder of Duncan. Like Lady Macbeth, the finacée encourages Georg to adopt a course so rash, yet so inviting in its possibilities, that he had not dared to admit it to himeslf. Like Macbeth, however, Georg had betrayed his obsession by talking about it with noticeable frequency to the person he regards as his firm ally. The movement of this paragraph throws new light on the oddly tense language of the previous paragraph describing Georg's last dealings with the friend: "And so it happened to Georg that three times in three fairly widely separated letters he had told his friend about the engagement of an unimportant man to an equally unimportant girl...."[11] Nothing merely "happens" to people in fiction, least of all in Kafka's fiction; when writing to the friend, Georg cannot stop referring to the term "engagement", just as, when talking to the fiancée, he cannot stop talking about the friend. Georg presents to his fiancée the reconstructed image of his relationship with the friend with such obsessive frequency that she comes to accept his version of matters as "true": not only is the friend in a very bad way, but Georg cares for him exceedingly and thinks only of how to alleviate his condition. Thus does Georg's imagined order of things tip over into reality, and the unacknowledged, insanely bold ambition of winning friend and fiancée simultaneously is forced out into the open by the fiancée's innocent remark: "If you have such friends, Georg, you shouldn't ever have got engaged at all."[12] All she means is that the friend seems to occupy Georg's thoughts more than she does. But Georg's reply thrusts the matter immediately into the atmosphere of *Macbeth*: "Well, we're both to blame for that (Ja, das ist unser beider Schuld)." His constant mention of the friend has had all along the unacknowledged purpose of provoking her into just such a remark; now that she has made it she moves, in his mind, into the position of close ally (or, as the word "blame" implies, accomplice). At last he feels the strength to move from barely acknowledged imaginings to a real act of hubris; this will be the easier, so he thinks, as the movement into reality (the friend's mind) will be a gradual one, mediated by a letter over which he retains complete control. The sheer impudence of Georg's final cliché to rationalize his change of direction reminds the reader how completely mental constructs have replaced any kind of self-awareness: "That's the kind of man I am and he'll just have to take me as I am (So bin ich und so hat er mich hinzunehmen...)."

The scene in the father's room can be divided into two sections, the first ending with the father's leap from under the bedclothes. During this first part the reader sees the progressive hollowing out of Georg's consciousness and is prepared for the total dislocation of the final pages. The story is still very much a "game", but suddenly Georg is not in control of the game. We have seen that the basis of Georg's game with reality is physical and mental distance; as the father says, he locks himself in his office and there he spins the web of controlled relationships into which he has been trying to incorporate the friend. What the father does is trap Georg into sheer physical closeness to reality, so that, when he finally launches his attack, Georg will be unable to retreat (retreat was in fact available to Oskar, the hero of "The Urban World": under attack from the father he opened the door, albeit with difficulty, and left). The father's strategy is, by his pretended obtuseness over the friend, to give Georg the illusion that he can still win and so draw him irrevocably into the conflict. From the ordered theater of his subjectivity Georg is compelled to act on the father's stage of total unpredictability; accustomed to absorbing each successive event into his mental scheme of things, he reacts anxiously to each statement of the father's, desperately hoping to restore some kind of order. But with every remark the father opens up new areas Georg had thought sealed forever; because Georg's "assets" have been totally absorbed into his ordered world, with the destruction of that order they drain away from him instantly, leaving him with "nothing but his awareness of the father (nichts mehr als den Blick auf den Vater)."[13]

From the moment of entering the room, Georg is afflicted with involuntary thoughts—"My father is still a giant of a man (mein Vater ist noch immer ein Riese)"—that loosen his control over his own actions. Indeed the immediate physical impact of his father in his own dark room—whether or not we choose to gloss the point psychoanalytically—causes Georg to submit, as it were, to his father's movements: "vacantly" (*verloren*) is a doubly significant word when applied to so self-controlled a character as Georg. As Georg spells out for the third time (previously to himself and to his fiancée) his "reasons" for not telling the friend of his engagement, the reader feels the accumulated feebleness of the clichés; Georg is still following his own script, but even he seems to feel its hollowness, judging by his overelaborate responses to the father's abrupt questions.

The father then draws Georg more deeply into the conflict with his deliberately "moderate" rehearsal of Georg's faults, culminating in the "trivial affair" (*Kleinigkeit*): "Do you really have this friend in St. Petersburg? (Hast du wirklich diesen Freund in Petersburg?)." By this question the father encourages Georg to think that his mind is wandering and so draws Georg into solicitous physical contact; at the same time the question goes to the central weakness of Georg's position—Georg used to have a friend, he hopes to regain the friend on his own terms, but it is debatable whether at this moment he actually "has" a friend. Georg falls into the trap: from this point he seems less and less able to "think", being aware only of physical groupings. He loses his sense of proportion to the point where he seeks "victory" on a purely physical level, through putting the father to bed: "Meanwhile Georg had succeeded in lowering his father down again (Während dessen war es Georg gelungen, den Vater wieder niederzusetzen...)." But the physical is the father's element; by choosing to fight on the father's terms, Georg dooms himself. The father's toying with Georg's watch chain has been interpreted variously, and I do not wish to argue with symbolisms that have meaning in the context of a different overall approach. In relation to Georg's life as he has organized it, his "dreadful feeling (schreckliches Gefühl)" is a response to the total intimacy of the gesture, the antithesis of the wholly controlled aloofness which is the foundation of Georg's adult life. We have seen Georg "putting to bed" the friend metaphorically, through patronizing letters; to attempt to do the same thing in actual physical terms is to forfeit the "distance" upon which Georg's power depends.

Upon the father's resurgence Georg, for so long a puppet-master, is now himself a puppet who can do no more than react to the father's thrusts, on both the physical and the verbal level: "'But attend to me!' cried his father, and Georg, almost distracted, ran towards the bed to take everything in, yet came to a stop halfway."[14] There is no "logical" connection between the father's command and Georg's response. Georg's mind, accustomed to order, attaches itself to the disorder of the bed; he rushes to put things right, stops as if afflicted by the absurdity of taking refuge in a world of things so long despised. But now everything is concentrated into physical images. He who had systematically detached his friend from all recognizable individuality can now see only a physical image of the friend; despite everything, the friend is *standing*, an action symbolizing his survival—all Georg can do is to run convulsively. "A long time ago he had firmly made up his mind to watch closely every least movement (Vor einer langen Weile hatte er sich fest entschlossen, alles vollkommen genau zu beobachten....)"; a symptom of Georg's total dislocation is that this resolve, so characteristic of what used to be his approach to all situations, comes into being merely as a memory of a past receding so rapidly that it already seems "a long time ago".

Georg's last independent act of self-expression is the utterance "You comedian! (Komödiant!)." Only on the most superficial level, as he at once realizes, is this a defiant remark; in all other respects it is a final surrender. Georg, by definition an "actor" playing his own life according to a script, hands this last attribute to his father. If the father, and not he himself, is the actor, then he has no refuge left; the only hope of recovery lay in Georg's withdrawing from the scene, whether physically like the hero of "The Urban World", or mentally by somehow absorbing the father's attack in his own game plan. Now he has not only played the father's game and lost, he has explicitly acknowledged his father's superiority. All Georg's remaining thoughts, words, and reactions express this final crumbling of his mental theater. With the vain hope that the father will fall and the mental incantation about the father's pockets we are in the realm of primitive magic; as the immediacy of the objects under the father's control overwhelms him, Georg lunges for some ritual potency in them that might yet save him. The helpless line "Georg made a primace of disbelief (Georg machte Grimassen, als glaube er das nicht)" and the exclamation "ten thousand times! (Zehntausendmal!)" reduce the magic to a still more rudimentary level; long unaware of the substance of the father's speeches, Georg responds like a circus clown, hoping that a mere negative grimace or its counterpart, a feeble exaggeration, will somehow divert his father from the assault. The theatrical theme comes into the open once again, with Georg's last response: "So you've been lying in wait for me! (Du hast mir also aufgelauert!)" As the father pitilessly points out, this sentence is a cliché that would have fitted into the script earlier. It has no relevance to what the father has just said; it is a phrase plucked by Georg from some melodrama in what remains of his memory, uttered as if to show merely that he is not yet dead. At most it is, like the earlier "You comedian!" a confirmation that the father has defeated him at his own game.

Sokel regards Georg's last words, "Dear parents, I have always loved you, all the same (Liebe Eltern, ich habe euch doch immer geliebt)," as expressing a genuine reemergence of the "innocent child (unschuldiges Kind)" from under the layers of the "devilish human being (teuflischer Mensch)." To me, Georg is an actor to the last. His death signifies no more than the final negation of his existence, an unravelling of time back through childhood to a starting point before the onset of consciousness. The rhythm which is to be codified into the ritual structure of *The Trial* is here presented with radical starkness: if consciousness implies manipulation, then the collapse of the mental theater involves the extinction of every trace of consciousness. Georg's last words are merely a corollary of his acceptance of the father's death sentence; having lost the struggle, he adopts the victor's point of view wholeheartedly, that is, his personality is simply eliminated by the father's will, so that at the end he says what the father wants him to say. There is no reconciliation here, just final defeat. In death Georg plays the role at the farthest remove from the role he had adopted in life, that of dutiful son. Georg has denied himself (as he denied his friend) to such an extent that his death does more than negate his life, it replaces it with an image—"innocent child"—of his father's choosing.

NOTES

1. Sokel: *F.K.*, 19-24.
2. Ryan: "'Zum lezten Mal Psychologie!'," 165.
3. *Tag*, 296/*D 1*, 278. Subsequent phrases of commentary quoted in the text are also taken from this diary entry for February 11, 1913. Sometimes, where Kresh's version seems to miss the immediacy of Kafka's self-analysis, I have substituted my own efforts.
4. The Muir translation misses this resonance, offering instead "dreamy".
5. Sokel: *F.K.*, 24.
6. My translation. Muir renders "richtete sich ein" as "resigned himself", thereby weighting the neutral verb in the direction of Georg's own bias. It is my contention that Kafka is deliberately conveying information at this point for which neutral language is appropriate.
7. The term is Walter Benjamin's; his remarkable essay on Kafka is printed in his *Illuminations*, 111-140. The phrase "swamp world", discussion of which begins on p. 130, refers to what he sees as the "prehistoric" quality of the novels, the anonymous instinctuality of so many of the characters; but the interdependence of the hero and his world suggests that the ruthless rationality engendered by modern civilization is itself a renewed manifestation of the swamp world, a breaking-down of the precarious human balance.
8. "Von dem Todesfall von Georgs Mutter... hatte der Freund wohl noch erfahren und sein Beileid in einem Brief mit einer Trockenheit ausgedrückt, die ihren Grund nur darin haben konnte, dass die Trauer über ein solches Ereignis in der Fremde ganz unvorstellbar wird." *E*, 55.
9. Again, Muirs rendering, "of course", dispels some essential shadows. The word may be untranslatable—clearly the friend *did* hear of the event but, equally clearly, Georg was not his source. "Surely" might be preferable.
10. "Er wollte nichts anderes als die Vorstellung ungestört lassen, die sich der Freund von der Heimatstadt in der langen Zwischenzeit wohl gemacht und mit welcher er sich abgefunden hatte." *E*, 56.
11. "So geschah es Georg, dass er dem Freund die Verlobung eines gleichgultigen Menschen mit einem ebenso gleichgültigen Mädchen dreimal in ziemlich weit auseinanderliegenden Briefen anzeigte." *E*, 56.
12. "Wenn du solche Freunde hast, Georg, hättest du dich überhaupt nicht verloben sollen." *E*, 57. Again I have altered Muir's phrasing, which reads: "Since your friends are like that..."; throughout this story he seems concerned to establish a logical, coherent "tone", whereas the pregnant neutrality of the language, the abrupt shifts in focus, have a vital part in suggesting the abyss that is about to open up.
13. Again the phrase is from Kafka's own commentary. *Tag*, 296-297/*D 1*, 279.
14. "'Aber schau mich an!' rief der Vater, und Georg lief, fast zerstreut, zum Bett, um alles zu fassen, stockte aber in der Mitte des Weges." *E*, 64.

Charles Bernheimer

Letters to an Absent Friend: A Structural Reading

"The Judgment", Kafka told Felice on December 4, 1912, about six weeks after he had written the story, "is a bit wild and meaningless and if it didn't have inner truth (which can never be established universally but must be acknowledged or denied every time by each reader or listener in turn) it would be nothing."[1] The first reader to try to elucidate this "inner truth" was Kafka himself. In a diary entry for February 11, 1913, he wrote out an extraordinarily coherent structural interpretation of the story, proofs of which he was correcting at the time. This interpretation is, I believe, well enough known that it need not be summarized here. Less familiar are Kafka's subsequent comments on the story, comments which indicate that, despite his claim to privileged hermeneutic authority, this birth that had emerged after a night-long labor, in a "complete opening of the body and the soul",[2] remained mysterious and slippery to its own mother. "Can you find any meaning in 'The Judgment'," he asked Felice on June 2, 1913, "I mean any straightforward, coherent meaning that one could follow? I can't find any, nor can I explain anything in it" *(BF, 394/LFe,* 265). Eight days later he declared once again that "'The Judgment' cannot be explained", though he offered to show

146

Felice his diary entries about it. Then he focused on the figure
of the friend as the primary source of confusion in the narrative:
"The story is full of abstractions, though they are not admitted.
The friend is hardly a real person, perhaps he is more that
which the father and Georg have in common. The story is
perhaps a journey ["Rundgang"] around father and son, and
the changing figure of the friend is perhaps the perspectival
change of the relations between father and son. But I am not
sure of this either" (*BF*, 396-7/*LFe*, 267).

This suggestion that the friend is a purely abstract relational
concept linking father and son has largely been ignored by
critics of "The Judgment". The only interpretation which
moves in this direction identifies the friend with Kafka the
writer for whom bachelorhood, solitude, asceticism and
alienation were necessary conditions. This view depends on an
appeal to Kafka's biography: we need to know *a priori* that he
felt a conflict between writing and marriage, that this tension
had recently been intensified by his encounter with Felice
Bauer, to whom he was later twice engaged, and that he
thought of writing in terms of an isolated, barren, lonely
existence. Further support for this interpretation is drawn from
a supposed analogy between the friend's stagnating business in
Russia and Kafka's stagnating writing in the years prior to
1912.[3] All this extratextual evidence needs to be mustered
because the friend's portrayal in the story as an unsuccessful
small businessman provides little basis to view him as symbolic
of the writer or of writing itself. Even the argument that Kafka
associated Russia, where the friend lives, with the kind of
extreme solitude necessary for writing is undercut by his
definition of Russia, in a diary entry, as the very absence of
representation: "The infinite attraction of Russia. It is best
represented not by Gogol's troika but by the image of a vast,
unoverseeable river of yellowish water on which waves—but
not too high ones—are everywhere tossing. Wild, desolate
heaths upon its banks, blighted grass. But nothing can
represent it; rather everything effaces it."[4] Just as Kafka speaks
of the friend as "hardly a real person", so he sees the blighted
grass of the Russian heaths as an image obscuring an essential

absence. The friend's existence is Russian only in so far as his image is effaced.

What is surprising is that critics with a sense that this story is somehow self-reflective, that it inscribes a commentary on the writing process, have paid so little attention to the writing activity that actually occurs in the narrative. It opens, after all, with Georg sitting at his writing table having just completed a letter to his friend while near its conclusion the father claims that the friend has never read Georg's "lying little letters" (64; 59)[5] but only those he himself has sent. Thus "the perspectival change of the relations between father and son" occurs through a transfer of the power to communicate in writing with the friend. But if, as Kafka maintains and as I propose to argue in this paper, the friend is nothing more than "that which the father and Georg have in common", then these letters appear to be communications to the very structure of the father-son relationship. Pursuing this argument with the help of psychoanalytic concepts introduced by Jacques Lacan, I shall interpret the story as dealing crucially with the link between writing and oedipal structure, a link that, in my view, extends significantly to Kafka's own writing about the composition of his story.

The story begins just at that moment when Georg has made a crucial change in the content of those letters in and through which he creates his relationship to his friend. Prior to his change, Georg's letters have had as their primary purpose "to leave undisturbed the idea of the home town which the friend must have built up in the long interval [of his absence] and with which he had come to terms" (56; 52). Because of the friend's peculiar sensitivity, Georg thinks to himself, "no real news" (54; 51) can be sent to him. It is best for him that he "stay abroad, just as he was" (54; 50) and that he be given "no inkling" (55; 51) of the improvements that have occurred in Georg's business affairs or of his intention to marry. Thus the conscious motivation for Georg's writing is the creation of an illusion that nothing has changed at home. Georg believes that he has invented that fiction out of consideration for his friend but, in a deeper sense, that fiction *is* his friend and its unconscious function is to preserve Georg's own illusion that sameness prevails at home.

In effect, the friend acts as a mirror image for Georg, one in which he sees himself as childish (were the friend to return home, he might appear as "ein altes Kind" [54; 50], Georg speculates) and sexually inactive (having next to no social intercourse with Russian families, the friend has resigned himself to permanent bachelorhood). The friend is Georg's *alter ego* constructed on a narcissistic model, a model best understood, I believe, in terms of Jacques Lacan's description of the "mirror phase".[6] In this pre-oedipal phase, which may be viewed as a permanent psychological structure as well as a genetic stage, the ego is constituted by means of identification with the other's image as a unified whole (or with the self as specular other). Being the product of an identification with another's image, the ego, in Lacan's view, is as fictive, as imaginary, as is the image in the mirror. But the narcissistic ego refuses to acknowledge this interdependence. Instead it aggressively resents the other's existence as constituting a breach in the perfect autonomy and omnipotence it desires. Georg's aggression is amply evident in his characterization of the friend as difficult, sickly, envious and incompetent. Aggression also contributes to Georg's ambivalence about the friend's proximity or distance. In his meditation at the beginning of the story, Georg seems to be playing a kind of *fort-da* game with his double's image. In a lordly manner, he decides that the friend is best off away (*fort*) given that, were he to return home (*da*), he might well be "niedergedruckt" (oppressed), "not intentionally", Georg adds, but through force of circumstances" (54; 50).

Freud interprets his grandson's game of making his toy disappear and reappear (accompanied by sounds resembling "Fort!" "Da!") as a strategy to gain active mastery on the symbolic level over his mother's power to leave him arbitrarily.[7] According to this theory, the absence of the child's mother causes him to initiate a game in which a toy signifies the mother (or, more likely, a part of her, her breast for example) and language repeats on an imaginary plane the experience of loss and recovery. This structure of linguistic mediation, a direct development from the mirror phase, reveals the maternal associations inherent in the specular image. "The precursor of the mirror is the mother's face" declares D. W. Winnicott.[8] Applying this information to Georg's case, we note first of all that Georg's mother had died two years previously and secondly that the friend, on being informed of this event, "had expressed his sympathy in a letter phrased so dryly that one could only conclude that the grief caused by such an event was quite unimaginable abroad" (55; 51). This associates the friend with the absent mother, but in a negative manner, one typical of Georg's ambivalent feelings towards his friend and, by extension, towards his mother. For the dual relationship, based on narcissistic identification, is extremely unstable. Proximity, though desired as bringing comfort and communion, is also feared because of its potential to annihilate either the self or the other. Distance, while it is painful and alienating, yet preserves the ego's illusory sense of autonomy. On one extreme of this oscillating diadic structure is the destruction of otherness by an imperialistic ego, on the opposite the destruction of the ego by an imaginary (m)other.

Georg has managed to maintain his sense of narcissistic control up to this point, but only by inventing a specular image which excludes difference, specifically sexual difference. Writing was the medium through and in which he conceived his double as an isolated bachelor ignorant of sexual desire. The stimulus for Georg to end this effort to deny difference is not so much his engagement as his fiancée's remark: "If you have friends like that Georg, you should never have gotten engaged at all" (57; 53). This acute observation reflects the fiancée's perception that Georg's primary allegiance is to an essentially intrasubjective dual relationship which excludes any third party. Firmly denying this, Georg decides to announce his marriage plans to his friend and invite him to visit for the occasion. Thereby he asserts his separate identity: "That's how I am and that's how he must accept me; I can't cut myself to another pattern that might make a more suitable friend for him" (57; 53). Surely a deluded statement, if not a conscious lie, since for many years Georg has been using his letters to cut himself to a pattern of sameness suitable to his own narcissism.

"So bin Ich" declares Georg, but it seems evident that his identity at this moment is in a state of confusion, poised between two different relations to the father: the narcissistic and the oedipal.[9] The narcissistic relation excludes the father and, in the Lacanian analysis, its purely specular character excludes language as well. Kafka moves outside this analysis by associating narcissism with a particular attitude towards writing, one that attempts to make it a tool of subjective intention. Writing is the instrument with which Georg simultaneously creates, and communicates with, the fiction of his self-identity.

The oedipal relation entails quite a different attitude towards language and, by extension, towards writing. It is Lacan's linkage of the access to both sexual and linguistic difference with what he calls the "metaphor" or "name" of the father that makes his interpretation of Freud so illuminating when applied to Kafka.[10] Both writers privilege the father as the symbolic originator of the dynamics of desire and of signification. In fact, for Lacan the *Nom-du-Père* (pun intended, of course), constitutes the law of the entire symbolic order. This law structures an open series of displacements and substitutions. In the field of desire, the series of potential love objects is initiated through the son's being barred from his primary object choice, the mother, still reflected in the specular image. In order to become a father himself, the son can identify with his father only in a privative mode: he must be like his father in possessing a woman but the woman in question must be other than the one possessed by the father. To resolve the oedipal complex is to accept that every father has been a son and experienced the threat of castration and that every son may become a father once he has surmounted that threat. The power of the father is thus purely transitory, inscribed in a temporal process bringing displacement and substitution.

In the field of signification, this process provides access to an awareness of language as expropriating the subject rather than

providing him with a means of self-definition through control
of the other. The father's place in language is not a presence but
a name, a name that designates a purely symbolic space itself
empty of meaning. Signification is generated in what Derrida
calls a "movement of supplementarity".[11] The supplement is
that addition which comes about by the signifier's temporary
obliteration, effacement, of the constitutive symbolic absence.
In Kafka's terms, the image of Russia as "a vast, unoverseeable
river of yellowish water" can be meaningful only because it
effaces and occults what is essentially outside representation
and meaning. The effacement of absence operates as an in-
facement, a production of images, and this production has
always-already been set in motion by the absence of any center
or origin, intentional or metaphysical, which might anchor its
freeplay. Thus Lévi-Strauss speaks of the signifier as "floating", as "a symbol in a pure state, hence susceptible to being
charged with any possible symbolic content".[12] Each semantic
"charge" is a supplement which takes the place of a lack and is
thereby inscribed into a chain of substitutions and displacements. The subject can no more control the freeplay of this
system of differences than he can situate himself outside the
linguistic order itself.

Kafka's extraordinary achievement in "The Judgment" is to
have found images to illustrate just this displacement of the
subject, this putting-into-process. It is given literal figuration
by Georg's leaving the writing desk in his own room and
crossing the corridor into his father's. In so doing he abandons
a space where up to now he had felt in full command of his
relation to the Symbolic for one where he recognizes a prior
authority with a regulatory function over that relation. Georg's
purpose in entering his father's room is to submit his letter for
paternal approval, that very letter which for the first time
announces his oedipal project. Having allowed himself to
assert his sexual desire in his writing, he feels compelled to seek
approval for that writing from the father whose function his
earlier letters had suppressed. Thus Georg is caught in a double
bind: he recognizes his father's absolute priority even as he

desires to inscribe that privileged position into a cricuit of substitutions that would deny any notion of priority.

This conflict affects the very presentation of "reality" in the father's room. Everything here appears to be simultaneously inside and outside Georg. The darkness of the paternal residence seems to signify the darkness in which Georg has kept the father figure within his own psyche. His perception of his father as "still a giant of a man" (59; 54), though apparently based on a response to the father's physical appearance, seems to reflect Georg's awareness of a purely internal domination. The old man's playing with Georg's watch chain might indicate his actual senility or his symbolic power over the son's life in time. Finally, the father makes this double mode of reference explicit in his punning question as to whether he is adequately "covered up" (63; 58). Symbolic meanings lurk behind every element of the "real", questioning its status, forcing us to see the external as internal and vice versa. It is as if the world had suddenly been affected by that "seasickness on land" which prevents the supplicant in "Description of a Struggle" "from being properly satisfied with the genuine names of things."[13] Now the very notion of a "genuine name", a signifier linked in a non-arbitrary fashion to a signified, is exposed as an illusion. In the father's room, the arbitrary reigns, the signifier floats, meaning is suspended.

This sense of arbitrariness is, of course, most dramatically experienced by Georg and the reader in the father's denial of the friend's existence. Critics have generally seen this denial as part of the sadistic game the father is playing with the son. But our premise that the friend is a fictional creation filling the space of an absence enables us to read this part of the story quite differently. In suggesting that Georg has invented his friend, the father is opening the way for the son to give up his narcissistic double and recognize the critical function of absence in structuring desire. The father, who is as much inside as outside Georg, is indicating that the Symbolic, that is, the very condition of being simultaneously inside and outside, subjective and objective, real and illusory, is generated only on the basis of a fundamental lack. By disclosing the absence that structures the movement of supplementation active within Kafka's text, the father opens his own position to the play of metaphor.

Georg's writing has attempted to arrest this play, to prevent the signifier from floating by closing off its polysemic overdetermination. Now he finds himself in a world which mirrors this overdetermination in its very structure. To respond at all positively to it would require certain qualities which Georg, like all of Kafka's heroes, eminently lacks: ironic distance, negative capability, a self-mocking appreciation of the comic, and, above all, the willingness to espouse what Derrida calls "the Nietzschean *affirmation*, the joyous affirmation of the freeplay of the world and of the innocence of becoming, the affirmation of a world of signs without need, without truth, without origin, offered to an active interpretation".[14] Faced with a father who presents himself both as potent giant and as senile invalid, Georg reacts with none of Kafka's sense of the joke involved in metaphor. "Metaphors", writes Kafka, "are one among many things which make me despair of writing.... Writing is helpless, cannot live in itself, is a joke ("Spass") and a despair" (*Tag*, 550-1/*D 2*, 200-1). Georg certainly sees the father as helpless and quickly recognizes the despair of his position. What he is unable to recognize is that the father is also a "Spassmacher", a joker or trickster, and that he is inviting Georg to acknowledge this quality in himself. "You have no friend in St. Petersburg", says the father. "You have always been a *Spassmacher* and you haven't even restrained yourself in relation to me. How could you have a friend in just that place. I can't believe it at all" (61; 57).

The essence of the joke is the absence of the friend, that is, the absence at the non-center of symbolic structure. To enter this structure is to be displaced from any originating authority and to enter a state of suspension in which power and impotence, guilt and innocence, knowledge and ignorance are purely differential and relative terms in an unstable, shifting metaphoric activity. In this sense, the father's dark, ill-ventilated room resembles those stuffy rooms and corridors in

The Trial where Joseph K. is kept in suspension between the inconclusive possibilities of "ostensible acquittal" and "postponement". Whereas Joseph K. never seems to consider ironic laughter as a way of dealing with this desperate situation, K. in *The Castle* is provided (as in Georg's case, by the paternal figure who guards the Symbolic absence) with a suggestive clue as to its critical importance: the assistants are sent by Klamm's deputy to "amuse him" because "he can't understand a joke ('Spass')" and "takes everything too seriously".[15]

The cornerstone of both Georg's and K.'s seriousness is their insistence on what Derrida calls "the metaphysics of presence". K. is fighting to obtain a face-to-face interview with the elusive Klamm, Georg tries to persuade his father of the actual existence of the friend. However, the image of a revolutionary priest which Georg conjures up in this connection betrays the repressed desire behind his effort to obtain paternal recognition for his friend. The Russian revolution was, after all, aimed at unseating the "papa" Czar and the radical priest who cuts a cross in blood on the palm of his hand signifies thereby the self-contained power of the father who sacrifices a son who is also himself. It is this narcissistic self-containment that Georg, despite his intention to marry, continues unconsciously to desire. Georg wants his father to acknowledge the friend as presence because this recognition would involve the father's abdicating his generative function in structuring the paternal metaphor, the relation to absence. Georg tries to suppress the Symbolic by treating the old man in purely physical terms. Having removed one paternal garment after the next, Georg carries his father to bed and tucks the blankets closely around him. He appears to be concerned only about the father's bodily well-being and is (deliberately?) oblivious to the metaphoric resonance of his twice-repeated question: "Am I well covered up?" Yet a cover-up is just what Georg has been attempting, and now, suddenly, he is confronted with the consequences of its failure.

In the story's third structural configuration, the paternal signifier, repudiated by Georg through his fictional mirror relationship with the friend, appears as the specular other within the same dual structure. Having been unable to respond to the father in terms of metaphor, Georg cannot perceive his desire to marry as part of an ongoing process active from generation to generation. Fatherhood is defined for him once and for all not as an alienable name but as the inalienable quality of the biological father. In his desire for a woman, the son puts himself in direct confrontation with the father whose position, in the son's unconscious judgment, gives him exclusive privilege over all women, a privilege which, according to Freud's myth of origins, once belonged to that tyrannical prehistoric father who was killed by the horde composed of his sons. This primal father, Freud writes, was "of a masterful nature, absolutely narcissistic, self-confident and independent... [with] few libidinal ties; he loved no one but himself, or other people only in so far as they served his needs."[16] It is such a father who now "springs erect", in totemic fashion, as an hallucinatory "Schreckbild" (literally, "picture of fear") opposed to Georg.

This experience is "uncanny" in the full Freudian sense of that term. Even the ambivalent meaning of the German word "heimlich", which Freud discusses at the beginning of his essay, is operative here. For it is at the heart of the familiar home and through the agency of the well-known figure of the father that the eerie, hidden and obscure suddenly explodes. And it explodes in accordance with Freud's observation that "an uncanny experience occurs either when repressed infantile complexes have been revived by some impression, or when the primitive beliefs we have surmounted seem once more to be confirmed".[17] In Georg's case, it is the castration complex that has been revived, or rather activated for the first time, through the psychotic mechanism Lacan calls foreclosure or repudiation (Freud: "Verwerfung"). This mechanism operates through a primordial expulsion of the threat of castration from the subject's symbolic universe. In the resolution of the oedipal complex, the subject unconsciously recognizes this threat as initiating the freeplay of the differential structures, sexual, linguistic, and cultural, into which he is being displaced. In psychosis, on the other hand, castration is not introduced into the subject as metaphor but is instead cast out into the external world where it reappears in an hallucinatory mode. Hence Lacan's famous revision of the Freudian formula: "What has been foreclosed from the Symbolic reappears in the Real."[18]

Georg's strategy to accomplish this foreclosure was his invention of an imaginary dual structure which effectively excluded the father's symbolic function. The entry of sexual desire into the medium of this invention, writing, precipitated the crisis in the father-son relation. Though exposed, in the father's room, to an enactment of symbolic structure, set in motion by the liberating recognition of the friend's non-existence, Georg persisted in maintaining the fiction of the friend, that is, the fiction of his own self-sustaining identity. This persistence in repudiating the paternal metaphor, in rejecting the father as both internal and external, causes Georg's psychotic break. Now he hallucinates the father as a purely castrating authority opposing him from the outside.

The father's first hostile move is to claim that he alone has authorized the fiction of the friend. Georg's great mistake, says the father, was to have forgotten to remove his writing things. Here the old man is simply taking over, for his own narcissistic purposes, Georg's conviction that writing creates a coherent, unified self in so far as it invents an imaginary double. Next, the father asserts his control over the *fort-da* game, pointing out that his son's belief that he may approach or retreat at will is an error since he, the elder, is still by far the stronger of the two. Meanwhile, Georg stands in a corner as far as possible from the father and attempts to deny the "psychical reality" of his primal authority by making fun of his physical appearance and mocking the extravagance of his claims. But of course it is just this extravagance which constitutes the phantasmatic quality of the father's ex-istence, his being outside of Georg's mind as an hallucination of that mind.

Huddled in his corner, Georg remembers that "a long time ago he had firmly made up his mind to watch everything closely so that he could not be surprised in some indirect manner from behind or from above" (64-5; 60). This "long

forgotten resolve" coincides with what I have called Georg's
foreclosure of the primal phantasy of castration. Now that
threat becomes all but explicit as the father asserts his ability to
sweep the son's bride away from him, reviles the sons' sexuality
as mere animal lust, accuses him of disgracing his mother's
memory, demands credit for all Georg's business successes, and
absorbs into his own orbit that specular other in terms of which
Georg had built up his narcissistic ego. The uncanny effect is
not unlike that which Freud ascribes to the hypnotist (note how
the father insists that Georg look at him—"aber schau mich
an!"—64; 59) whose relation to his patient, says Freud, is like
that of "the individual member of the primal horde to the
primal father".[19] Georg is hypnotised by his own hallucination, the vision of a paternal narcissism so sweeping that it
includes and absorbs sexual difference.

That is, in effect, just what Georg has desired for himself: the
accommodation of his imaginary, narcissistic relationship to
an active heterosexuality. Such an accommodation, as we have
seen, denies the paternal metaphor and blocks access to the
Symbolic. Georg's attempt to achieve this denial of oedipal
structure prompts his unconscious return to an archaic
paternal image, an image which, though repudiated by Georg
as son, actually forms the ideal model for his conception of
himself as father. The problem with this identification is that
the primal image is conceived entirely from the son's
perspective. Looking at it as a model for fatherhood, Georg
finds himself thrown back into that very filial position he had
rejected from symbolization.

Thus, at the end, the foreclosed father condemns the son for
desiring the very mode of being which he, the father,
exemplifies: "So now you know what existed outside of you,"
screams the father, "till now you've only known about
yourself! You were truly an innocent child, yes, but still more
truly were you a devilish human being" (67;62). Narcissism is
innocent in the child, cruel and tyrannical in the adult, as the
father's own actions demonstrate. His remark that Georg now
knows what is outside himself is highly ironic, for it is precisely
Georg's inability to accept difference that has precipitated the

hallucination now presenting itself as "other" before him. The father observes that Georg delayed a long time before becoming mature. But what he fails to add is that Georg's maturity, like his own, is in form only, purely a matter of possessing a woman, a certain social position, and the instrument for illusory domination over the Symbolic, writing. He is as unwilling to accept his name as metaphor as is Georg himself. Thus his sentence of his son to death by drowning can be understood only literally by Georg, as it might be by certain patients under deep hypnosis. What appears outside of him has all the power of an inner "drive" (cf. "zum wasser *trieb* es ihn"—67:63) and, in fact, seems to collapse as soon as that drive takes over (while Georg feels himself driven out of the room, the father crashes down on the bed behind him).

In order to preserve the illusion of his autonomy, Georg had kept his friend at a distance. But when the position of the specular double is taken over by the primal father, Georg's effort to maintain a separation fails and his continuing impulse towards unity finds fulfillment by dissolving the gap in a fusion with the paternal will. The aggression which had been directed outwards in the service of sadistic mastery is turned inwards in a masochistic self-destructive impulse. Instead of imagining that he has the father "within him", as Kafka's diary entry says he does at the beginning of the story, Georg now feels driven to become a part of the father, hallucinated though this figure may be. The landlady's outcry as Georg rushes down the stairs is thus perfectly in accord with his own earlier evocation of Christian imagery: like Jesus, he is being sacrificed by a father who is, in a sense, a product of his own mind and with whom he imagines uniting through death. His final thought is of his love for his parents; the component of fear has been entirely forgotten; the water receives him in a kind of maternal embrace. Internal and external, active and passive are at last made one. "Drop quietly into the river", Kafka wrote in a diary entry. "Dropping probably seems so desirable to me because it reminds me of being pushed" (*Tag*, 419/*D 2*, 76).

This brings us to the final sentence of the story: "At this

moment a downright unending stream of traffic (*Verkehr*) was going over the bridge" (68; 63). On one level, this statement stresses the total insignificance of Georg's fall which, like that of Icarus in Breughel's painting, takes place in the neglected margin of everyday activity. In Ferenczi's psychoanalytic interpretation the bridge symbolizes "the male member which unites the parents during sexual intercourse, and to which the little child must cling if he is not to perish in the 'deep water' across which the bridge is thrown".[20] Such a view may help to explain Kafka's remark to Brod that in writing this closing sentence he "had thought of a strong ejaculation".[21] This ejaculation would then refer to the active "Verkehr" (which in German may refer explicitly to sexual intercourse) from which the suicidal psychotic is excluded. But this concluding image has perhaps a more important function in terms of the structural dynamics of the text. As Ferenczi notes, the bridge symbol may be seen as "autosymbolic",[22] that is, as referring reflexively to the very function of the symbolic. We have noted that it was Georg's "crossing over" into his father's room which initiated that never-completed process of crossing which is the essence of metaphoric structure.[23] Such a crossing occurs in the temporal dimension of Kafka's final sentence: in one moment the traffic is unending. Here the infinite is compressed into the momentary, the momentary is expanded into the infinite. The normal course of time is suspended by a simultaneous movement in opposite directions. This suspension reflects the very condition of the text itself, a condition which Georg has rejected within the text but which Kafka affirms as its necessary ontology. During the composition of the story, he may have felt, as he notes in his diary, "as if [he] were moving forward in a body of water" (*Tag*, 293/*D 1*, 276), but the completed text constitutes a bridge over that water, one on which the writer traffics between a finite moment and an infinite expansion.

Although Kafka's attitude towards the nature and value of this scriptural traffic vacillated greatly throughout his career, "The Judgment" remained his favorite work, one that he called "more of a poem than a story".[24] Complimenting Milena on her translation of the closing sentence, Kafka remarked: "In that story every sentence, every word, every—if I may speak this way—musical note is connected to 'Angst'; the wound broke open then for the first time in one long night."[25] As I hope my analysis has demonstrated, this breaking open achieves the extraordinary coherence Kafka cherished by dramatically integrating the sexual and the textual aspects of oedipal struggle. On the textual level the story illustrates the necessary independence of writing from intentional control. It is his need to obliterate the Symbolic by filling in the figure of the friend with letters that causes Georg's breakdown when he wishes to cross the bridge to fatherhood.[26] The friend, like the castle in the novel of that name, is an idol created in an attempt to give stability to a textual world whose essential being-in-process undermines all dualisms. Maurice Blanchot calls this idolatrous figuration "the perceptible form of error" and explains its genesis in terms of that impatience, often deplored by Kafka, which causes one to "grasp as the immediate, as the already present, the profundity of the inexhaustible absence". "Man wants unity at once", comments Blanchot; "he wants it in separation itself; he pictures it for himself, and that representation, the image of unity, immediately constitutes the element of the dispersion in which he is lost more and more; for the image, as image, can never be attained, and it hides from him, moreover, the unity of which it is the image, and separates it from him by making itself inaccessible and by making unity inaccessible."[27] In "The Judgment" the image of unity— which Blanchot so rightly perceives as structured through separation—does its damage less by obscuring the inevitable proliferation of mediative figures than by closing off access to the very principle of metaphor.

No such closing-off, however, occurs in Kafka's own writing. For him the Symbolic is that absence which structures the world into which every literary beginning forms a bridge. Such, in exemplary manner, is the significance of the bridge in the very first paragraph of *The Castle*, on which K. stands gazing up into the "illusory emptiness" above him. The ambiguity of this phrase, which may connote a momentarily absent presence or the permanent void of an illusion, determines the very structure of the typical Kafka text, a structure which he first discovered in writing "The Judgment". At the apparent center of each of these texts is an image determined in some crucial way by its relation to the father—the torture machine in the penal colony, the court system in *The Trial*, Klamm and the castle bureaucracy in *The Castle*. The protagonist actively explores the meaning of these images in terms of the father's presence within them. The action of the text, however, undermines this assumption of presence by showing that the paternal image has authority in name only and is actually a metaphor for the play of metaphor.

"The Judgment" illustrates the psychotic consequences of a foreclosure of the father's metaphoric function. In the later works, this function is not so much foreclosed as it is aggressively combated. The dynamics we saw operating in the central section of "The Judgment" are elaborated to structure whole dramatic conflicts. The protagonists enter the text with a language and mode of thought not unlike those exemplified by Georg's writing: mimetic, controlling, repressive of unconscious motives, searching to establish presence. The world in which they find themselves, however, cannot be decoded using their habitual methods. It is inherently unstable and duplicitous, governed by the substitutive activity of metaphor itself, an activity which suspends the differences between active and passive, above and below, inside and outside, in a theoretically endless play of supplementation and interchangeability. Gregor Samsa cannot read his metamorphosed body as a significant revelation about his life because, as Stanley Corngold has pointed out, the metamorphosis is an ongoing process in which the relations between the literal and the figural, between Gregor's human consciousness and his insect being, are constantly changing.[28] No more can Joseph K. possibly understand the meaning of innocence within his *Prozess* because, as the painter Titorelli explains, accounts of definite acquittal are to be found only in legends; all written documents relating to the case, even the acquittal itself, are destroyed. Innocence exists solely outside the text, never as a presence within it.

Now Kafka himself felt, perhaps more acutely than any other writer, that his own being was determined by the deferring and suspending activity of writing. "It is not death, alas," he exclaimed, "but the eternal torments of dying" (*Tag*, 420/*D 2*, 77). The disjointed, fragmentary quality of his writings was, to his mind, the visible manifestation of this torment. Especially in the diary entries for the years 1911 and 1912, he repeatedly stated his desire to achieve a unity between the "fullness" of his conception, the "tremendous world" he had in his head, and the written expression of that "restrained harmony" (*Tag*, 162, 306, 75; *D 1*, 152, 288, 75). "I have too little time and quiet," he complained, "to draw out of me all the possibilities of my talent in their totality. For that reason it is only disconnected starts that always make an appearance. . . . If I were ever able to write something large and whole, well shaped from beginning to end, then the story would never be able to completely detach itself from me and it would be possible for me calmly and with open eyes, as a blood relation of a healthy story, to hear it read" (*Tag*, 142/*D 1*, 134). This is Kafka's own imaginary version of the mirror phase: the fantasy that a creation of language can have the same ontological status as a creature of the flesh. "The Judgment" was the only story he ever wrote which seemed to fulfill this fantasy, hence the fact that it remained his favorite work throughout his life. He recounts in his diary that no sooner had he finished writing the story than he entered trembling into his sisters' room and read it aloud to them (*Tag*, 293/*D 1*, 276). His action parallels that of Georg; here literature provides the script for life. Only, instead of bringing his writing to his father for approval, Kafka brings it to his sisters. A few months earlier he had remarked in his diary that the reason he so loved to read to his sisters was that their rapt attention allowed him to feel that he had actually merged with the work he was presenting (*Tag*, 231/*D 1*, 213). Thus Kafka's reading "The Judgment" to his sisters served to confirm the blood relationship he felt with this story, the composition of which he associated with the labor of birth.

"The story came out of me," Kafka noted in his diary as a preface to his interpretation of the work, "like a real birth, covered with filth and slime, and only I have the hand that can reach the body and the desire to do so" (*Tag*, 296/*D 1*, 278). This image of himself as both mother and (hermeneutic) midwife appears to counter that of the "Blutkreis" (circle of blood relationship) which, by Kafka's own account of the story's structure, was so tightly and destructively drawn around father and son. If this is so, then the ejaculation Kafka associated with the final sentence may have its genesis in the victory he felt his writing act had achieved over the spectre of hostile paternal narcissism that prevailed in the story's narrative. In the terms in which Kafka metaphorizes his creative process, the feminine experience of release through birth is prior to, and may even trigger, the masculine experience of release through ejaculation. Thus it would seem that, for Kafka, to mother a text is to triumph over that paternal threat of castration which structures the text's signifying function.

The exhilarating experience of giving birth to "The Judgment" remained a focus for Kafka's nostalgia, but it could not erase his penetrating lucidity about writing being a process of dying rather than a celebration of potency. To identify himself with writing, as he increasingly did, meant to experience his life as structured like a text. He could not emerge from this text to take a place outside it any more than Joseph K. can extricate himself from his trial. Thus the metaphor of the father, which Kafka saw as determining the displacements and substitutions of textual production, continued to dominate his life as it did his writing. He mothered no other texts after "The Judgment" because he found it impossible to consider his literary products as continuous with his biological existence. Moreover, none of his subsequent writings were brought into the world in the continuous labor of one long night. His life was like a text, but his texts were not life.

"The writer," Kafka wrote to Max Brod, "has no ground, no

duration, is not even made of dust…[his] existence is really dependent on the writing table, and if he truly wants to avoid madness, he must never go away from the table but cling to it with his teeth."[29] The writing table is Kafka's bridge, the locus of his unrealizable crossing, of his suspension in process. "The Judgment" is the first text he wrote in which this suspension is effectively imaged and directly linked to the notion of a decentering absence. But, from the metamorphosed metaphor named Gregor Samsa to the "illusory emptiness" named the castle, Kafka subsequently explored in more and more complex elaborations the structural function—as floating signifier, as supplement, as name-of-the-father—of that absence obscured in "The Judgment" through the letters to the friend.

NOTES

1. *BF*,156/*LFe*, 86-87. Henceforth abbreviations, with page numbers, included in the text. Unless otherwise indicated in these notes, all translations in the text are my own.

2. *Tag*, 294/*D 1*, 276. Henceforth abbreviations, with page numbers, included in the text.

3. This analogy forms part of the interpretation of the friend as Kafka the writer first put forward by Kate Flores in her seminal article "The Judgment." *FKT*, 5-24. Martin Greenberg in his *Terror of Art*, 60, believes that this interpretation corresponds to Kafka's intention, but then he argues that "the necessity for…biographical references indicates Kafka's failure to realize *in the story* the meaning he intended the friend to have." Evidently, this appeal to intention reveals Greenberg's own interpretive choice: Kafka himself was far more uncertain about the function of the friend than is his critic.

4. *Tag*, 463/*D 2*, 115. Henceforth abbreviations, with page numbers, included in the text.

5. The first of these two page numbers refers to the German text as given in *E* (1935 ed.); the second to the English translation in *PC*.

6. Jacques Lacan: "Le stade du miroir comme fornateur de la fonction du Je" in his *Ecrits*, Paris: Seuil, 1966, 93-100.

7. Sigmund Freud: *Beyond the Pleasure Principle*. New York: Liveright, 1961, 8-11.

8. D. W. Winnicott: "Mirror-role of Mother and Family in Child Development" in his *Playing and Reality* New York: Basic Books, 1971, 111. In italics in Winnicott's text.

9. The meaning and structure of these two relations as they are found in literary texts is the subject of Jeffrey Mehlman's brilliant and stimulating book, *A Structural Study of Autobiography: Proust, Leiris, Sartre, Lévi-Strauss*. Cornell University Press, 1974. My thesis in this article is indebted to the close examination of Mehlman's argument I undertook in a review-essay, "Structuralist Plots and Counterplots," *Boundary 2* (Spring 1976).

10. Unfortunately, Lacan has never given a full exposition of the difficult concept of the name-of-the-father. The most complete explanation is to be found in "D'une question préliminaire à tout traitement possible de la psychose," *Ecrits*, pp. 531-583.

Anthony Wilden's discussion helps clarify matters somewhat: *The Language of the Self*. Johns Hopkins Press, 1968, especially 270-284.

In this essay I will be making use of the three terms by which Lacan designates the essential orders of the psychoanalytic field: the Real, the Imaginary and the Symbolic. Briefly, the Real is whatever exists outside of symbolization; the Imaginary refers to the dual relationship of subject and counterpart characteristic of the mirror phase (of which, more later); the Symbolic, to borrow the cryptic definition adopted by Laplanche and Pontalis, "covers those phenomena with which psychoanalysis deals in so far as they are structured like a language." *The Language of Psycho-Analysis*. New York: Norton, 1973, 439.

11.   Jacques Derrida: *L'écriture et la différence*. Paris: Seuil, 1967, 423. This passage has been translated somewhat differently in *The Languages of Criticism and the Sciences of Man*, ed. Richard Macksey and Eugenio Donato. Baltimore: Johns Hopkins Press, 1970, 260.

12.   Claude Lévi-Strauss: "Introduction a l'oeuvre de Marcel Mauss" in *Marcel Mauss: Sociologie et Anthropologie*. Paris: Presses Universitaires de France, 1973, XLIX-l. 13.   *BK* (1954 ed.), 43.

14.   Derrida, 427; *Languages of Criticism*, 264.

15.   *S* (1935 ed.), 270; *C* (1964 ed.), 302. Walter Benjamin remarks of the assistants that they belong to a recurrent group of characters in Kafka's work, "the unfinished and the bunglers," none of whom "has a firm place in the world, firm, inalienable outlines" but whose "intermediate" existence, both "comforting and silly," provides the only token of hope for an exit from the paralyzing family circle. "Franz Kafka" in his *Illuminations*. New York: Harcourt, Brace & World, 1968, 116-118.

16.   Sigmund Freud: *Group Psychology and the Analysis of the Ego*. New York: Norton, 1975, 55-6. Walter Benjamin stresses Kafka's uncanny ability to evoke a "prehistoric world" and notes that "as the father [in "The Judgment"] throws off the burden of the blanket, he also throws off a cosmic burden. He has to set cosmic ages in motion in order to turn the age-old father-son relationship into a living and consequential thing," 113.

17.   Sigmund Freud: "The 'Uncanny'" in his *On Creativity and the Unconscious*. New York: Harper and Row, 1958, 157.

18.   Quoted by Laplanche and Pontalis, 168.

19.   *Group Psychology*, 59, "The hypnotist," Freud remarks "awakens in the subject a portion of his archaic heritage which had also made him compliant towards his parents and which had experienced an individual re-animation in his relation to his father; what is thus awakened is the idea of a paramount and dangerous personality, towards whom only a passive-masochistic attitude is possible, to whom one's will has to be surrendered,—while to be alone with him, 'to look him in the face,' appears a hazardous enterprise." The difference with Georg is that, having repudiated rather than re-animated the archaic conflict at the oedipal stage, he lacks the patient's "knowledge that in spite of everything hypnosis is only a game, the deceptive renewal of these old impressions."

It should be pointed out that to look the father in the face is not equivalent to perceiving the father's threat to be specifically castrating. As Samuel Weber has observed in his sophisticated critique of Freud's essay on "The Uncanny": "What is designated by the term 'castration' is precisely the impossibility of seeing directly, right on or straight ahead. . . . What should have remained concealed and what has nonetheless, in a certain manner, emerged engenders the uncanny because its very appearance eludes perception, its being is not to be had, because it side-steps and side-tracks. . . . by repeating, doubling, splitting and reflecting." In a similar manner, Georg is blind to the way the father doubles him and reflects the fears of his own past: "He kept on forgetting everything" (66; 61). Though the father's power remains ultimate, Georg seems unable ever to bring it into focus. "The uncanny," Weber continues, "is thus bound up with a *crisis* of perception and of phenomenality, but concomitantly with a mortal danger to the subject, to the 'integrity' of its body and thus to its very identity, which—if we accept the psychoanalytic theory of narcissism—is based upon this body image as its model." Samuel Weber: "The Sideshow, or: Remarks on a Canny Moment," *MLN*, LXXXVIII, No. 6, (Dec. 1973), 1122, 1131.

20. Sandor Ferenczi: *Further Contributions to the Theory and Technique of Psycho-Analysis*. New York: Basic Books, 1952, p. 356. (I am grateful to Murray Schwartz for having drawn my attention to this essay as well as to that of Winnicott mentioned above.) There is a striking biographical analogy here. Two months before he became engaged to Felice Bauer, Kafka, in despair about his ambivalence in her regard, imagined committing suicide by jumping from a balcony. "My place is down below," he wrote in his diary, "I find no other solution" ("Ausgleich," literally, "equalization") *Tag*, 360; *D 2*, 20.

21. Brod: *Uber F.K.*, 114.

22. Ferenczi, p. 355.

23. It is significant that in Kafka's marvelous parable "On Parables" the debate centers on the sage's advice "Gehe hinuber," "Go over." Literature in Kafka is always a movement of crossing but, as this parable illustrates, the space on the other side can be entered only through absolute "loss"; writing is a never-ending approach from the position of exile.

24. *Br*, 148.

25. *BM*, 214/*LM*, 191.

26. Though he was a prolific letter-writer, Kafka remarked to Milena that "all the misfortune of my life...derives, one could say, from letters or from the possibility of writing letters....The easy possibility of letter-writing must—seen merely theoretically—have brought into the world a terrible disintegration of souls. It is, in fact, an intercourse with ghosts, and not only with the ghost of the recipient but also with one's own ghost which develops between the lines of the letter one is writing and even more so in a series of letters where one letter corroborates the other and can refer to it as a witness." BM, 260; LM, 229. Just this kind of invention of a fiction of the self in terms of an imaginary other occurs in Georg's correspondence with his friend.

27. Maurice Blanchot: "The Diaries: The Exigency of the Work of Art," FKT, 213. Originally in *L'Espace littéraire*. Paris: Gallimard, 1955, 92-93.

28. Stanley Corngold, "The Structure of Kafka's 'Metamorphosis'" in his *The Commentators' Despair*. Port Washington: Kennikat Press, 1973, 1-38.

29. *Br*, 386.

Kate Flores

The Pathos of Fatherhood *

Kafka's story "The Judgment" has been analyzed so often and in such scrupulous detail it would seem not a word has been left unexamined. There is, however, one word that so far as I know has been neglected, as if it held no significance; and lest it be overlooked I should like to accord it the consideration given most other words in this story. That word is "alone".

"Alone—" Georg Bendemann says to his bride-to-be of his bachelor friend in Russia, "do you know what that means?"

Georg Bendemann is evidently a man sensitive to what it means to be alone. He hesitates to invite his friend to his wedding out of fear that his loneliness in his exile might be intensified by attending this event celebrating the end of his own aloneness amidst his old friends in his native surroundings. He worries about the loneliness of his friend in the vastness of that foreign country where he has no contact with either the natives or the colony of his compatriots there. He seems to miss him, noting the lameness of his excuses for returning home so rarely; yet wonders about suggesting that he give up his exile for fear he might not be welcomed back to the

---

* This is a new essay on "The Judgment" by Kate Flores. The one referred to by other contributors to this book is "Franz Kafka and the Nameless Guilt" (_QRL_, 1947; _FKT_, 1958).

circle of his old friends; there might be a certain estrangement which, Georg thinks, might prove so painful the friend would go back into his exile, lonelier than before. Georg seems nonplussed by solitude, vaguely afraid of it, as we are of hermits, haunted houses and lone wolves; if others give no evidence of minding it he thinks something must be wrong (did his friend not have signs of some disease on his last visit home?) He is a sociable man with what he clearly regards as normal social instincts. In the evening he sits for a while with his widowed father and then goes out with friends or, more recently, to visit his bride-to-be.

While Georg Bendemann's aversion to solitude is not explicitly stated, it can readily be deduced from the narrative text, which is presented in such dry, emotionally bare prose that one is put off from delving into any substratum of human feeling, as if this would be not quite polite or politic—a prose Kafka cultivated, evidently, in writing accident reports for his insurance office, in which he would describe the most awful mishaps as ordinary matters of course, in faceless tones devoid of any trace of sympathy for the unfortunate victims. Yet the lean narrative related in this detached, seemingly casual style is obviously only the tip of a huge hidden iceberg of which one is aware the more keenly because of the care with which all mention of it is avoided.

The fear of aloneness to be perceived in this story is another of those typically human traits distinguishing men from animals which fascinated Kafka in all his work. One might almost say his subject was the contrast between the human and the animal condition. He constantly portrayed animals with human attributes: intellectual dogs, mice who sing, apes who give lectures to academies. And in depicting human beings what intrigued him were peculiarly human problems that animals for some reason are not required to cope with: existential meanings, the intricacies of laws men are supposed to abide by but which are never explained; syndromes of guilt; the need to marry, have a home, be a father. The burdens of being human he found oppressive to the point of being laughable. To probe into the substratum of some of his stories, therefore, means to trace that mysterious line between the animal and the human, even to go back to some of the origins of the human emergence from the animal state. Yet such probing may, I think, be illuminative of some of the apparent obscurities of his tales which for all their strangeness seem to hold some buried truth we do not quite understand.

The fear of aloneness is a typical human trait which owes its intensity to the long period of helplessness of the human infant—longer than that of any other species. This long helplessness is due to the size of the human brain, which is only partially developed at birth and requires several more years to reach full development; if the brain were any larger at birth the infant could not be delivered of its mother. Thus the dread of aloneness which is one mark of distinction between the human and the animal is traceable to the largeness of the human brain, the principal physical attribute distinguishing the human species, and the exceptionally long period of helplessness this extraordinary size necessitates.

The human child is not only born helpless; he instinctively knows he is helpless, dependent on others around him; hence his instinctive cry, his instinctive need for contact and constant touch, and his instinctive fear of being abandoned even temporarily. If left alone even momentarily he cries; upon his elder's return he cries even harder to indicate that leaving him is a betrayal of him in his helplessness. No mother is unaware of her infant's sense of betrayal at being left alone, or of her own sense of guilt at abandoning him even temporarily; it is the foundation of her human morality. As the child slowly matures he may not cry but still resents absence deeply; he may cry only when she returns—the sense of betrayal remains.

Thus when he comes to learn about the fact of death, usually from someone other than his parents, the child fears death as a terrible betrayal—his parents are going to die and leave him alone forever. Though he may realize it is something his parents themselves dread and do not care even to mention, the knowledge that some day they will leave him never to return is a traumatic experience, another instance of the faithlessness of his elders whom he has learned to suspect to the extent they are constantly trying to escape from their trust to seek respite from his care in adult activities from which he is firmly excluded. To a child the discovery that his parents will one day die is final proof of their perfidy which sinks into his consciousness even though he may give it little thought or actually try to conceal it, from his parents particularly. But it remains an unspoken strain between the generations, part of a widening gulf of non-understanding between them.

And the child, whether knowingly or not, tries ever after his discovery to prepare himself for this eventual loss. He seeks, for example, closer bonds with his contemporaries who are not going to die and leave him alone. It is thus usually about the age of discovery of death that children form close friendships with their peers, much closer than such ties had previously been. These childish bonds of friendship are their first rejection of a generation too old for them, their consolation for their parents' anticipated desertion, insurance against the aloneness they will one day have to face.

These friendships of childhood and early adolescence are parent-substitutes in more ways than one. The friend provides the child with a mutuality of interest his parents in their oldness cannot give—the friend will play with him indefinitely, all day and every day; while parents are busy with their adult affairs. The child thus revels in his new friendship—the parent-substitute is better than the parents. With his friend he forms almost an alliance against both sets of parents, the entire adult generation, who constantly spoil the fun with tiresome admonitions about keeping clean, being careful and such. Sometimes these alliances are taken rather seriously. Pre-adolescent boys especially will vow eternal loyalty; often they will tell one another they are never going to marry—women particularly are a nuisance. Meanwhile the parents encourage such friendships, realizing the child requires more play than they can possibly engage in with him; and the child recognizes this encouragement as further proof, if any were needed, of their already proven unfaithfulness—a quality they detest.

It may be supposed that Georg Bendemann's friend in Russia, whose face he says he has known since childhood, is such a friend, the male-bonding friend of boyhood and adolescence who often becomes best man at weddings—a stopgap friend between the bondage of parents and the bondage of marriage. Clearly the continuance of the friendship has been important to Georg; he has maintained it all these years and tried even after the friend's departure to correspond despite their increasingly diverging interests and attenuating contact. "What can one write to a man like that?" he muses; but he writes him nonetheless, not out of nostalgia for his youth and sympathy for him in his exile, which he has no wish to share—his friend has invited him to no avail—but for a more important reason: at the urging of his fiancée in a moment of passionate embrace he has decided to break the news of his engagement to his friend. This decision has been difficult because he apparently feels, despite his self-reassurances that his friend will still be his friend after his marriage, that this announcement will announce the end of his friendship as well.

For marriage with a young woman of his own age who will be his companion for life is another of those substitutions comparable to the substitution of his friend and boon companion for his parents at a time of dissatisfaction with the quality of their companionship and of realization that the closeness they were providing was only temporary since ultimately they were going to die. The bride-to-be is another contemporary substitution replacing both his parents and his friend as insurance against aloneness.

Thus it is that he has felt a certain guilt toward his boyhood chum whose companionship he once enjoyed so much: he is in a way betraying him and forming an alliance with his bride-to-be just as he once, no doubt, formed an alliance with his friend against his parents. Like his parents, however, one of whom has already deserted him, his friend has gone abroad and left him "at home," at home with his now elderly father. And he refuses to return. Nor is there any assurance that his companionship would be the same even if he were to return; most probably it would not, Georg has come to think; there would be an unavoidable alienation. Thus the quality of his friend's companionship, like that of his parents, has deteriorated; and by abandoning him for such long periods he has almost forced Georg into finding another contemporary protection against aloneness. The bride-to-be, he has decided in a moment of closeness, will be as superior to his absent friend in this respect as his friend was superior to his parents; and it was in that moment of intimacy, when he was not only sure of the bride-to-be but also certain that his friendship was irretrievably impaired, that he had made his decision definitively to end this friendship in favor of marriage.

Thus he seals the letter to his friend feeling that even if it seals his friendship he is still secure against aloneness because he has already sealed the compact of his engagement. Yes, he can end this friendship with impunity. This relic of his boyhood must be left behind; he must give up this youthful attachment, and step into manhood at last.

And yet, and yet....

Why, after finally finishing this letter he has been trying for so long to avoid having to write, is he so pensive? Why is he so dilatory, toying with it for a while before slowly, dreamily, inserting it into its envelope? Why does he then linger with this letter in his hand "for a long time," lost in contemplation, apparently, and, with his elbow propped up on his writing table, sit gazing out the window at the river, the bridge and the greening hills in the distance?

Can it be that he is reluctant to cross that bridge to manhood?

Can it be that he feels regretful now, that he has doubts about his decision, that he wonders if anyone can ever take the place of his absent friend of so many years—certainly not the "passing acquaintance" whose greeting from the street below he has "barely acknowledged" with an "absent smile," as if the smile were for the absent friend?

Why does he at last put that letter in his pocket and, instead of going out to post it, cross over to his father's room, where he has not been for months, to ask his father's approval of this particular letter? Can it be that this is another procrastination; that he thinks, perhaps hopes, his father may put obstacles in his way, and thus spare him the need of really mailing it off? Why does he need his father's opinion about informing his friend of his marriage? He does not seem to need his advice about other matters; in the business he seems relieved that his father has given him free rein to do things his own way, to be a man at last.

In his protracted deliberations about friendship and marriage, Georg's father has not figured at all, except negatively in the sense that since his semi-retirement the business has flourished as never before. Georg has dwelt upon this, evidently taking great satisfaction in it, almost giving figures to prove it. The additional profits for which he feels he is responsible would seem to be an added incentive to marriage, as the unprofitableness of his bachelor friend's business has meant, according to Georg, that "he is wearing himself out to no purpose."

Georg Bendemann is the typical vacillating Kafka hero, one of those earnest, solitary young men who, apparently innocent of having done anything wrong, try desperately to be extremely moral men but find themselves enmeshed in hopeless quandaries because of rules of human society they do not quite understand. They have no idea how they came about, why or by whom they were made, on what criteria of right and wrong, even at times what they are; they seem to be unspoken codes which everyone but themselves either knows or is not concerned with in the least. In this existential dilemma men differ, of course, from animals, who never have such problems.

Actually the social codes in which the human male becomes involved at maturity have their origins in the distant emergence of the human from the animal state, and are for this reason mythic and arcane, to the human male particularly, whose emergence from the animal state was much more complex than the emergence of the female.

Thus the basic unit of animal society, such as it is, is the mother and brood. Whatever animal morality there is is based on the mother bringing her brood to maturity. This is in all cases a relatively brief and temporary period—at most, in the case of the apes, a few years, after which the mother-offspring identity lapses; it rarely lasts into a new bearing period. In this primitive "ethic" the male is hardly involved; his role is almost always purely sexual.

Except that the human mother bears even when she still has a dependent youngster, the period of dependence being considerably longer and her identification with all her offspring lifelong instead of seasonal, essentially the animal family unit, animal society and animal morality are comparable to the matriarchal system of the early human emergence, when children were not identified with their male parents; there was matrilinear descent. This was before the cognizance of paternity.

For paternity is a relatively recent discovery of the human race; even the anthropoid apes are unaware of it. Indeed among human beings there are tribes who until fairly recently never associated the sexual act with infants born nine months later and for several months not evident in the mother's body. The human discovery of paternity had the profoundest repercussions. It might almost be said that civilization began with this discovery. For whereas previously the role of the male was very fleeting, with discovery of paternity the male gradually became a permanent part of the basic family unit of society: mother and father both caring and providing for their progeny and identifying with them for life. The basis of morality thus shifted from mother-child to father-mother-child association and responsibility, the patriarchal system.

The shift to the new moral code, however, was not quickly made. For while maternal identification with her offspring is easy, encoded in her genes, as it were, paternal identification is exceedingly far-fetched; it is not encoded in the genes of the male; only his sexual role is encoded. The idea of a father—a male with a more than purely sexual association with a female and with responsibility for his progeny, is almost an abstraction, requiring an intellectual leap; and has to be taught. It cannot be taught to animals because their brains are physiologically incapable of cognizance of things not immediately impinging on their sense organs; they must live almost entirely in the present and cannot be aware of such things as origins or destinies. The "metaphysical" awareness of past and future is peculiarly human because of the associative powers of the human brain which develop in those years of helplessness after birth that distinguish the animal from the human infant. Nevertheless the teaching of fatherhood required thousands of years of indoctrination. The human male did not readily accept paternal responsibilities; a whole new framework of laws had to arise to impress it upon him, often, at first, in a very heavy-handed way. Thus with discovery of paternity the worship of goddesses as source of life slowly shifted to worship of male gods. The father, mother and infant were held up in religious myth as the "Sacred Family" which must hold together for life; unless this basic social unit held together, society as a whole would disintegrate, men were told. The socio-religious-legal establishment of early civilization was dedicated at first almost entirely to the task of making males identify with their offspring and, at maturity, assume the burdens of paternity. Numerous means were devised including rituals such as weddings at which the woman even took the man's name and agreed to give it to her children. This shift from matrilinear to patrilinear descent was only a small part of the monumental efforts of patriarchal society to bind the male not only to the woman but to their offspring for life. Thus the human wedding rite is attended by eyewitnesses certifying to the identification who represent powerful institutions—the religious establishment, the law, her family and friends, his family and friends, the whole human power structure, as it were. The emphasis upon virginity at such rites was a way of reassuring the male that her children would be his; and the religious and social proscription of pre-wedding-rite sex as a "sin" had the double advantage of reassuring males of their paternity and pressuring males to wed, since only after thus publicly acknowledging their identification with the bride's children was sex permissible as no longer a social and religious "sin." All this intense social, religious and legal pressure is of course unknown to non-human males. Only human males had to assume fatherly responsibilities as the price of socially acceptable adulthood; for this reason they often feared and evaded it in ways animals never do. Among many early social groups, including the Jews, all males were forced to marry; males who refused to do so were usually ostracized from the group, or at least regarded as anomalous, abnormal if only because they could bear the loneliness of alienation from their family and friends.

The life Georg Bendemann's bachelor friend leads in his exile is perhaps what Georg conceives himself as having to endure were he to fail to marry; and in his normal aversion to aloneness and need for social acceptance he of course chooses marriage.

But not without misgivings. Like all Kafka heroes, he is plagued with indecision. For he seems to have an aversion to marriage almost equal to his aversion to aloneness.

This aversion to marriage, like his aversion to aloneness, is never stated. For it is a complicated emotional problem; and in Kafka emotions are painful and, as a rule, suppressed. Nevertheless Georg's attitude toward marriage may be read between the lines of this story.

Of Georg's fiancée as a person we are told very little; we know much more about the individuality of his friend. This in itself tells us something. And as compared with his intense absorption in the personality of his friend, almost to the point of obsession, there seems to be something perfunctory about his relationship with his fiancée. We are twice informed, once in his letter to his friend, that she is "a girl from a well-to-do-family," as if this were her chief identity and characteristic, and he attached more importance to her family and their affluence than to any personal qualities she might have. There is something revealing too about her being described twice in exactly the same way: "a [or "one"] Miss Frieda Brandenfeld." She seems a bit boring; is there nothing else to say about her except that she is "a Miss"? Even the use of the indefinite article is indicative; one uses it to describe people one feels uninterested in or detached about: "a [one] Mr. Joseph Smith," someone with whom one is not involved and knows little about but the name, the implication being that there is little else of interest to mention. What is she like, then? We are told she "breathes hard under his kisses;" but otherwise are given no inkling of her nature except what can be gleaned from two remarks which would seem to indicate she is possessive, demanding and rather illogical: "Still I have a right to know all your friends. . . . If you have friends like that, Georg, you should never have got engaged"—surely one of the oddest non sequiturs in this story. He then reminds her that she is "to blame" for this as much as he himself; evidently he feels she made advances and got him involved in something for which they are now "to blame," as if it were some not altogether fortunate situation.

In any event Georg seems worried not about this "Miss Frieda Brandenfeld" as an individual—apparently he feels women are all pretty much alike and one must resign oneself to their foibles; but about the whole prospect of marriage itself.

It would seem to trouble him, to loom as a large undertaking requiring the most elaborate preparations, something he agreed to mainly for family and social reasons, in a moment of passion, perhaps, but is rueful about in moments of coolness, though he is willing to go through with it now because of his extraordinary conscientiousness and need for social acceptance. He knows his vulnerability. "That's the way I am made," he tells himself, almost apologetic about what he seems to regard as a weakness in himself to which he has succumbed. Defensively he adds that his friend will just have to take him the way he is. How strongly he seems to feel that his friend will not forgive him for succumbing!

And indeed it is in his uneasiness about his friend that his uneasiness about marriage is most clearly revealed.

Thus he goes to extreme lengths to avoid having to "confess" his engagement to his friend, preferring merely to hint at it in three separate letters, and finally telling his fiancée he would prefer his friend found out about it by hearsay, or in some other way.

Moreover in his long soliloquy he seems, rather oddly, to equate his friend's decision to remain abroad with a decision to remain a bachelor. It is as though those who stay at home and are sociable and conformist marry, while those who go abroad are anti-social, non-conformist and remain single. So that the friend's refusal to return is equivalent to a refusal to marry.

Why then is he so unaccountably reluctant to suggest that his friend return home? In his soliloquy the entire third paragraph, the longest in the story, is devoted to a rather labored rationalization for not trying to persuade him to come back, whether permanently or even for a visit to attend his wedding. Can it be that long ago they had a compact between them not to marry, and that the friend, in staying abroad a bachelor, is showing that he has not forgotten that compact, and intends to honor it? Can it be that Georg realizes that to urge him to return is to urge him to forget their old covenant, to renounce it and betray it, as he himself now wants to forget it and renounce it, to grow up now and stop being a "big kid"? Can it be that the friend's integrity in remaining single is a silent accusal, a reminder of Georg's bad faith; and that rather than have him return now that he is reneging he would prefer him to stay abroad, where he will not have to face him in dishonor?

At all events it seems clear that when Georg enters his father's room to consult with him about his letter he is ill at ease and ambivalent. On the one hand he wants his father to help him decide to mail the letter, marry and become mature, assume the burdens of manhood. But on the other . . .

Thus the excruciating dilemmas of the maturing human male, problems peculiar to human society and human morality—problems of the human condition which animals in their animal condition need not and cannot cope with. Some of these are problems which we have not solved partly because we still do not quite understand them.

No animal, for example, ever knowingly faces its male parent; this facing is peculiar to the human species. When a human son knowingly faces his father and the father his son, the facing is complex and often uneasy, laden with the weight of the millennia of human emergence from the animal state, including the early religious emphasis upon the father as creator and hence object of worship, for example. Some of this

background can be sensed in the facing of father Bendemann—
he is given no first name—and his son Georg, who is in all ways
a human son, child of a human family who wants to be a
"moral" accepted member of human society. He sincerely
respects and "loves" his father with a love that includes fear of
his authority over him. But although the ancient background
of father worship can be sensed in the Bendemann facing, it is
sensed only ambiguously because of Kafka's cold, emotion-
cleansed style. Thus even though Georg kneels before his
white-haired father and gazes up into his eyes, on the whole the
old man is described with a clinical detachment bordering on
distaste, with references to his toothless mouth, defective
vision, soiled linen, his war wound on his upper thigh; and the
father's age and decrepitude are made so clear he can hardly be
taken for immortal. So that despite the faint religious echoes
here of the father worship of the early human emergence, the
relationship between the two Bendemanns is portrayed as a
specifically human relationship fraught with all the exquisite
uncertainties of the human condition, neither animal nor
divine.

Thus this human father and his mature son face one another
not only in recognition of their fatherhood and sonhood; they
face each other across a tremendous gap of time, the gap of an
entire human generation, manhood to manhood. This gap
puts them in two different worlds, unlike all animal
generations, which either have no contact at all (the earliest
animals merely divide in two and *become* the new generation),
or at most a brief and passing one.

Kafka makes it clear that in crossing that passageway from
his own room to his father's Georg Bendemann is entering a
different world; but it is also clear that Georg is either not quite
aware of the difference or wishes to ignore it. It is partly because
of this obliviousness that he finds himself in the difficulty
which in his ambivalence he surely seeks.

The father is sitting alone in a corner decked out with
mementoes of his dead wife, his breakfast almost untouched
before him on dishes which his wife would surely have removed
had she been there to share it with him. He is reading an old,

apparently now-defunct newspaper by a window overlooking a narrow courtyard bordered by a high blank wall which darkens the room even on this sunny day. Georg in his aversion to solitariness seems repelled. "It's unbearably dark in here," he remarks, adding, "And you've shut the window too," to which the father replies, "I prefer it that way."

This opening exchange is a foreboding of the conflict to come.

For there can be no doubt that what we are about to witness is a power struggle between these two grown men, a struggle involving not only the two protagonists but the dead wife and mother, Georg's fiancée and of course the exiled friend. The background of this struggle is the entire history of the relationship of these five persons in the context of the family. And like a tribe or nation, a family is basically a power unit joined in a struggle against loneliness and the outside world. The unit, to survive in this struggle, must hold together in mutual protection, "love" and domination. Between these three there runs a very thin line, and it is across this perilous line that all involved must walk. Where does one end and the other begin? Does one protect because one loves, vice versa, or both? One must dominate a child in order to protect him; at what point does protection cease and domination begin? The child, like a pet dog, is "good" if he obeys, allows himself to be protected-dominated and therefore loved; he then loves in return; but does the love cease if he no longer needs protection-domination? One can assert one's domination by withdrawing love if he is not "good" (obedient, or submissive to protection-domination); but does the child by the same token no longer "love" when, mature, he no longer needs protection and expresses his wish to end domination as well? As the permutations are endless, the questions are infinite. The male animal, happily, is never faced with such alternatives. Only the human male is a family man, with family cares, family responsibilities, and father-son confrontations.

In the Bendemann confrontation the father is manifestly a very much stronger character. He is the indomitable male of the patriarchal society, who feels he must be dominant to love, dominant to protect, dominant over everything and everybody around him; and they must love him for being so; for is he not protecting them because he loves them? Undoubtedly he dominated his wife, now totally muted in death and missed as an object of domination as much as an object of love. But he can still dominate Georg; and he does. This is evident in his first response to Georg's opening gambit observing, with ever so gentle a demurrer, that his father's room is intolerably dark and airless; though of course it probably seems more so by contrast with his own room. Does the father play the gracious host, open a blind, raise the window, try to make his guest comfortable? No, no one is going to tell him how to keep his room; he is the master here, not Georg. Warily Georg retreats, without exactly apologizing, by offering a face-saving non-critical rejoinder, "as if it were an appendix to his previous remark," though of course it is not: "Well, it's quite warm outside;" so that he is back on neutral ground, instead of aggressively on his father's. But he has been made to feel almost an intruder, and quickly, defensively, states the purpose of his call: "I really just wanted to tell you. . . ." He lifts the letter out of his pocket slightly, then, as if intimidated, vulnerable, lets it drop back.

There can be little question that of these two men Georg is the weaker personality; if he has difficulty facing the prospect of marriage it is partly the difficulty of conceiving himself ever becoming as masterful as this father. His extreme gregarious-ness and fear of solitude is only one indication of this weakness. Unable to prevail upon his friend to return home, he gives up almost in fear of even trying; and though he wanted almost desperately not to inform his friend of his engagement he finally does so reluctantly at the behest of his fiancée, who manipulates him easily. Both in will and physique the father is overpowering, evidently huge compared with Georg, who would not observe "My father is still a giant" were he not smaller. And all the somewhat fussy qualms that beset his delicate sensibility are clearly not to be shared with this giant of a man who would undoubtedly brush them aside with a raucous laugh at their silliness.

Old Bendemann obviously still feels toward young Georg the same patronizing condescension he has had since Georg was a baby, and which Georg has always, no doubt, felt keenly in his presence; he quails before him. For his father never fails to put him down, make him feel insecure, pull the rug from under him to demonstrate his paternal superiority. And somehow, as Georg now observes, he is even more overbearing when they face one another alone. "In business hours he's quite different," he thinks. "How solidly he sits here with his arms crossed." Obviously he is no man to be trifled with; and Georg takes him very seriously, too seriously. For Georg is an extremely serious young man, even prim and proper; a square who follows in his father's footsteps; though the father later accuses him of being a jokester, he is not one to play jokes, especially on his father. Rather it is the old man who in his paternalistic manner loves to tease Georg in his ingenuousness, and play jokes upon him.

Thus when Georg tells him, "I am sending the news of my engagement to St. Petersburg," the father asks, as if uncomprehendingly: "To St. Petersburg?"

How equivocal Georg is about that friend! "To my friend there," he specifies, "trying to meet his father's eye."

When the father then says "with peculiar emphasis": "Oh yes, to your friend," and puts down his paper, his glasses on top of the paper and his hand atop his glasses, one can surmise that he is going to seize upon this friend in his ensuing offensive.

Georg is now frankly apologetic, explaining in painstaking detail his sensitive considerations in not having told his friend of his engagement before.

The father seems unconcerned with these compunctions as he asks, with a trace of sarcasm, perhaps: "And now you've changed your mind?"

Doggedly Georg outlines why he has changed his mind; finally asking his father's approval of mailing off the letter.

But the father is clearly interested in neither the friend nor the letter. He is interested only in taking control of the situation, in seizing the center of the stage, in dominating Georg, in telling him off.

It is thus significant that this story takes place on a Sunday, when the family business is closed and the employees not around. For during business hours the father has to play the role of loving father bequeathing his business to his son; lately he has even been deferring to Georg, "keeping himself more in the background," instead of "insisting on running the business in his own way"; for the employees, especially the new employees, must be made to feel that Georg is in charge; and he must keep up appearances before them. But Sunday is the one day he can give vent to his grievances. And these are many.

We can believe that Georg, in his anxiety to conform, to be accepted, is something of a prig, in business as well as everywhere else. One can indeed picture him, in the words of old Bendemann, "stalking away from his father in the impassive mask of an honorable man" as he concludes business deals prepared for him by his father without bothering to give him credit explicitly. It would of course be awkward if not impossible to do so; Georg would lose face; and even if his father established the business in the first place, Georg has been dutiful in carrying on. Nevertheless, even though the father's retirement is inevitable if Georg is to succeed to the business, he seems to want to hang on. He has put all his life's work into this business and naturally feels resentful, unfairly ignored and rejected, however unfair to consider it unfair.

Moreover old Bendemann, like all human parents, knows that when his only child reaches maturity his intergenerational role is over and his nuclear family disintegrating, the wedding being in one aspect the ritual of this disintegration, when the nuclear family breaks up just as a cell breaks up on reaching mature size to re-form into two new ones. Georg's announcement, therefore, that he is sending this letter to his friend signifying his maturity announces what the old man does not really want to hear: the sealing of that letter has sealed his end as a father dominating-loving-protecting his nuclear family.

Georg, however, seems oblivious of this and of its emotional implications. In his desire to observe the proprieties he tries to ignore emotions, just as he does in business hours; emotions are to be contained, never recognized or stated. It would be too painful, too embarrassing.

But the father resents this attitude. He feels it is hypocritical, a pose that serves to keep Georg on top of him. Hitherto he has suppressed his resentment; but the slights have been adding up. Most are attributable to his age and imminent retirement which he associates with his imminent death—all hard to accept, especially for a man once as dominant as he. In the unaccustomed solitude since his wife's death he has been brooding on all this, wondering how to surmount this situation in which Georg is assuming control while he himself is being relegated to a back seat, literally, the back room. When Georg walks into his room he has already decided that at a propitious time he would call Georg to task, make him get off his high horse, expose his whole lifestyle of pretence once and for all. The time has come for a showdown. And this Sunday morning is the moment he has been waiting for.

Characteristically, when Georg starts talking about "St. Petersburg," he decides to shake him up—play a little joke on him as ridiculous as Georg's pretensions: he flaunts "St. Petersburg" in his face by querying the very existence of the friend. What friend? You have no friend....

It is the sort of patronizing game one plays with a three-year-old (Do you have a nose? What nose?), to amuse oneself, to feel superior, to make some sort of contact across the years.

But Georg in his earnestness and vulnerability about his friend is terribly disconcerted; he fails to find it funny in the least. "Georg rose to his feet in embarrassment."

Is he embarrassed because of his guilt; or because his father, if taken seriously, must be in his dotage?

He acts now as if he thought the latter; if only to cover his guilt-feelings.

"Never mind about my friends. A thousand friends can't take the place of my father."

Needless to say, this sudden almost emotional declaration of devotion after months of cold neglect the father in his cynicism takes to be insincere, as Georg tries abruptly to switch the subject from consideration for his friend to consideration for his father: "Do you know what I think? You're not taking good care of yourself," following this with a long barrage of proposals for a complete change of regimen ostensibly intended to restore his beloved father to health, but so insistent they seem designed not only to change the subject but to prevent all further mention of his friend.

The father would seem to be not nearly so far gone as to warrant all this, even if he in fact could not recall the friend; he has even said he prefers shade to the sun and air Georg is recommending. Nevertheless he allows Georg to have his say.

As he finishes they are standing close together. The father has let his tousled white head sink to his breast. He says "Georg" in a low voice, without moving, and Georg kneels down at once beside him, looking up at the old man's weary face. One almost expects tenderness now; there has been no hostility thus far. Perhaps he will put his hand on Georg's head; now there may be some closeness. It is too much to expect. Not only is the father described with chilly impersonality ("the pupils, overlarge, fixedly looking at him from the corners of the eyes"); but it is clear that having thrown Georg off balance the father intends to press on with his advantage.

Completely ignoring Georg's elaborate plans for arresting his decline, about which he is himself vulnerable, of course, he returns to the patently sensitive subject Georg has been trying so transparently to avoid.

"You have no friend in St. Petersburg.... How could you have a friend out there of all places? I can't believe it." And he, the leg puller, accuses Georg of pulling his leg.

Poor Georg! He takes his father at his word, and begins to expostulate about the reality of his friend's existence, taking off his father's clothes meanwhile as if the fact of his friend's existence were proof of the necessity of undressing the old man and putting him to bed.

He notes his soiled linen, another sign of his missing mother, reproaches himself for neglecting his father. He had supposed that his father would stay on in the flat when he married, but now, with his usual sensitivity to loneliness, firmly resolves to bring him along to his new home. And like an adoring son he lifts his father up and carries him in his arms to his bed, just as the father once carried him in his arms to his bed; though he realizes with a terrible sensation that the old man is clutching his watchchain so tightly he can hardly put him down.

Acutely conscious of his waning powers, the father is no doubt envious of Georg's youth and strength, in which, however, Georg has overestimated his father's frailty. Nevertheless, in spite of being perfectly able to walk—he stood up to greet Georg when he came in—and not even ill, the father allows himself to be carried to bed just as children sometimes let themselves be carried to bed pretending to be asleep: as a typical delicious little trick.

Thus he not only allows Georg to put him to bed, but even covers himself up exceptionally well, drawing the blankets high over his shoulders, as if to cover his face. Then, savoring his delightful wit, he looks at Georg "with a not unfriendly eye." One is reminded of the big bad wolf snickering under his covers as Goldilocks wonders at her "grandmother's" big eyes, big ears, big teeth. And Georg, the naif, is relieved. "You remember my friend now, don't you?" nodding encouragingly as if thinking "Yes, he belongs in bed; what a relief to have him out of the way." But now the father turns the tables. Ignoring this question about the friend he reverts to talk of his "health". "Am I well covered up now?" feigning concern that his feet be properly tucked in. And Georg, falling ever more deeply into the trap, gloats: "You find it snug in bed already?" tucking the blankets tightly around his father who persists:

"Am I well covered up?"

"Don't worry. You're well covered up."

How melodramatically now the father springs his little surprise. He throws off the covers as if arising from the dead; even the blanket, rather than falling limply, unfurls for an instant flat in the air as he shouts "No!" sending the answer "resounding against the question".

"You wanted to cover me up, that I know, my young scamp, but I'm not covered up yet...."

It is the black joke of a morbid old man, obsessed with thoughts of death, his wife's death and his own, a brooding, embittered, self-involved old male, self-important, self-righteous, self-pitying. After all his years of sacrifice for his little family she, the binding energy of the nucleus, as it were, has dealt it a crushing blow by dying and leaving him without her to dominate-love-protect; and now their son is about to give it the coup de grace by going off on his own to marry and leave him alone utterly. "The happy day!"

Thus the pathos of the human father who must bring his son to maturity only to find that his son's strength is his own debility, his son's joy his own despair, his son's manhood the end of his own.

Whom will he dominate now? There is only Georg, absorbed in his fiancée, his business successes, his friend in Russia.

As he stands there on the bed steadying himself gently with one hand against the ceiling, he is tasting power for possibly the last time; it is as if it were his final moment of glory; and he is not about to let it slip by. Now for once he will let himself go, demonstrate indubitably his lifelong supremacy, show up this young squirt. And all his pent-up rancor he projects upon Georg, twisting his finally-expressed tenderness to viciousness, transforming all his benevolent intentions to baseness. He will expose everything—the rottenness under it all.

For he is not the man to go gentle into that good night; he will rage, rage against the dying of the light.

Nor in his rage will he be logical. For this is an emotional moment, and emotions are not logical. Logic is for gentlemanly discourse, when one wants to persuade without playing on the emotions. But this is war, war to the death, and one must catch one's adversary by surprise, the surprise of non-rationality. The secret of the father's power to confound Georg completely is the shock of his total illogic.

Thus the friend whose existence he has just pretended to doubt he suddenly claims to know well, better than Georg, and he even prefers him to Georg and Georg knows he prefers him and for that reason has been deceiving him "all these long years". How well the old man knows what wild accusations will cut through Georg's armor.

Georg is dismayed. How does his father know he has been deceiving his friend?

What does Georg do? Does he smile, does he put up an argument, offer a contest? No, he is completely at a loss, so shaken he takes his father's words with absolute literalness, and believes that in truth his father suddenly knows his friend well.

Seeing that he has thrown Georg off his guard—he starts to run toward his father but stops halfway—the father now with uncanny dramatic sense displays his utter revulsion at the carnality behind Georg's outwardly proper engagement, hitching up his shirt around his legs as if in imitation of the way she allegedly raised her skirts to seduce Georg, and accusing Georg of all sorts of treachery in "taking his pleasure with her"—desecrating his mother's memory, betraying his friend, and putting his father to bed so he couldn't move. "But can he move, or can't he?"

In his decorous vulnerability Georg is aghast. He shrinks petrified into a corner as far away from his accuser as possible. Exultant at his strategy, the father now reverses himself again: "But your friend hasn't been betrayed after all! I've been his representative here on the spot!"

Georg in his petty rationality is no match for this glorious irrationale. But he has been touched so deeply he becomes slightly irrational too. He finds his father "radiant with insight". The phrase is sarcastic but the sarcasm loses its edge. Weakly he tries to mock his father but finds his own ridicule turned against himself. "You comedian!" he cries. It is true that the essence of the old man's effectiveness is the farcicality of his assertions; but how easily he turns the thrust aside: "A comedy! Just the word for it!" as he describes with harrowing precision the tragedy of his "comedy", ending with the most poignant of all his remarks: "Do you think I didn't love you, I from whom you sprang?"

The word "love" is used in this story only in the most anguished of all possible contexts, as when Georg, dropping to his death, declares he has loved his parents all along. It is as if a word so charged with emotion cannot be used except in an ultimate extremity.

And it is when the father, perhaps for the first time in his life, declares his "love" for Georg that Georg gives his first explicit though unspoken wish for his death: "Were he to fall, and smash himself to bits!"

But he can neither wish his father away nor discredit him with derision. The father, noticing him stopped dead in his tracks, as if in a paralysis of will, taunts him with lacking even the strength to approach him, as compared with his own strength; and Georg realizes the veracity of his father's claim that if it is his last strength it is enough for this son, more than enough. When he announces he has Georg's customers "here in my pocket" Georg takes the metaphor literally and tries to ridicule the idea of pockets in his shirt, "as if that could make him a laughing stock before all the world"—thus the futility of his feeble attempts at scorn. And when his father proclaims in his fervor "a splendid alliance" with his friend he tries pitifully to outdo his father's rhetoric but fails again; the exaggeration he hopes will demolish his father's exaggeration proves more accurate than his father's.

He not only has no answer. He finds his father omniscient, accepting everything he says as revealed truth.

Once, no doubt, his friend was his ally against his parents; does he know that too?

And of course in becoming engaged he has found a replacement for his dead mother whom he had long ago betrayed by replacing her with his friend; so perhaps he *is* defiling her memory.

Now his father's revulsion at his sensuality becomes his own revulsion—how could he have allowed "a Miss Frieda Brandenfeld", who recently came to town, to lure him into betraying his absent friend whom he has loved for so many years?

Too late he perceives that his sudden gestures of concern for his father's well-being were all unwitting reminders of his physical decay, serving only to show the old man that he considered him on his last legs—though he is not on his last legs, as he is now proving by standing there above him, kicking his heels. How far he is from being helpless, ready for the death Georg has been preparing for so long, for which he is indeed now much more prepared than his father. For in his maturity he no longer fears his father's death; he is resigned to it; though resigned is perhaps an understatement; in a way, no doubt, he would welcome it.

For it is now clear that his father, like a guest who has overstayed his welcome, is living too long. Certainly the business would continue to prosper even more than with his father around; he is superfluous there, excess. And he has outplayed his role as husband-father too; his dead mother no longer needs this man, just as he no longer needs him, especially with a wife who, it may well be, would find him an unpleasant burden, particularly with no wife of his own to look after his needs. Alive the father cannot possibly be the asset to his marriage and his friendships—the security against aloneness—that he would be if he died. Georg's unuttered death-wish for his father adds to his guilt-sense as he realizes that his sudden apparent solicitude made all the more unmistakable the suppressed desire which he has just expressly though inwardly stated: "Were he to fall, and smash himself to bits!"

Did his father hear it?

In the radiance of his insight has he suddenly apprehended that for all these years Georg, an "innocent child but a diabolical human being", on the assumption that his father would die before him, has been girding himself for that now wished-for event?

By now the father is overwhelmed with his perception of the misery of his fate: Not only must he as well as his wife die, but this son and heir in whom once they both took pride will go on merrily without them, enjoying their departure and all they have given him, without so much as remembrance.

Yet Georg has still neither married nor posted that letter. He is still in control of this son not yet quite a man and obliged to obey his every command.

And he decides that for the last time he will teach this boy a lesson, avenge himself with a final ghastly joke: trip him up by not living up to his expectations and dying before him. Let this heir die first. Only then will he have nothing more to lose and, quite alone, be able to accept the horror of his own death. So he sentences Georg to death by drowning as his last defiance of his inexorable end, his final pathetic demonstration of his paternal love-protection-dominance.

It is something he does only because his wife is dead. If she were alive and the family nucleus intact, he would never do it, not because she would physically prevent him but because human morality would prevent him, the binding energy of the nuclear family. With that energy gone, his energy is gone and his human morality destroyed.

Thus he collapses on the bed as Georg obeys him dutifully, even gladly. For as he drops from the bridge to the river below, his letter to his friend is still in his pocket, and he knows he will never betray him, will never have to reach maturity, to give up his carefree youth for the sacrifices of manhood.

Georg's mad rush to carry out his father's judgment—his own death-wish visited upon himself—expresses in a way the anguish of the human family of two generations who must recognize one another for life. What can one do about an aged father for whose death one has steeled oneself, guiltily, ever since one's childhood and which one at last feels ready to face? If the guilt is exposed, if one realizes finally that for all those years between the generations one has wanted one's own father to die, how can one face that father, how can one make amends for all those years of guilt, how can one live with it? The only way one can wash away those years of human guilt is to die before him.

Walter H. Sokel

Perspectives and Truth in "The Judgment" [1]

"The Judgment," the work of Kafka's "breakthrough" of
September 1912, is thematically, i.e., in terms of mythos or plot
content, a continuation of his earliest extant work, "Description of a Struggle" (1904-05). In the frame story of that work, an
engaged young man comes to grief under the influence of a
bachelor. In the inner story, the Fat Man is separated from the
girl he dates by the appearance of a weird, solitary figure, the
Praying Man. He comes under the latter's spell and is
subsequently drowned—a striking anticipation of Georg
Bendemann's fate. Six years after "Description of a Struggle,"
in a diary entry of July 1910, Kafka describes an encounter
between a party-going, socially "engaged" young man, who is
the narrator, and a hideously pathetic bachelor in whom the
narrator anticipates a perilous eventuality for his own
development. The threat of drowning appears here as an
analogy to the bachelor's dangerous clutch on the narrator.
"The Judgment" carries this theme farther. Here the engaged
protagonist, Georg Bendemann, actually drowns himself as a
consequence of his bachelor friend's "alliance" with the
protagonist's father. Proclaiming himself the "representative"
(SE, 30)[2] of his son's bachelor friend the father accuses Georg
and ultimately condemns him to death by drowning.

---

* Some of the ideas expressed in this paper were first presented in my book *Franz
Kafka: Tragik und Ironie* (1964) and monograph *Franz Kafka* (1966), but have been
thoroughly revised, reformulated, expanded and combined with new ideas.

The introduction of the father into the conflict between bachelor and engaged man ties "The Judgment" to an even earlier period of Kafka's writing. In a diary entry of January 1911, Kafka outlines the plan of a novel, conceived in his childhood or earliest youth, which was to relate the fate of two brothers, one of whom had emigrated to America, while the other stayed at home, imprisoned (Tag, 39f.).[3] The two childhood friends of "The Judgment" easily appear as a later variant of the two brothers of the early project. Like brothers, Georg Bendemann and his friend descend from the same womb—shared native city and common past. Corresponding to one of the two brothers, Georg stayed at home, while his friend, counterpart of the other brother, emigrated into exile. In "The Judgment," the empire in the East, Russia, replaces the Western continent of the planned novel, which reappears at the same time as "The Judgment," in Kafka's new novel, *Der Verschollene* which Brod called *Amerika*. But what in particular connects the two friends of "The Judgment" with the brothers of the early plan is the presence of the father.[4] While no father is mentioned for the planned novel, in "The Judgment" Georg and his friend function like old Bendemann's two sons. Old Bendemann says of the friend that he would be a son after his own heart, while he terms his actual son a "devilish human being," who has to be condemned to die. We learn nothing about the friend's family. For all we know his only ties are to Georg's family. Nor are we supplied any reasons for his original discontent that made him "flee" to Russia. He functions only as an alternative to Georg's way of coming to grips with a frustrating home situation which he had experienced prior to his mother's death. In a letter to his fiancée-to-be, Felice Bauer, Kafka himself pointed out that the friend should not be seen as an autonomous character, but as the common element between father and son.

The story is perhaps an inspection tour around father and son, and the changing figure of the friend is perhaps the perspectivistic change in the relations between father and son. (BF, 397)[5]

Both in the early planned novel and in "The Judgment," one member of each pair is "good" and the other "bad," but the criteria of evaluation are reversed. In the early novel plan the brother who stayed at home in prison was to be the good one, while the one who had left would be bad. Now, if we take Old Bendemann's perspective as our standard of evaluation, the opposite prevails. The friend who emigrated into exile is the ideal son; his exile and misery serve as equivalents for the good brother's imprisonment at home. But the stay-at-home, Georg, now corresponds to the "bad brother." According to the father's judgment, he is a bad friend and a diabolical son. This shift in moral evaluation is easy to explain. The two friends, read "brothers," represent two alternative attitudes toward home and origin, translated into two contrasting life styles.

Georg and his friend started out with an identical discontent with their situation at home. The word "discontent" is explicitly mentioned only in reference to the friend. However, as we are cursorily told, his father's overpowering, self-willed nature which forced his own opinion on everyone around him had overshadowed Georg's youth; profound "discontent" is thus implied in his life, too. The two young men's reactions to this discontent, however, are markedly different. The friend "practically fled" his native land. The word "fled," Georg's word, only slightly weakened by the qualifier "practically" (*förmlich*), implies extreme frustration, even fear. Usually one "flees" a scene posing danger. Georg too could have removed himself from his father's domain by following his friend's example and explicit invitation to join him in exile. The friend had urged Georg to come, for the last time when Georg's mother died. But upon his wife's death, the father's powers began to wane. The giant's apparent decline permitted Georg to rise rapidly in the family business and he began to take it over. Given the father's self-willedness, an

Oedipal combat seemed likely to result from the son's option to stay in the father's domain. The friend showed a possible way out which Georg chose not to follow.

Georg and his friend, it must be said here parenthetically, correspond to the two sides of the fundamental choice that Kafka had seen confronting him all his life. Kafka presented himself as split between the bachelor's ascetic hermit-like withdrawal from the world and the wish to engage himself fully in it, with particular stress on the obligation to marry and raise a family. In "The Judgment" he depticted this split most clearly in the two representative antagonists—Georg's friend, the bachelor in Russia, and George himself, engaged to "a girl of a well-to-do family" (SE, 25).[6] Essentially Kafka himself veered toward the friend's way.[7] In his "Letter" to his father, written more than seven years after "The Judgment," he depicts himself as one who had to withdraw from his father's realm and presence. Given a progenitor as tyrannically self-righteous and as brimming over with robust vitality as Herrmann Kafka, the weakling sensitive son's only possibility for survival was flight. In his diaries, Kafka also compares himself to one exiled by his father from Canaan, the land of fertility and life, to the desert, a region not dissimilar to the desolate solitude of the friend's Russian existence. Only eight months prior to his writing of "The Judgment," Kafka links the terms "Russian" and "friend." "Russian" describes the most extreme loneliness which results from having removed oneself from one's family into an isolation more thorough "than the most distant journeys can achieve." Then, he adds, "you have lived through an experience of solitude so extreme by European standards that it can only be termed Russian" (Tag, 233). The link to the friend is expressed in the paradoxical afterthought that this loneliness is heightened by dropping in late at night on "a friend" to see how he is doing. In this strange link of "Russian" and "friend" we can see the seed of this enigmatic figure of "The Judgment."[8]

But Kafka's own engagements distinguish him from the friend and link him to Georg. The writing of "The Judgment" followed soon upon Kafka's first meeting, in August 1912, with

Felice Bauer, about whom he noted in his diary that he had formed "an unshakeable judgment." (Tag, 185) As Politzer points out, it could not have been a judgment about her, but only "a judgment of himself" in relation to her.[9] The story is dedicated to Felice Bauer and carries her initials in the name of Georg's fiancée, Frieda Brandenfeld. This name is also an allusion to Felice's residence in Berlin, as Berlin is the capital of the province of Brandenburg. Kafka's professional career as an official in an insurance agency which kept him in daily touch with the world of industry, his helping out in his family's factory and his, albeit most reluctant, partnership in it, his staying in his native city and continuing to live, as an adult of marriageable age, in his father's household—all these facts point to close analogies with Georg Bendemann. Kafka made his identification with his protagonist clear when he pointed out that "Georg" had the same number of letters as "Franz," the "Bende" had as many letters as "Kafka," and that the vowel "e" is repeated in "Bende" exactly at the same place as is "a" in Kafka.

In this connection, a striking structural analogy between "The Judgment" and one of Kafka's autobiographical observations should be mentioned. Georg's fall from a considerable height of achievement, repeated later by Josef K., and to a lesser extent Gregor Samsa, has its analogue in Kafka's recounting of his forebodings of doom in the face of any success of his, no matter how modest. Shortly before writing "The Judgment," he records in his diary that as a child and adolescent he had been convinced of having only temporarily postponed disaster whenever he had managed to pass an examination or was promoted to the next grade in school. Any success had to be short-lived because it was based on a "swindle" (Tag, 225), and entailed catastrophic exposure to come. For him "the great manly future" appeared as an impossibility and any provisional sign of it must be a facade hiding a terrifying failure soon to be revealed. Kafka thought he would be "found out" sooner rather than later, but in any case eventually, and would marvel that he could have come as far as he had. In the "Letter" to his father, he attributes this utter lack of self-confidence to his father's threatening presence in his life, a circumstance which establishes an even closer analogy to "The Judgment." The difference between the author's forebodings, as described by him, and his protagonist's fate is of course even more significant. Kafka expected the "unmasking" that Georg experiences as an unforeseen blow. Unlike his creator, Georg does not perceive the provisional facade, which all wordly success axiomatically represented for Kafka; he lives it.

Although its roots can be traced to Kafka's own life, the juxtaposition of Georg and the friend must be viewed in more universal terms. The friend functions not only psychically, as a rejected possibility for Georg, but also socially, morally, and existentially as the choice of a non-economic way of life, an existence defined by the rejction of the struggle for power as its guiding principle. It is Elias Canetti's merit to have pointed out the drive for power, and its radical condemnation, as Kafka's central concern.[10] It is the conflict between the son's drive for self-assertion and the father's insistence on the absolute dominance of his will which ended the golden age of harmony that had at one time existed in the Bendemann family. The origin of discord in "The Judgment" offers a significant parallel to Kafka's "Letter" to his father. The letter is an indictment of the father's stifling and crippling influence on the son's natural need for independence and ego-development. By the sheer weight of his personality and largely unconscious "pedagogy," the father had thwarted and deflected the son's growth as a person. In "The Judgment" this deflection of the will to assert himself is split off from the protagonist and embodied in the friend. Georg, on the other hand, asserts the will to attain his "great manly future" and takes up the struggle for succession to the father's role with a directness which his author never dared or desired to assume. He represents an unrealized tendency lurking in the writer of the "Letter" to his father.

By the same token, the two hostile "friends" or "brothers" of "The Judgment" represent two universal possibilities for human existence. These possibilities can be expressed in terms borrowed from Freud's *Totem and Taboo*, a work written almost simultaneously with "The Judgment";[11] but they can also be couched in socio-economic, existential, and religious terms. In the terms of *Totem and Taboo*, the friend's way parallels the wifeless sons whom the father of the Primal Horde to whom all the women belong deprives of sexual fulfillment and casts out into the wilderness, while Georg corresponds to one of the unsuccessful challengers of the primal father who, too weak to covercome him, is defeated and killed before the father in turn is killed one day by the band of rebellious brothers. Transcending the framework of the Oedipal combat, the friend represents the way of the ascetic and holy man, the way of the monk loyal to the three vows: poverty (his business failures), chastity (his bachelorhood), and obedience (his self-removal from any chance of rivalry with the fathers). He comes in touch with the sphere of spirit and religion. It is in connection with the friend that Kafka introduces into "The Judgment" the single reference to a priest. Moreover, this priest embodies a religion of self-mortification. He cuts a "broad cross of blood into the palm of his hand" (SE, 29). The image adumbrates Georg's self-punishment in obedience to his father. The attribute "broad" unites the cross and Georg's father whom Georg sees as "broad"—"How broad he is sitting there" (SE, 27)—until it forges the semiotic link between the symbol of martyrdom and holiness on the one hand, and Georg's father whom Georg's ultimate act of obedience reveals as being "the cross" his son bears. At the same time the image also points to a larger tradition in which the religious life entails celibacy, asceticism and mortification of the flesh. It likewise alludes to the existential exposure into which the friend ventured when he took the step of exiling himself and "fleeing" the bourgeois circumstances in which Georg has opted to remain. For the friend's Russia, which, as Georg insists on reminding us, is not identical with the actual country of that name, is a realm of disquiet, turbulence, savage mobs, and spiritual fanaticism. It is a place far too unstable for the friend to leave in order to journey back home into the snug comforts of Central or Western European respectability.

In all these respects, Georg at first seems to be the opposite of the friend. By choosing to stay at home, trying to succeed his father, he has followed the ways of the modern bourgeois. His engagement is a token of his socio-economic success, as the emphasis on the financial standing of his fiancée's family clearly underlines. To put it more precisely, both the socio-economic and the sexual realm represent areas of the—in the broadest sense—"political" sphere, the arena in which the struggle for power takes place. The appearance, in contrast to the substance, of a woman's love is essential for the exercise of power in Kafka's world, as is evident in "Description of a Struggle," where the mere mention of being engaged, or the mere thought of being loved by a girl, suffices to boost the combatant's position decisively. Marriage then is the sign of physical power and worldly success; it is the most visible evidence of male strength and a primary means of its exercise. Georg has to wait for his mother's death to make his ego felt in the father's business, because immediately upon the loss of his wife, his father weakens and begins to decline. Yet, the socio-economic aspect of power has priority over the erotic in "The Judgment." Georg's apparent supplanting of his father in the firm antedates his engagement. The economic sphere determines the nature of the Oedipal conflict. It is as economic man that Georg stands in opposition to his father and to his friend. It is in the business that he first perceives his father as one who blocks him; and by his economic success he automatically assumes an antagonistic position vis-à-vis his father whom he threatens to overshadow. It is from the vantage point of his bourgeois success that Georg looks down upon his childhood friend and senses his increasing alienation from him.

Georg has assumed a patronizing stance toward the friend. In his reflections on their relationship, which initiate the story, Georg dwells on the friend's poverty, economic ineptitude, and social isolation, from which his other pecularities and above all his "adaptation to permanent bachelordom" derive. In Georg's eyes resignation to remaining a bachelor only crowns an existence of total failure. His friend had ended in a cul-de-sac, as we might translate Georg's term *"verrannt."* It is from the perspective of the successful bourgeois that Georg judges his friend's life to be a failure. As he looks down physically upon the world at his feet—street, river, bridge, and nature at the opposite bank—he looks down socially upon the friend's exile. Separating him inwardly from the childhood friend, his bourgeois outlook alienates Georg from his own childhood and past which, in a certain sense, stay embodied in the distant friend. Precisely because of his total failure in bourgeois terms, the friend has remained in touch with the characteristics of childhood. His lack of means would make him a dependent if he were to return home, his celibacy keeps him in the condition of sexual immaturity, and his social ineptness illustrates his unfamiliarity with the conventions which rule adult society. The ultimate sign of this permanent immaturity is of course his inability to found a household of his own. The German word for bachelor, "Junggeselle," includes the word "young" and thus graphically conveys the friend's near-childlikeness. In the friend is preserved Georg's link to his own childhood, otherwise apparent only in his tie to his father. Everything points to the friend's emblematic connection with childhood. Although he wears a "fremadartige Vollbart," (foreign-looking beard) this token of masculinity can only poorly conceal "the face well-familiar since childoood days" (SE, 23). For Georg the friend has remained "an old child." Like a child, he would simply have to obey his successful friends who had remained at home (SE, 23).[12] This condescension toward the friend betokens the loosening of Georg's bonds to his own past. This self-alienation surfaces in the frequent occurrence of the word or syllable "fremd" ("alien" and "strange") in the two paragraphs describing Georg's thoughts about his friend.

Georg's bourgeois perspective on the friend, and therewith on his own childhood, with which the story opens, also establishes Georg's life as a facade existence hiding unacknowledged realities. To show this fully, it will be necessary to return for a moment to the earlier versions of the bachelor-engaged man conflict. In the frame story of "Description of a Struggle," the narrative perspective is still that of the bachelor, who also functions as the narrator. In the inner story, which the Fat Man relates to the narrator, the perspective briefly shifts to the "engaged," i.e., dating, partner of the struggle. This shift is fully worked out in the diary entry of July 1910. There the socially engaged, party-going narrator views the lonely bachelor with distaste and anxiety, and yet with fascination. With the same apprehensive concern, Georg Bendemann looks down on his bachelor friend in Russia. In both diary scene and "The Judgment," a sense of mortal danger emanates from the bachelor. However, in the diary scene, the engaged protagonist explicitly acknowledges the danger; it forms the topic of his conversation and reflections. The decisive switch in "The Judgment," two years later, lies in the protagonist's failure to admit the peril which the bachelor's existence constitutes. The shift from first to third person narrative facilitates the presentation of a rift between admitted and unacknowledged elements in the protagonist's attitude toward the bachelor. This rift between conscious acknowledgment and actual behavior constitutes the real "breakthrough" toward the narrative structure which we have come to call "Kafkaesque" and which, among other things, is a masterful and unique exposition of the bad faith lodged in consciousness.

Georg Bendemann's fear of a menace from the exiled bachelor can only be inferred, but never proved. It can be inferred from Georg's attempts to keep the friend away from himself. However, George never admits this as his motive. Instead he claims that it is his solicitude for the friend's feelings which makes him wish he would not come back. He reasons that his friend's self-esteem would be shattered if he were to return and witness the successes achieved by his friends at home. But the friend's presumed feelings of offended self-respect are only attributed to him by Georg. They are feelings imagined by Georg but not necessarily felt by the friend. Georg, however, fails to make this thought process clear to himself. Neither does the narrator ever intervene to inform the reader of Georg's mental manoeuverings. Georg's arguments resemble a sleight-of-hand. He projects onto his friend what he wants to prove, and then reasons as though his projections were fact. By imputing to his friend his own bourgeois criteria for self-esteem, he persuades himself and us that it would be in the friend's interest to stay away. He builds up in his mind a bogus "friend" for whose sake he displays great delicacy of feeling which, by the nature of the case, has to be spurious. For Georg persuades himself that he tries to spare feelings which, as far as the text shows us, exist only in his imagination.[13] The friend's real feelings remain unknown to us. Georg, however, utilizes these imagined feelings to argue against the real friend's reappearance.

Georg's deliberate self-deception, which is the essence of bad faith in the Sartrian sense of the term, arises from his ambivalence toward the friend. Despite his wish to keep him in distant Russia, he continues to write to him regularly. Something in Georg attaches him to the friend and prevents him from making a clean break with this exiled remnant of his past. But something else in him disallows this channel to the past to remain honestly open. This unadmitted and unresolved conflict between two tendencies in Georg, one for keeping the bond to the friend and the other against it, makes for a structure of his behavior which closely resembles the structure of the human psyche as Freud described it in *The Interpretation of Dreams*, *The Psychopathology of Everyday Life*, and *Wit and its Relation to the Unconscious*. There is no evidence that Kafka had read any particular work or works by Freud; but there is no doubt that he had absorbed Freudian thought by the time he wrote "The Judgment," particularly as he noted "thoughts of Freud" as "naturally" accompanying his composition of "The Judgment" (Tag, 294).[14] Georg's behavior toward the friend resembles the quasi-ludicrous character of Freudian "slips" or accidents. Georg cannot bring himself to tell the friend of his engagement. He conceals the fact from the friend, thus acting like the repressive Freudian "censor." Yet he cannot help writing to him three times in a row about the "engagement of an unimportant girl" until the friend, made curious by this "slip," begins to show interest in it.

Georg also conceals his economic success from his friend. As in the case of his engagement, he thereby inadvertently reveals his own unadmitted negative thoughts toward both tokens of success. While pretending that he would find these negative thoughts in his friend's mind (for instance wretchedness and "discontent" if informed of Georg's forthcoming wedding), he suppressed the fact that these thoughts are only in his own mind, since we get no evidence of the friend's actual thoughts on these matters.

This highly critical view of both business career and impending marriage is a part of himself that Georg will not acknowledge. At least to his friend, Georg still seeks to appear as the unsuccessful bachelor he had once been. His letters perpetuate the image of a son innocent of the recent successes that have made him his father's threatening rival. Having chosen to challenge his father by following the route of economic man and sexual maturity, he yet wants to retain a realm in which his earlier, pure, child-like self can be preserved. Georg's bad faith lies in his unwillingness either to allow this bachelor self to persist as a true reality or to give it up entirely. Instead he abstracts this self to an idea in the mind of his friend. As the course of the plot shows, his tie to his friend will prove, in the end, much stronger than his desire for marriage and his ambition to succeed economically. But as the story opens, Georg seeks to indulge adult and bachelor self simultaneously by the device of keeping his actual life separate from the idea of his "pure" self. Reflecting the constancy of "existential symbols" in Kafka's work, the abode for this image of the bachelor self is the vast Northern empire of Russia, associated with those regions of cold, winter, and snow in which, from "Description of a Struggle" to The Castle, Kafka's bachelor figure finds his being.

By insisting on this split Georg exhibits bad faith in both directions. He indulges the adult's sexual appetite, but only furtively, shamefacedly, keeping it hidden from his "pure" friend, while at the same time degrading his friend by attempting to keep him as the mere receptacle for his own self-image. In this light his father is right when he accuses Georg of having known "only of yourself"; (SE, 32) of having approached his fiancée only "because she lifted her skirts," (SE,

30) i.e., for sheer lewd self-gratification, and of having tired to "get his friend down" so that he could "sit on him with his behind" and immobilize him.* This is precisely what Georg does. He "sits" on the actual person, whom he shuts out from visibility, and substitutes for him a carrier of his own idea, feelings, and desires.

Georg's "repression" of the friend manifests itself most obviously in the form of the deception which his letters perpetrate. Georg omits from them the essential truth of his present life—his financial successes and his intention to marry. His correspondence is a false facade, a "cover-up." His relation to his friend, and through him to his own past and "pure self," has become profoundly inauthentic. Georg is able to write only about "unimportant matters," making his "literature" an inessential enterprise. For Kafka only the most conscientious comprehensiveness could ever hope to approximate "truth" in literature, as in life, and truth alone was the ultimate, although practically unattainable, vindication for both. By having his protagonist practise in his letters the kind of deceit, based on self-serving selectivity, which Kafka attacked in other writers and above all in himself, he conveyed his condemnation of this character. The father's "judgment" of his son merely puts in explicit terms the author's "judgment."

In "Wedding Preparations in the Country," the giant beetle into which Raban transforms himself in his dream sends his human facade out to do his work in the world. In "Description of a Struggle," the bachelor-narrator reduces the engaged man

---

* The sentence to which I refer is ambiguous because the third-person personal pronoun in it could refer to the father as well as to the friend. "As you thought just now that you had got him down, so far down that you could sit on him with your behind and he won't move, at that moment my fine son decided to get married!" (SE, 30). The father could have himself in mind here as Georg's presumed victim. With at least equal likelihood, however, he might be referring to the friend. His tirade, although it began with himself, switched, in its second sentence, to the friend. Two sentences earlier the father still talked of Georg's "false little notes to Petersburg." Furthermore, Georg himself seems to relate the father's harangue to the friend. In the paragraph following it, his thoughts are focussed entirely on the friend. All this points to the friend as the "him" and "he" of the above-quoted sentence. The reader's inability to make a clear-cut decision for the friend or the father as the exclusive object of the sentence is in itself significant. The ambiguity of the text makes the partners in the "alliance" against Georg literally indistinguishable. I am grateful to Kate Flores for having pointed out this ambiguity.

to the status of a horse which transports him into a landscape that reflects the wishes of his imagination. In both cases the imagination debases physical reality by making it serve as the intrument of its self-gratification. In "The Judgment," Georg Bendemann repeats the process, but reverses the roles. He, the engaged man, exploits his bachelor friend, to be no more than the repository of the dream of chastity and purity which his actual life has betrayed. The narrator ironically highlights Georg's unacknowledged subjectivity in regard to the friend's feelings, when he lets us have that rare glimpse into the actual friend's behavior, which we have already mentioned. By making the friend evince an unexpected interest in the "engagement" of "an unimportant girl," which Georg had mentioned to him three times in a row, the narrator suggests that the real friend might be less hostile to the idea of engagement and marriage than Georg makes him out to be. There is here also the innuendo of a possible revenge threatened by the friend, which would account for Georg's "disquiet" at the friend's interest.

Typical of Georg's hidden repressive design on the friend is his unwitting self-revelation in musing about the friend's possible return. No one, he thinks, would "intentionally suppress" him—or "repress" or "oppress" or "depress," since the German word "niedergedruckt" has all four meanings—if he were to come back. The insertion, "not intentionally," gives Georg away. It shows that he has to defend himself in advance against the accusation that "someone" might "oppress" his friend "on purpose." It is easy to see that this "someone" is of course George himself. He literally anticipates his father's subsequent charge of his having tried "to get his friend down." We might add that Georg never denies the charge. His final answer to it is suicide.

The other side of the coin is his concealment of his engagement, which makes the latter appear as something shameful for which he feels guilty, at least toward that aspect of his existence which the friend represents. Indeed, in his conversation with Frieda Brandenfeld, as remembered by him, he admits that their engagement was their "guilt" (SE, 25). "If you have such friends, Georg, you should not have become engaged at all," Frieda tells him, whereupon he answers: "Yes, that is the guilt of both of us" (SE, 25). (The English translation fails to bring out the word "guilt" present in the original German.) J. P. Stern raises the question: "Is (Georg) guilty because he intends to get married?" and then claims that we cannot answer because we know too little about Georg's relationship with his fiancée.[15] However, he overlooks the crucial fact that it is Georg himself who "answers" the question, first by hiding his engagement from his friend and then by literally declaring it to be "guilt." It is of course Georg's view alone that counts as the criterion for judgment in Kafka's tale.

Georg immediately covers up this admission of "guilt" by kissing his fiancée with an ardor which threatens to "choke" her. This scene is also structured in a manner reminiscent of a "Freudian slip." Georg has just concealed his guilt feeling about the engagement. He now seeks to erase the impression by adding an afterthought in which he emphatically affirms his engagement. "But now I would not have it otherwise," he adds. The ambivalence of his protagonist, which Kafka himself eminently shared, as his *Letters to Felice* show, requires the cancellation of any "truth" by the assertion of a "counter-truth." However, the now suppressed "truth" continues to have its effects. It manifests itself in the very act of being denied. Georg's kisses which are to bury his guilt feeling about his engagement turn out to be so excessively impetuous that they threaten to "suffocate" his fiancée and thus to do away with the object and cause of his "guilt." That is, the real intent of Georg's feelings expressed in the word "guilt," but repressed by his "change of mind"—"now I would not have it otherwise"— re-emerges in the guise of an overzealous display of affection. The very manifestation of his love acts as both a cover-up and an unacknowledged expression of his true hostility toward the fellow conspirator in his "guilt."

Even prior to this, the text, as we have seen, revealed a "Freudian slip" of Georg's feelings about his engagement. We have already remarked that Georg, instead of informing his friend about his own engagement, reported the engagement of an "unimportant fellow" to an "unimportant girl" (SE, 25). By the narrator's choice of the word "unimportant" ("gleichgül-tig") in describing Georg's thinking, the unimportance of his engagement is inadvertently revealed. For what the use of the word "unimportant" lets show here obliquely will later emerge as Georg's truth. In the decisive confrontation with his father, Georg can no longer think of Frieda but only of his friend. The father ironically challenges his son to summon Frieda to his aid, but Georg cannot even live up to the challenge. Frieda fails to move him in the crucial encounter in contrast to the friend who "gripped him as never before" (SE, 30), but whom he has lost. The father boasts that he will simply "sweep" the girl "off (Georg's) side." But Georg himself has already accomplished what the father predicts. He fails to have Frieda in his heart and therefore does not have her by his side to call on her for aid. Not his bond to Frieda but his tie to his friend is shown to be Georg's true or essential self. His engagement turns out to be no more important to him than the engagement of the "unimportant" couple he had reported to his friend.

By entering his father's room instead of sending off to his friend the letter that was finally to announce his engagement, Georg obtains the verdict of "guilty" on this engagement, which he himself had uttered spontaneously, but then had failed to face and acknowledge. We note a phenomenon of crucial importance for the structure of "The Judgment"—the two-layered duality of perspectives linguistically expressed by the coincidence of literal and figurative, or basic and derived, meanings of certain crucial words. Georg seeks to give to his word "Schuld" ("guilt") a superficial and casual meaning according to which it would convey something like "that was our fault." The father, however, applies the full force of the literal meaning of "Schuld" as a debt that has to be paid and an offense that has to be atoned for. This layered semantic duality of perspectives corresponds to the multiplicity of layers comprising Georg's attitude toward his father which the encounter with him lays bare.

First of all, we discern a striking parallelsim in Georg's

relationship to the two figures that dominate each half of the
story—friend and father. The earliest points discernible in each
relationship represent an era of closeness and harmony. In
Georg's early youth, he had been the true friend of his friend. At
the same time, his father had loved him; he had been the pride
of his parents, and had loved them in return, as we learn at the
end of the story. That was a happy, harmonious time; the
natural order of things, an original state of paradise, seemed to
prevail. The beginning of Georg's alienation from both his
friend and his father marked the fall. Georg's contempt for his
friend's failures has its complement in his growing indifferent
toward his father which marks the period between his mother's
death and his entrance into his father's room. He had separated
his life from his father and seems to have become autonomous.
For a young man preoccupied with the rapid progress of his
business and his own career, there is no reason to set foot in an
aged father's room. His father has simply receded from Georg's
consciousness, and significantly he is mentioned only once in
the story prior to Georg's abrupt and apparently unmotivated
entrance into his room. Before that, the son had paid scant
attention to his father's physical decline, was unaware of the
sorry state of his cleanliness and bodily care, and had not
realized the gloom enveloping the room in the back of the
apartment. Occupying the bright and wholesome front room,
George had not bothered to look after his father's condition. It
never occurred to him to question the propriety of the
occupancy of the two rooms; this spatial structure eloquently
expresses the change in status between father and son. The
father is literally relegated to the back, pushed into the
background, and the son has literally become the front, the
representative of the family toward the world. It is he, and not
his father, who is greeted with respect from the street below, a
sign of deference to family and firm which is no longer given to
the father, but to the son.

Yet this reversal of roles is not a conscious rebellion. That is,
Georg does not permit himself to view it as such. His
indifference to and neglect of his father are allowed to appear as
explicit revolt and hatred after the father literally "uncovers"

them as such. A thoughtlessly accepted development, the "natural" pushing aside of the aged parent by the ambitious child becomes a rebellion with a parricidal wish only after the father's perspective is focussed on it. It takes the father's accusatory "resurrection" in his bed to make the son's potentially murderous hatred explicit. Implicitly the Oedipal displacement of father by son had been present as soon as the father withdrew his full energies from the business and the son jumped, "decisively", to use his own word, into the power vacuum thus created. From the perspective of the son this was a natural assertion of the normal adult ego. From the perspective of the father, it entailed a criminal displacement of the rightful chief of family and firm. The father accuses Georg of having perpetrated, or at least having caused or allowed "certain things" to occur in the business "that were not nice" (SE, 27). The father alludes to information having been withheld from him and his rightful control over the firm having been undermined. The reader cannot determine the factual "truth" of this. Nor is that the point of Kafka's story. The point lies in the father's automatically assuming an accusatory view of the natural succession of the generations. Important is not the factual and legal question. Whether or not "things that aren't nice" have actually occurred is not important. What matters is Georg's "decisive" stepping into his father's shoes. That by itself is "the thing that isn't nice," the change that should never have occurred, and which cries out for retribution, "some day—sooner than you think" (SE, 27). In Kafka's world, natural man, who is identical with economic man, stands condemned by the paternal perspective. The father in "The Judgment" assumes the perspective of Shakespeare in *King Lear*. For all his foolish caprice and self-willed stubbornness, the old king is justified as soon as the rebellion against him breaks out, precisely because this rebellion, as Edmund sees it, is an assertion of mere nature—"Thou, nature, art my goddess; to thy law my services are bound" (I, 2)—against the sanctified law that protects the privilege of feeble old age as it espouses lawful wedlock against natural lust. As in *King Lear*, nature in "The Judgment," stands condemned from the perspective of a higher law. In nature the brute strength of youth prevails over the wielders of authority who are weakened by age. But in the eyes of another law, external to nature and opposed to it, the natural process itself becomes guilty. Georg's neglect of his father is "natural" and to be expected from a young businessman intent on the pursuit of the battle for survival and success, in that extension of Darwinian nature that is modern capitalist society. But it literally becomes a crime when looked at by Georg's father. Decisive is Georg's taking over and incorporating into himself his father's accusatory view of natural self-assertion. A declining father's displacement by an energetic son, sanctioned and justified by the natural order of the Darwinian age, will then be revealed as Luciferian revolt and parricide.

It is this duality of perspectives that has to be kept in mind if we are to understand what makes the father's "uncovering" a revelation of the truth, and what kind of truth it is that is revealed. The coinciding of two perspectives—one "natural" and the other parental—is inseparably linked to the division within Georg between his "natural" wish to assert his ego at his father's expense and his original self which lived in love and approval of his parents.[16] It is surely significant that Georg remembers once having been the object of his parents' pride. Side by side then with his growing independence and the neglect of his father, a solicitude persists which makes him accuse himself for his neglect. We encounter here the same dichotomy which we have seen displayed in his relationship to his friend. But since he does not acknowledge his negative feelings toward either father or friend, and fails to face his ambivalence honestly, its unacknowledged existence tends to make the positive feelings a facade in his mind which covers up the unacknowledged presence of negative sentiments. For instance, no sooner has Georg allowed himself to believe that his mother's death facilitated his rise by weakening his father, than he takes back the thought and covers it up by "blaming" accidental factors for his rapid ascent. Or as soon as he comes up against the damning thought that he had not set foot in his father's room for months, he at once adds the exculpating afterthought that there had indeed been no need to do so, since he meets his father regularly at meal times and also spends some evenings with him in the shared living room. Ironically, however, we learn that these evenings spent with his father can only nominally be viewed as time together, since each is absorbed with his own newspaper. The close parallel to Georg's letters immediately suggests itself. In both cases Georg maintains the semblance of a relationship, but its essence, its soul—genuine communication—has departed. His life with his father, outwardly a sign of filial loyalty, has become a facade hiding their essential isolation from each other. Georg's neglect of his father has become the actual and effective state of affairs, while his continuing solicitude literally appears as an afterthought. When he discovers the unclean condition of his father's underwear, he reproaches himself for having neglected the old man. His former affection still appears but it is now something negative—self-accusation. As with the letters to his friend, the unacknowledged simultaneous presence of two opposed wishes constitutes bad faith. Georg's continuing cohabitation with his father, like the continuing letters to the friend, has become a cover-up for his wish to be free. And his living a life of facade is expressed in terms of spatial logic by his occupying the *front* room of the common dwelling.

As in the relation to the friend, Georg's marriage would act as the final decision for a severance of the umbilical cord—his final separation from his father's household. Georg and his fiancée had tacitly assumed that they would leave his old apartment to his father. However, upon entering his father's room, and seeing his apparent decrepitude, Georg has to change his mind. His "duty" makes him decide to take his father along into the new household. There the son will be head and master, and his father a child-like dependent to be looked after. Georg's solicitude paradoxically causes his father's subjugation. With this, the meaning of his forthcoming marriage also changes. From a mere affirmation of the son's independence, it becomes the father's reduction to dependence, his unmanning, as it were. Georg's plan in itself constitutes a disenfranchisement of the old man. For the young man makes the decision without consulting his father's own wish and preference. Georg disposes of his future fate as though his father had no will and mind of his own, and his solicitude ironically turns into the instrument of its own negation. Loving care in intent, it is overthrow in effect. The nature of Georg's intended marriage is thus revealed as Oedipal revolt aiming at a reversal of roles between father and son, a symbolic slaying of the old by the young. Filial devotion turns out to be the cover-up under which displacement of the father may proceed.

This reversal of roles and the subsequent cover-up are literally enacted by Georg as he undresses his father, carries him to bed in his arms, and covers him "well." This covering of the father calls to mind the premature burials of still living fathers by impatient heirs, as exemplified in Schiller's drama *The Robbers*. Georg literally lays his father to rest and when his father lies finally "covered" it "seems" "well" done to Georg. The real meaning of this "covering" emerges soon thereafter when Georg explicitly wishes for his father's death. "If he were to fall and get smashed! This word hissed through his head" (SE, 31). The subjunctive used in the German text expressed Georg's thought as a wish now unrestrained by the appearance of filial duty. The facade has burst open and bares the inner truth of his presumably solicitous actions. By uncovering himself and rising in his bed, the father explicitly refutes the son's cover-up as working well. At the same time, he uncovers the true content of Georg's devotion as murderous revolt.

The reader, sharing Georg's perspective, would object by insisting that the text shows that Georg has no intention of subjugating his father, that he is motivated merely by understandable alarm at his father's apparent deterioration, and that his subsequent thought of his father's death is only the reaction to the old man's "irrational" accusations, which in turn can be attributed to his senility.[17] We must therefore take a look at the father's appearance of senility as the crucial clue to the interpretation of "The Judgment."

The father's senility is seen by the reader from Georg's perspective. What is it then that makes us feel that Georg is

justified in treating his father as though he were in need of
special care and had, because of senility, lost the right to be
consulted about his own fate? That he is toothless is a physical
fact and does not necessarily entail mental decline. His
"peculiarities" appear as the symptoms of an enfeebled
organism when seen through Georg's eyes. They do not
necessarily require such explanation, as we shall see. To be
sure, old Bendemann himself admits his loss of vigor, his
weakening memory, and decreased ability to pay full attention
to the whole range and complexity of the business. However,
the very insight allowing him to make such an admission also
shows that he may yet be far from senile. The main impression
of senility derives from one particular circumstance more than
from any other. It is the father's question: "Do you really have
this friend in Petersburg?" (SE, 28). It is, however, Georg's
reaction to the question rather than the question itself that
suggests the father's senility.

The question is ambiguous. It could mean: "Is there a
person in Petersburg whom you call your friend?" In that case,
the question would address itself to a fact, and the father's
asking would indicate loss of memory. For we know that Georg
has been writing to such a person, and we also know that this
person has visited the Bendemann home in the past. However,
the question can also have another meaning. "Is this person
whom you call friend truly your friend?" Then it would not
relate to fact, but to meaning and to truth, if truth is, as Kafka
often assumed it was, in regard to his writing, an adequate
relationship between word and feeling, name and thing,
language and existence. If taken in that deeper meaning, the
question would imply not a loss of memory, but a search for
truth. The text shows that truth rather than fact is the purport
of the father's question. For before asking, he urges Georg to
tell him "the full truth." Understood with this demand in
mind, his question would have this sense: "Is there a person in
Petersburg, whom the term 'friend' applies in truth?" Then the
answer must be negative. We have seen that Georg has stopped
treating his friend as a true friend; he looks down upon him
with patronizing contempt, has tried to forestall his possible

return, and has deceived him. But Georg, and with him the reader, fails to perceive the other meaning of the father's question; i.e., he chooses to relate it only to the factual location in Petersburg of a person whom he _calls_ "friend."

We see in these two interpretations of the father's question a bifurcation of perspectives that broadens and generalizes the semantic duality we have already touched upon in relation to the term "Schuld." The difference between Georg's and the father's understanding of the meaning of "friend in Petersburg" amounts to the distinction between an empiricism or positivism for which truth is fact and a spiritualism or idealism that searches for agreement between language and essence. Georg understands "friend" to be nothing but a person _called_ "friend." His view of language is nominalistic. The conventionally accepted label suffices to designate the truth. The father, on the other hand, is concerned about the essence of "friend." Does the name correspond to "friendness," a view which implies the presence in language of a moral ideal or command to which we should conform and aspire?

The discrepancy between the two understandings of the word "friend" is closely relevant to Kafka's view of language and literature. Kafka aimed for an ideal of complete "correctness," i.e., the complete agreement between the emotion and the word used to convey it (Tag, 11). The agreement should be so thorough that no gap whatsoever would open between speaker and speech, or writer and sentence. Any distracting, extraneous element inserting itself between the speaker and his sentence or word, such as the aim for rhetorical effect, vitiates meaning and makes the statement untrue. Ideal speech and writing would reveal a truth in the sense of an intimate connectedness, an indissoluble link of every word with the speaker's or writer's life (Tag, 39). One should be able, Kafka says, to take one's writing to his breast, or be carried from his place by it (_Ibid._). He felt the word to be part of his flesh, part of himself (Tag, 77). It is in this sense that the father's searching question for Georg's meaning of the word "friend" has to be understood. Does a total agreement prevail between Georg's existence and his use of the word "friend"? Is there a friend in Petersburg to whom the word applies not as a mere rhetorical designation, or a cliché employed by habit, or a pretense of feeling no longer felt, but as a living reality equal to Georg's total being? The father asks for "the full truth" of Georg's friend *qua* friend, not for a label to which an incomplete or contradictory reality corresponds. Such a discrepancy would make the word "untrue." A speaker uttering a word for which he cannot supply in himself all the emotions corresponding to its meanings would, according to this perspective, be a liar.

The thought might suggest itself that we are dealing here with something akin to Platonism in which the word should be adequate to the concept or archetypal idea. Such a connection would be misleading. Kafka demands the total coincidence of the linguistic unit—word, sentence, paragraph, speech, story— not with a universal idea, pre-existing and external to the speaker, but with the speaker's individual existence. At most one might call this an individuated, existential Platonism, if such were not a contradiction in terms. Yet precisely such a paradoxical formulation would be necessary to do justice to Kafka's view of language which is bound up with his idea of truth. A good example which closely relates to the dialogue between father and son in "The Judgment," is Kafka's stricture against the German-speaking Jews' false relationship to language which implies a false relationship to themselves and their total existence. Not long before writing "The Judgment," Kafka reflected in his diary on his loveless attitude toward his mother. He tried to understand his lack of true love for her at least partly in a linguistic context. Between his actual Jewish mother and his feelings for her, the German language had interposed an alien emotional complex contained in the German word "Mutter." *Mutter* is associated with a very different world, a different "feel" and contrasting actuality of human relationships. Its use distorted the relationship between Franz and his Jewish mother which it was supposed to express. The word "Mutter" carried for Kafka a coldness, hauteur, and reserve alien to the warm affectionate atmosphere of the Jewish family. On the other hand, it brought with it also a kind of sentimentality incongruous with the particularly Jewish emotionalism which the speaker would intend to convey. "Christian" feelings were conjured up whenever the word "Mutter" was used. These imported a falsifying tone into the talks between Jewish mother and son. Eventually they marked and covered the original emotional reality of the Jewish son's life with his Jewish mother. "We give to a Jewish woman the German name "mother," but forget the contradiction [between them] which then sinks all the more heavily into our feeling . . ." (Tag, 116). Since Kafka ties mind intimately to language, inauthentic language, i.e., language that inadequately conveys the speaker's external and inner life, makes for an inauthentic, inwardly divided existence. Expressing, as it does, the uprooting of the Westernized Jew, the use of German creates a facade which first covers and later alienates him from his original Jewish self. The significance of the friend's Russian, i.e., Eastern, domicile for the Judaic implications of "The Judgment" cannot be gone into here. But we can emphasize the analogy between the language-related duplicity the Western-ized Jew assumed for Kafka, and the bad faith underlying the concept of his protagonist George Bendemann.[18] Georg's linguistic nominalism, evident in his superficial understand-ing of the word "friend," reveals his restricting himself to his facade existence, to a way of looking only at surface meanings and to his avoidance of the deeper issues and responsibilities involved in the use of language as communication, not only between human beings, but also within each person, since language is the medium of one's dialogue with oneself.

The contrast between Georg's empiricist nominalism and the father's "existential Platonism," for which "absolute morality"[19] or spirituality might be a more appropriate term, forms the essence of the entire confrontation scene. Entering his father's back room, Georg confronts a world, new and strange to his bourgeois ego, but familiar, as we shall see, to a forgotten and repressed layer of his self. Unconsciously, without explicit and deliberate challenge or claim, he embarks on the quest in which Kafka's later protagonist, K., will engage when he penetrates the village of the mysterious Castle. He enters a counter world, different from and opposed to empirical nature and bourgeois society. Immediately upon his entrance, he notes the darkness of his father's room, which is caused by the interiority of its location.[20] A high wall cuts off the view of the external world. Shut off from the light of nature, the room affords no opportunities for observing external phenomena. It tends to draw the occupant inward to himself and to the inner reaches of his mind. Georg, on the other hand, has occupied the front room. He has been accustomed to looking out into and over the world, surveying it from his window (anticipating in this respect, too, the land surveyor), enjoying the external light of nature. He finds the darkness of his father's habitation unsettling and slightly menacing. He praises the bright airiness of the front room and asserts that his father's health will improve by a move to the front. He is intent on promoting the benefit of light, wishing to spread it to the dark regions and to save his literally "benighted" old father from himself. This "crusade" for light and open windows, nourishing food (he implicitly criticizes the abstinence of his father who has hardly touched his breakfast), and cleanliness and hygiene (we know that his father's unclean underwear greatly disturbs him) mark Georg as a representative of a perspective which could be termed one of "enlightenment." The family firm has benefited from his management, he has achieved great economic progress measurable in statistical terms, and the employees side with him against his father, as we learn from the elder Bendemann's complaint of a disloyal staff. Georg does not merely wish to take his father's place. He wishes to outdo the old man and move the world ahead to a richer, healthier stage than his predecessor bequeathed him. He even wishes to reform his father's life. These "reforms" are all directed toward the body, toward physical health and comfort. But like any enlightened despot or any revolutionary vanguard in the forward march of history, Georg will not consult the desires of the presumed beneficiary of his reforms. The father is to be moved, a doctor is to be consulted, fresh air is to be let in, all without ascertaining—and sometimes even going against—his specifically expressed preference.

In Georg and his father two perennial antagonists of Kafka

and of the world confront each other. Georg initiates the procession of rational, empiricist, rebellious, and ultimately self-defeating protagonists, son figures, representatives of the modern liberal-progressive and bourgeois outlook. The father heralds the "counter-world," of obscure and archaic organizations and power structures, hidden away and irrational, apparently obsolete and decrepit, yet in a sinister and mysterious way all-powerful. We meet a later development of the son/father confrontation in the New Commander and the old penal system of "In the Penal Colony," in Josef K.'s fight against a court's lurking in filthy attics and dark cathedrals, and in the land surveyor's reputation of bringing reform and a breath of fresh air into the timeless, snow-covered, and frozen corner of the world in which the Castle holds sway. In "The Judgment," the opposition between hero and "counter-world" is least explicit, because it is contained in a family setting and thus obscured by the appearance of a "realistic" frame. But even here the allegorical implications of this opposition are clearly discernible. When the father complains that the employees have become "disloyal" to him, siding with the usurping son and "persecuting" the legitimate chief, Georg's ascent to the top of the business assumes the nature of a displacement of ancient legitimacy by a progressive and efficiently capitalistic force. The father's counter-world, his conspiratorial "alliance" with Georg's friend, with the spirit of Georg's dead mother, and the loyal customers, is cast in the corresponding role of a reactionary party seeking to regain the rights of dethroned power. Between the father's alliance and the Habsburgs' desperate rearguard action in the empire whose subject Kafka was, a subtle connection cannot be ruled out. But it is the spiritual-philosophical and ultimately religious context in which the father-son conflict must be seen. What makes such a context discernible is the combination of spatial and temporal terms in the structure of "The Judgment."

As Georg enters his father's room he moves back not only in space from front to rear, from wide-sweeping vision to blocked vision, from light to darkness; he also steps back in the time dimension from his forward-looking, future-bound career to a backward-looking realm in which mementos of the dead mother and archaic newspapers seem to mock and stubbornly resist all change. In this dark back room, time seems to have stopped. The newspaper in which his father has been pretending to read is so ancient that Georg cannot remember it. As the father, deprived of the love and physical presence of his wife, has nothing but the past to sustain him, the son has everything to expect from the future.[21] Further success is imminent and marriage beckons to him on the near horizon as the crowning of his ascent. As if to emphasize the "modernity" of his fiancée and the opposition to the past she signifies, Georg pointedly mentions to his friend that she did not settle in their town until long after the friend's departure. Like the oppressive new Pharoah in *Exodus* who knew nothing of Joseph, she comes from a new generation that knows nothing of the friend. Inasfar as a reader of "The Judgment" himself comes from an intellectual climate that shares the "progressive" outlook, Georg's orientation toward the future would appear to him to be correct and worthy of approval, while the father's attachment to the past would seem to be a pathetic sign of a wrongheaded, demented condition. All the more disconcerted and astonished must this "progressive" reader be when he later sees Georg carrying out his "mad" father's verdict.

What this reader would fail to see is another aspect of the temporal structure of the confrontation scene. By living in the past, the father also lives outside the sensory world in a realm of inwardness in which feelings refuse to bow to the onward march of time. Memory creates, as in the universe of Proust, a purely spiritual realm in which the aged widower has his being. The father's loyalty is extended over spatial separation as well when he cultivates the bond with Georg's distant friend, while for Georg physical distance has meant dilution and corruption of friendship. The temporal opposition between past and future thus takes on the additional meaning of a confrontation between the power of the invisible, the power of spirit, and reliance on physical and empirical strength. If this is recognized, then the father's clinging to a dead past will no longer appear merely as a pathetic oldster's sentimentality or a reactionary's nostalgia, but also as a confident assertion of the primacy of inner bonds over physical change, including death. This confidence in the invisible enables the father to draw, as he says, on his dead wife's support from beyond the grave. His power is rooted in a constancy of spirit and emotion which, in Rilke's term, comes from "the world's inner space."

Against the possibility of such strength, Georg's initial strategy in the struggle is the attempt to view the spiritual itself as a sign of senility. Initially, seen through Georg's eyes, old age appears as toothless enfeeblement, loss of rational control, as utter decline—in short as the breakdown of human dignity and personality. Later, by virtue of the father's "revelation," it emerges as a fearful and mysterious power confounding and overthrowing the rational and empiricist perception of the world. It has to be stressed, however, that in the beginning Georg chooses to impose a negative interpretation on his father's behavior. This behavior would appear in a very different light if perceived from an "unnatural," spiritual, and transcendent perspective. But Georg uses his one-sided perspective to "declare" his father senile, i.e., to act toward him as though he were senile.

The first example of this use of perspective is seen in Georg's reaction to the "closed" window in his father's room. He finds this strange and objectionable since the weather is warm. The state of the external world determines his values. The father's answer that he prefers the window closed might indicate a primacy of personal will and choice, and his independence of external circumstances. The preference for shutting oneself off from the external world regardless of the weather, might point to a deliberate withdrawal into an interiorized life. It might express a determination to place the memory of his dead wife, and loyalty to her, above all considerations of physical health and hygiene. However, from a naturalistic perspective for which physical health and an outward-looking stance are *ipso facto* superior to withdrawal to an inner world, the father's choice represents the caprice of a mind slipping into dotage. It deserves the same apprehensive disapproval as the friend's asocial existence in Russia. Georg's perspective and its values subtly prejudice the reader who sees the father through Georg's eyes, and he is therefore likely to share Georg's feeling that there is something "queer" about the old man's insistence on keeping his window closed. Henceforth we are prepared to expect further signs of decrepitude and craziness from the oldster. Georg's perspective deliberately shuts out any possible spiritual and existential interpretation of his father's words and actions, and justifies in our eyes his treatment of the father as senile. Georg, we feel, is right in disregarding his father's wishes and in depriving him, presumably in the interest of the old man's health, of his right to self-determination. The son's naturalistic value system, implied in his perspective, then gives him the pretext to pursue a naturalistic, i.e., Darwinian, policy which places the aged, as physically unfit, under the tutelage of the young and strong. Power being a matter of the body, and the body being subject to time and to change, this subjection of the old is accepted and even espoused as beneficial. Moreover, the reader by his own conditioning in a naturalist-empiricist civilization, is in any case inclined to affirm Georg's course as the only "natural" and only sensible one to follow, and is prepared to disregard whatever might contradict Georg's view of his father. The younger man's deliberate ignoring of the deeper meaning of his father's question about the friend in Petersburg is likely to escape the reader.

The narrator, however, unmasks Georg's perspective as a cover-up. He does so above all by the subsequent plot and Georg's own behavior in it. In a more subtle way, however, he lets the textual structure of the passage immediately following the father's question reveal the cover-up. He describes Georg as "embarrassed" and shows him evading the answer to his father's question. Instead of addressing himself to the question regarding the friend, Georg answers: "A thousand friends do not replace my father" (E. 28). He distracts attention from the question to his father's presumed need for rest and care. By Georg's evasive manoeuvre and shifting of the ground, the narrator has him betray his uneasy conscience and dishonesty. At the same time, a hint is given that Georg is already thinking of his father's demise. Otherwise he would not allude to its possibility in his uncalled-for answer to the father's question. To be sure, the thought of his father's death is clothed in the guise of solicitous apprehension for his well-being. But soon it will, as we have already mentioned, erupt undisguised.

Typical of Georg's "cover-up" is the continued maintenance for the reader of the two perspectives throughout this scene, culminating in the actual "covering" of his father with a blanket. Georg's suggestion that his father retire from the business is sugar-coated by his addition that he would rather close the business than allow his father's health to be endangered. The brutal aspect of retiring the father without questioning his wishes in the matter is "covered up" by this display of seemingly unselfish, indeed self-sacrificing, regard for the father's well-being. Georg would rather sacrifice his own promising career than allow his father to continue to overwork himself to the point where, as Georg by his tactics insists, his mental health is giving way under the strain. Thus the son presents himself as the soul of consideration. But from another perspective this very consideration appears as a forcible elimination of his father from the business he had founded, in which he works, and from which, as he indicates, he has no desire to be removed. On the contrary, the father makes it plain that he resents being shut out from its control by Georg's deviousness. From this perspective, solicitude is a guise for taking away the old man's self-determination.

Undressing his father and putting him to bed can be seen as marvelous kindness and subordination of Georg's self to his father's needs. On the other hand, it is the father's crass reduction to the status of a small child. While carrying his father, as though he were a child, Georg is terrified when he notices him playing with Georg's watch chain. Thereafter Georg has difficulty in putting him to bed because the old man "held on so firmly to this chain" (SE, 29). Here the two perspectives follow each other in time. First we see the scene from the point of view of the anxiously solicitous child. What terrifies Georg is this new evidence of his father's apparent senility. The word "playing" seems a strong indication that the old man has finally lapsed into his second childhood.

However, immediately after that, when Georg finds it extremely difficult to put his father to bed, a very different perspective takes over. Now he has to face his father's powerful strength and ominous hold on Georg's life. The sequence clearly shows that the two perspectives do not have the same validity. By being able to displace the first perspective, the second shows its greater strength, which is moreover borne out by the plot. Already when he entered his father's room, the troublesome thought had fleetingly occurred to Georg that his father "was still a giant;" and the subsequent plot shows that Georg has every reason to fear not his father's senility but his powerful hold on him. In pre-World War I Europe, the watch chain represented a symbol of male maturity and bourgeois respectability. Thus we see the father weighing down with his full force on Georg's childhood, and his "playing" with Georg's watch chain now appears in the light of a deliberate and terrible irony.

Georg's fear of his father is now hardly disguised. Otherwise he would not be comforted by the observation that his father is looking up to him in a "not unfriendly way" (SE, 29). The use of the negation implies that he expected "unfriendliness" from his father. His consciousness is now literally the cover that he spreads over his fear. His perspective merges with an anxious desire to render his father harmless. The physical blanket with which he covers him acts as the "objective correlative" of the tendency to bury "the giant." Consciousness itself functions as the cover of the Oedipal rebellion. If taken literally, Georg in covering his father is only acting out the duty of a good son. But if "cover" is taken figuratively, his consciousness itself is the cover of the Oedipal wish for his father's final disarming. The two perspectivist levels of meaning correspond to what the father will later identify as "the innocent child" and "the devilish person" in Georg. "Actually you have been an innocent child..., but even more actually you have been a devilish human being!" (SE, 32). The "actually" expresses the literal, the "more actually" the figurative level of meaning on which Georg's act of covering his father is seen. The literal level is the son's and the reader's perspective; the figurative level is the father's and the narrator's.

The father's second decisive question in the dialogue is his: "Am I well covered?" It has again the two levels of meaning contained in his question, "Do you have this friend in Petersburg?" If understood as referring to physical fact, Georg is right in answering that his father is "well covered." But if referring to the figurative, metaphoric meaning of covered as being buried, retired, done away with and finished, Georg is proved wrong. With his resounding "no," his throwing off the wraps, and rising in bed like one "resurrected," the father establishes the figurative perspective as the only one on which the *mythos* will be conducted. The perspective of Georg's consciousness is now swept away and annulled.

Georg's immediately avowed open hostility toward his father shows that he too has accepted the figurative perspective, and that his former solicitude and unselfish devotion prove to have been a facade destroyed by the eruption of truth.

However, the Oedipal rebellion which the father uncovers is not Georg's ultimate truth. As soon as his antagonism toward his father is liberated from the cover-up of "duty" and solicitous concern, a still deeper force counteracts and defeats the Oedipal revolt. The father's "revelation" does not immediately bare a unified, authentic self in Georg, but a profound cleavage. The simultaneous presence of two perspectives in Georg's thoughts, speeches, and behavior, now stands revealed as an inner conflict. The terms of this conflict too have radically shifted. Prior to the father's "uncovering," dutiful devotion had been in conflict with a concealed Oedipal hostility. Now that the revolt is openly visible, it is challenged in turn by a still unacknowledged drive for self-defeat and adoption of the father's will as Georg's own. In the dramatic dénouement of "The Judgment," the father's will and the son's actions combine to smash Georg's ego, the conscious self-willed part of his self.

Georg's Oedipal revolt shows itself first undisguised as his explicit wish to defend himself against a father threatening from everywhere. He remembers a decision he had made long before to protect himself by constant wariness and close observation from a surprise attack. The text leaves it open when he had made this decision. "A long while ago" (SE, 30) might at first sight refer to the beginning of his father's present tirade. But since these accusations had just begun, it is much more likely that "the long while ago" is to be taken literally as a distant past. In that case, we see here the first open acknowledgment that Georg had been living in a state of war in his father's apartment, and that his now open hatred cannot be merely a reaction to what is happening at this moment.[22] The purposeful ambiguity of the text still hints at the two perspectives, one of which would view Georg's hostility as a reaction to his father's sudden attack of "madness," while the other would see it as a permanent state of hostile preparedness which had hitherto been concealed. But in either case Georg's resolve can only be seen as an act of self-defense of the ego and its integrity against the ever-lurking danger from the powerful Oedipal father. Elsewhere I have called this ego, armed with the powers of accurate observation and acute awareness, the ideal of the concentrated self, which occurring here for the first time in Kafka's entire *opus*, plays an important role throughout his work, from *Der Verschollene* to "The Burrow."[23] Connections between this ideal and one important aspect of Kafka's writing can be established. But what concerns us here is the immediate cancellation of Georg's posture of self-defense by a distracted-ness or absentmindedness which makes him forget the resolve of preparedness each time he remembers it. A force within him, hostile to his ego, disarms him before any defense against his father can get under way. His Oedipal struggle is nipped in the bud by something stronger within himself. Georg does not permit himself to gather strength against his father. Since it is this deeper force which prevails over his conscious will to resist, I propose to call this self-defeating force his true or effective self.

Georg's next assault upon his father is verbal. He shouts "Comedian!" at him. But immediately he regrets the epithet and as his first act of actual self-punishment, he bites his tongue so fiercely that "the pain made his knees give" (SE, 30). Thus he anticipates his final fate soon to come.

After Georg's wish for his father's death openly declares itself, the narrator informs us that the father now expected his son to approach him, but that he failed to come nearer. A physical assault upon the father would be the logical consequence of the son's murderous wish. His failure to realize his wish assures the father's victory. Rightly the father now exults and proclaims his triumph over Georg who, he declares, is deluded into believing that he still has the strength to carry out his own will. It is the father's strength that dominates now.

Finally, Georg's intention of mocking and undercutting his father changes, literally in Georg's mouth, into achieving the opposite effect of confirming and even outdoing his progenitor's berating statements. When the father jubilantly announces that Georg's friend knows everything "a hundred times better" and then "a thousand times better" than Georg, Georg multiplies this by another ten and says "ten thousand times." He raises his father's bombastic assertion to the second power "in order to deride" him—having even before wished to "make him impossible in the whole world"—"but even in his mouth the word assumed a deadly serious ring" (SE, 31). Georg's own mouth, Georg's body, now turns against his conscious will. A force inside him supports his father against himself. This force wins out and demolishes the self, even as Gregor's body transforms the salesman Samsa into vermin, and thus liberates his father from the son's rule in the household. Georg's true, i.e., effective, self has risen against him to do his father's work on himself. The alliance between father and friend extends to Georg's own innermost and ultimately prevailing self. Even as the facade of duty toward the father had given way to the Oedipal revolt, the latter in turn has yielded to the wish for defeat and surrender. Georg's last assertion of rebellious independence is to accuse his father of having lain in wait for him treacherously. Like Josef K., he views his downfall as resulting from a sneaky attack by an external foe. But actually he blames his father for something that has arisen against him from within himself. Because of this mistaken perspective his father calls his remark outdated, long overtaken by events. It would have fitted earlier when Georg's Oedipal ego still had seemed to have a chance of battling the father. "Now it is no longer a propos."

When Georg carries out his father's judgment, his father's command has taken the place of his autonomous will. Without applying any physical force, by the sheer spiritual power over, and psychic hold on the son, the father drives him out of the room, down the stairs, and into the river. His perspective has taken over Georg and become one with the core of his being, which in Freudian terms, we would call the Unconscious or Id. The grammatical structure which describes Georg's self-execution bears this out. Kafka changes the subject of Georg's act from the personal "he" the the impersonal "it"—"it drove him across the roadway, toward the water" (SE, 32). By his syntax Kafka shows that Georg's Id now executes and dissolves his person. Long before Freud's *The Ego and the Id,* but in close analogy to it, Kafka shows the alliance of Superego and Id doing away with the Ego.

Yet it is not the unconscious Id that remains as the last truth of Georg, but the articulate consciousness of his original self reaffirmed. His last words are a declaration of love for his parents, a conscious avowal of moral stance, a deliberate assertion of his return to what he had originally been. Climbing over the railing of the bridge, he becomes the reincarnation of the child who had once been the object of his parents' pride. With his statement, "Dear parents, all the same I have always loved you," he denies, cancels, revokes his Oedipal ego and rebellion, his years of dissatisfied ambition and attempted displacement of his father, and his alienation from both parents. That the dry tone which Georg had noted in his friend's words of condolence reflected Georg's own lack of proper sadness over his mother's death appears obvious from the context in which he dated his success from the moment of her demise. By proclaiming with the last sentence of his life that he had loved his parents always, he takes back and wipes out the entire intervening period between his original and his ultimate self. That is, he erases himself as an independent ego at loggerheads with its origin, since his ego had been the element contradicting the love for his parents.

To be sure, the moment of Georg's murderous wish for his father's fall seems to belie his claim of having loved his parents always. How is that earlier wish to be reconciled with his final statement? It can be reconciled if we see his ineffectual revolt itself as the instrument of his self-punishment and thus as the necessary station on his road to the reattainment of his original self. Georg's rebellion is its self-judgment. Only by bursting open and manifesting itself explicitly can his true self be freed from the oppressive facade—"the closed face of the man of honor," as his father calls it—of his hypocritical dutifulness with which he masked self-indulgence and ambition. Georg's dutiful devotion toward his father necessarily entailed bad faith as long as it was coupled with his existence as economic man. For the basic principle of economic man, hedonistic egotism, runs counter to the filial reverence and self-subordination which Georg felt bound to express as well. As long as the rebellion of the ego remained unconscious and covered up by the pretense of duty and devotion, it festered unchecked and corroded the self. As with an abscess, purification came only when it broke open.

This came about with Georg's final letter to his friend in which, at his fiancée's bidding, he openly acknowledged his engagement and invited him to the wedding. The letter was to establish Georg at last as the successful engaged adult he had apparently become. But instead of sending off the letter he entered his father's room. This entrance has initially two opposite aspects. On the one hand, it appears as the final step toward emancipation from the father as well as from the friend. By letting his father frankly know that his engagement is irreversible and marriage imminent, Georg flaunts before the father his liberation from his childhood bond. The bald and brutal spareness of tone with which he informs the father of the *fait accompli*, the use of the belittling word "only" ("Actually I only wanted to tell you") (SE, 27), the arrogance of the word "tell" with its decisive preclusion of asking for his father's opinion—all these point toward a defiant, humiliating triumph over both "bachelors"—father and friend. Georg seems to wish to "rub in" the fact that he has won the victory at last over his dependency. In fact, he appears intent on arousing his bachelored father's painful envy of the good fortune of the son. For we know, and Georg knows, how profoundly deprived the father has felt by the loss of his spouse. On the other hand, going to his father's room functions as a substitute for actually sending off the letter. It takes the place of the act which his fiancée had wished Georg to perform by writing the letter in the first place—namely to openly proclaim himself engaged and thus achieve the integrity of his divided self. By sealing the letter but not sending it, Georg first of all postpones and finally undoes what the letter was to bring about. And moreover, from the perspective of the end, we must say that Georg tacitly concedes his father's right to advise him and ultimately to judge his intention and prevent him from carrying it out. His stepping into the rear of the dwelling is also a stepping back in time to his childhood, when all his plans and acts were subject to his father's judgment, and his father's will was Georg's law. Walking into his father's room, in place of sending out the letter, he becomes implicitly what his self-punishment makes him explicitly—his father's obedient child. The Oedipal rebellion, the flaunting of his engagement, thus serves as the detour to and the very occasion for his punishment.

Georg's self-punishment, however, contradicts his father's judgment. His father had discerned the "innocent child" in Georg, but then expressly stated that the "devilish human being" in him was the more basic layer of his self, was in fact his "more actual" self; and he makes this analysis the reason for his death verdict:

> Actually you have been an innocent child, sure enough, but still more actually you have been a devilish human being! And therefore you should know: I now sentence you to death by drowning! (SE, 32)

But if the "innocent child" is to be equated with obedience and love, and "the devilish human being" with rebellion, then the order of layers in Georg does not conform to the father's diagnosis, but is its reverse. Loyalty to his father and self-punishment are, as we have seen, in every instance of the confrontation, more effective, still "more actual" than the devilish revolt. The very structure of the scene, and above all Georg's final act of carrying out his father's sentence, refute his father's analysis. Georg contradicts his father—this is the story's final paradox—by obeying him. His self-execution appears as a last act of protest and as a disproof of the justice of the judgment.

The paradox changes into a clear, albeit complex meaning if we realize that Kafka incorporated two perspectives into the story, both of which are ultimately found in Georg. The father's perspective uncovers and condemns the son's Oedipal rebellion and self-deceiving bad faith, and establishes these as sufficient reasons for justifying a death verdict. Georg accepts this perspective and identifies himself with it by acting in accordance with it. But his own perspective takes over and goes far beyond his father's. For he also sees his punishment as his vindication. Thereby he questions the basis of his father's sentence. He is, Georg seems to say and proves it by his obedient suicide, in his fundamental essence a loving innocent child, and no longer the devilish person the father condemns. His declaration of love for his parents denies his father's view of him as ultimately devilish. On the contrary, this declaration proves he is the very opposite of his father's view of him. While his father sees nothing beyond the villain in him, Georg looks upon himself tragically. To be sure, he implicitly admits by his suicide that his adult life had gone wrong, and therefore he consents to his death sentence. But he does not see in his punishment a mere erasure of his person. He considers it an atonement and therewith a symbolic reinstatement of the original harmony that, in agreement with the 'structure of tragedy, can only be achieved at the price of death.[24] His self-punishment is a self-sacrifice which calls to mind Nietzsche's view of tragedy in *The Birth of Tragedy*. The tragic action liberates and reaffirms the species as it slays the individual in the person of the hero. At the beginning of the story, the bridge, like the whole scene of the world surveyed by Georg from his window, had seemed empty and lifeless, except for an isolated sign of deference offered the mighty individual Georg, enthorned in his contemplative Apollonian repose above the scene. This mute and still Apollonian world is brought to life at the moment of his leap. Now it suddenly teems with "a well-nigh infinite traffic" (SE, 32). The individual's destruction calls the collective life into being.

The traffic collectivizes the family. It represents a symbolic broadening, a token of the universalization, of the family context. The German word "Verkehr" which Kafka uses in this last sentence of "The Judgment," means not only traffic, but "intercourse" which is its more basic meaning. It thus refers to the sphere of sex and procreation as well as to communication and commerce. "Verkehr" thus relates to Georg's parents and their intercourse to which he owes his life. It is to them he returns in his dying profession of everlasting love. "Dear Parents, all the same I have always loved you." Max Brod underlines this link between the intercourse on the bridge and that of the parents. In a conversation recorded by Brod, Kafka explained that the last sentence of "The Judgment" had evoked in him the thought "of a strong ejaculation."[25] The self-elimination of his hero from the life proceeding unendingly on the bridge above him, his letting himself fall under the "intercourse" of living, henceforth undisturbed by his presence, provided the author with the thought of intense pleasure. A later diary entry of Kafka's corroborates this meaning which self-punishment and death possessed for him. He writes that

> the best I have written is founded in this ability to die contentedly. . . . For me . . . such dying scenes are a secret game, in fact, I am happy to be in my dying protagonist (Tag, 448).

Behind the back of the overt text, as it were, or underneath it, embedded in the key word "Verkehr," a secret connection exists between the traffic on the bridge and the sexual intercourse to which Georg owes his being. The parallelism between commerical and sexual intercourse is established in the text by the coinciding of Georg's utterance of eternal love for his parents with the unending traffic which drowns out his fall. The attribute "unendlich," meaning both "unending" and "infinite," describes the stream of life which Georg restores by surrendering to the river beneath him. By drowning, he, too, re-enters that universal current, one form of which coursed through his parents' love, while another streams "unendingly" on the bridge, and a third flows in the river beneath. The stream of existence, which development into an autonomous, and thus separate, individual had interrupted, re-forms when the son returns to his father the love which his father had earlier extended to him. Just before Georg wanted him to topple and smash, the father had professed his love for him. "Do you think I had not loved you—I from whom you issued?" (SE, 31). His father's love was founded explicitly on his procreative powers, on the affection of the begetter for his offspring as for a part of himself. Then Georg had answered this love with his Oedipal wish for his father's fall and death. But that answer was provisional. The true answer is given at the end with Georg's own self-propelled fall. Literally echoing his father's "I love you," by his own, "Dear parents, I have always loved you," the son links himself directly to his father's love. In his own interpretation of the story, Kafka mentions "the circle of blood" "around father and son into which the fiancée cannot enter" (Tag, 296). This "circle of blood" is now allowed to flow once more, reuniting father and son in the "dialogue" formed around the verb "love."

However, this reunion is achieved only on a linguistic and symbolic level. It can no longer come about in the actuality of the story. River and bridge traffic are only signs, tokens standing for, but not identical with, the living blood stream, "the circle of blood...around father and son" which Kafka mentions. By restricting reconciliation to a symbolic act, to atonement in place of restitution, the narrator establishes the tragic dimension of the tale. For the broken law of an original harmonious state cannot be restored in actual life. It is achieved only in representation on a token plane, by the protagonists's sacrificial death. It is not the family that is restored but only its token, the intercourse on the bridge. It is not the actual stream of the generations that flows again, but only the current of the river symbolically accepting the son. And it is the bridge, mere sign of conjunction, rather than the actual re-embrace of parent and child, that is left in the end.

However, on this symbolic and representational level, Georg attains what all tragic heroes attain. By becoming a victim, he is vindicated as a martyr and symbolic savior. His sacrifice of self assures the infinite life of the bridge. It restores the intercourse between the divided parts of the world. In his death he goes beyond the friend, as Christ surpasses the mere ascetic who by renouncing the world merely removes himself from harm's way. What separates Georg from Christ is of course that which separates the tragic hero from Him—guilt. But what connects him with the savior is his sacrifice and its function in renewing the world. The cleaning woman's exclamation "Jesus!" as she sees Georg rushing past her, down the stairs, is both a cry to be expected under the circumstances within the conventions of realistic fiction and a strong hint at the universal implication of Georg's role. It is the son rushing to his self-sacrifice who is addressed by the name of the scapegoat and savior. Georg shares the scapegoat function with all tragic heroes in the Dionysian view of tragedy, in which the individual, a separating factor, is sacrificed for the higher life of Dionysian unity.[26] Georg Bendemann's scapegoat function emerges more clearly if viewed in connection with the other stories—"The Stoker," "Metamorphosis," and "In the Penal Colony"—to which Kafka saw "The Judgment" intimately linked (wanting to unite all four tales in two volumes, entitled *Sons* and *Punishments*.[27]) From Kafka's special perspective, Georg is a scapegoat figure as are all of his son figures. These protagonists are modeled on Kafka's view of himself as burdened with a sacrificial mission which precluded his participation in the life stream—marriage, procreation, family life. On the contrary, he has to sacrifice himself so that the happiness of families might prevail. One of his most revealing reflections expresses this view.

> He does not live for the sake of his personal life; he does not think for the sake of his personal thoughts. It seems to him that he lives and thinks under the compulsion of a family, which, it is true, is itself superabundant in life and thought, but for which he constitutes, in obedience to some law unknown to him, a formal necessity. (BK, 269 f.)

It is against such a law that Georg had sinned by seeking to realize his independent self and for which he atones by his death.[28]

Yet Kafka was very concerned with guarding himself and his protagonists from making a special virtue of the sacrificial exclusion from the life stream. At the end of "The Judgment," he makes sure that no perversion of self-execution into a martyr's cult occurs. Before taking his plunge, Georg espies a passing bus and waits for its sound to drown out his splash. He insists on a death that will go unnoticed. In this total self-obliteration of the ego in any guise, including even that of martyrdom, Georg's perspective merges with his father's. Both perspectives coincide as Georg's death is presented as necessary. Both father and son seem to unite in judging the "innocent child" preferable to the adult ego which stands in opposition to its source in the struggle for self-assertion and power. It is therefore most consistent with the meaning of his punishment that Georg's last statement and thus his ultimate truth—his declaration of love for his parents—should be united in the same sentence with a death that will not divert attention from the unending "intercourse" of life. Love and genuine self-erasure are one. This seems to be the ultimate statement in "The Judgment." Uncontradicted by the rest of the text, it represents a kind of "truth" which works of Kafka's later periods never arrive at.

NOTES

1. This paper forms part of a forthcoming study: *Franz Kafka: The Myth of Power and the Self.*

2. SE, 30. Henceforth abbreviations, with page numbers, are included in the text. Paul Raabe's edition is the most reliable text of Kafka's fiction, apart from his novels. Despite the in many ways fine quality of the standard English translations of Kafka, they frequently fail to convey the literal accuracy of his texts. Since the literal wording is an indispensable key to the understanding and elucidation of Kafka's art, I use my own translations of his German wherever I quote him.

3. Tag, 39 f. Henceforth abbreviations, with page numbers, are included in the text.

4. The story fragment "The Urban World," to which Kafka refers when he lists the associations occurring to him during his writing of "The Judgment," first introduces the father figure into his *oeuvre*. However, because of the unimportant and rather confused role which the friend figure plays in "The Urban World," discussion of this fragment would fit more properly into a study tracing the evolution of the father figure in Kafka's work. For an excellent analysis of the role of "The Urban World" in the evolution of Kafka's narrative technique, see Rolleston's *Kafka's Narrative Theater*, Chapter 3.

5. BF, 397. Henceforth abbreviations, with page numbers, are included in the text.

6. Cf. Kate Flores: "The Judgment," In *FKT*, 12. A very similar view of the split between the artistic side of Kafka, represented by the friend, and the "social" Kafka, represented by Georg, is held by Marson: "F.K.'s 'Das Urteil'."

7. Demmer: *F.K.*, 144 ff.

8. Binder: *Kafka-Kommentar*, 129.

9. Politzer: *F.K.*, 49.

10. Elias Canetti: *Der andere Prozess: Kafkas Briefe an Felice.* Munich: Hanser. 1969.

11. Cf. my *F.K.T.I.*, 59. A year later Greenberg also referred to *Totem and Taboo* in *Terror of Art*, 56 f.

12. In a letter to Brod, Kafka sees himself as "a child" in comparison to his successful married friends who stand firmly planted in reality. Cf. Br, 313.

13. Cf. J.P. Stern: "*F.K.'s* 'Das Urteil'," 121. Also included elsewhere in the present volume.

14. For Kafka's acquaintance with psychoanalytic thought, see Binder: *Motiv und Gestaltung*, 92-114.

15. Stern: *Op. cit.*, 122 f.

16. In *Motiv und Gestaltung*, 371, Binder also sees two perspectives at work in "The Judgment," but in a way that differs radically from the interpretation attempted here. Binder sees a "neutral" perspective, in which the father is actually senile (which is indeed the opposite of our view), and Georg's "emotional" perspective, in which the father becomes a "vision of terror." His approach completely ignores the fact that the father's actions and pronouncements are presented by the narrator as "objective" facts, and are perceived as such by the reader. That is, in contrast to the friend's feelings, as surmised by Georg, the reader gets a direct, "objective" view of the father's terrifying height and vigor. Although we experience the father's rising through Georg's sensibilities, the narrator nevertheless compels us to assume that what Georg perceives is actually happening and is not merely the result of his interpretation. This is, of course, particularly true of the father's pronouncements.

17. The father's senility, equated with madness, is the key to the interpretation of "The Judgment" by Claude-Edmonde Magny, *KP*, 85-106 (1975 ed). This interpretation is determined entirely by a perspective suggested to the reader by the protagonist's point of view. It therefore misses, as we shall see, the meaning of Kafka's story.

18. Cf. Kafka's letter to Max Brod of June 1921 (Br, 336f.), in which a very similar view of Westernized Jews is elaborated. Cf. also Seidler: "'Das Urteil': 'Freud Naturlich?'."

188; and Steinberg: "The Judgment in Kafka's 'The Judgment'."

19. J.P. Stern's term, 126.

20. Politzer rightly sees Georg's move into his father's room as a move into the interior "of his own mind." *F.K.*, 54.

21. Cf. Politzer: *F.K.*, 55.

22. Cf. Greenberg: *Terror of Art*, 57.

23. See my *F.K.T.I.*, Chapters 18-20.

24. Seen also by Politzer: *F.K.*, 60, but not elaborated by him.

25. Brod: *F.K. A Biography*, 158.

26. See my *F.K.T.I.*, 71-76. Erich Heller in his *F.K.*, 33-36 expounds a very similar view.

27. Cf. Br, 116, 148 f.

28. Stern: *Op. cit.*, 123, aptly calls this kind of "law" an "oxymoron," a "subjective law."

Peter U. Beicken

"The Judgment" in the Critics' Judgment

This story, whose "indubitability"[1] was always evident to Kafka, is the "spectre of a night".[2] After the first reviews,[3] critical interest was focused for a long time on Kafka's other works, until the publication of the biographical materials gave new impetus to the process of interpretation. Another factor very likely played an important role in delaying appropriate consideration of "The Judgment:" although the story marks Kafka's breakthrough to his mature writing, it does not yet possess the full authority of his later works. Kurt Pinthus objected to a particular difficulty, which, however, has to be accounted the critic's failure, since the question of psychological consistency in narration is a narrow standard for literary judgment. The felt absence of psychological consistency in "The Judgment" follows from the reader's expectation of a different narrative type. Pinthus thus reveals the limitations of his critical stance:

A young man, whose father has gone mad, is condemned by him to death by drowning for sins he did not commit. It is in no way apparent what compulsion drives the young

238

man immediately to throw himself off a bridge into the water.[4]

What here appears inscrutable is based of course on Kafka's mode of paradoxical representation. The question for him is not one of psychological realism.

Whereas Walter Benjamin read "The Judgment" as a demythification of the corrupt and parasitical world of the fathers, Herbert Tauber, while conceding the father's "senile stubbornness" nonetheless turned this invalid into "the God of Judgment".[5] Kate Flores rejected Tauber's religious constructions but also attacked Claude-Edmonde Magny for both declaring the father insane on the ground of his bizarre behavior and at the same time condemning Georg.[6] Kate Flores sees the real problem in the friend. In her view he represents Georg's other self, the feminine self; and the entire story is seen as the conflict between Kafka the writer and Kafka the social personality, in which the father figure corresponds to the wishful image of the poet-martyr. The writing self longs for an authority to decide the struggle between Georg, who is guilty and impure, and his virtuous friend, who is committed to literature and the authentic life, i.e. the life of writing. Kate Flores considers the father figure as the unconscious projection of a wish-image, resembling only superficially the real father but in fact his due opposite in the decisive matter of his judgment on the value of literature. Hartmut Binder writes similarly of the "inner father image."[7] This sort of psychological interpretation is based on the biographical method, that is, on the premise that Kafka carried over autobiographical materials into the story, as Rita Falke puts it, in a kind of "translation".[8] While her position depends on the reference to Freud in Kafka's own interpretation of "The Judgment," Eric L. Marson systematizes the inner structure of the story.

On the basis of the doppelganger-motif which recurs in Kafka,[9] he defines Georg as the social and the friend as the literary self of the author to whom he imputes the desire of putting himself, in a sort of wish-dream, on a par with his real father through the envisioned engagement with Felice Bauer and then of submitting himself remorsefully to the image of the friend out of his fear of losing his existence as a writer.[10] The real father, meanwhile, is transformed into a symbolical authority figure, who declares the friend's existence more authentic than that of the son rebelling in oedipal defiance. These issues are indeed Kafka's most passionate concern. Georg, who executes the sentence willingly and wholeheartedly as if driven by an unknown inner force, thus rescues the authorial existence of Kafka the writer and annuls the rivalry with the father, which threatens to overwhelm him with guilt. The social self is eliminated, its uncompromising emancipation destroyed by regression into infantile submission. Moreover, Kafka would have seen the prevention of the triumph over the father and its immediate consequence—a settled bourgeois existence founded on marriage and family— as a diminishment of the danger to the writing he considered as the last refuge of his autonomy. It should be stressed, however, that these consequences of Marson's thesis are based on biographical rather than on textual evidence.

Most interpreters have more or less explicitly followed the pattern of increasing the value of the father at the expense of the son. For Edmund Edel the son is an inadequate, self-centered sinner laden with existential guilt and separated from the "authenticity of spiritual existence";[11] he is condemned without question by the representative of the "spiritual world" or the "powers of the good" embodied in the father. This alleged "mythical process" is completely mythologized by Karl H. Ruhleder and stylized into the conflict of son (Cronus) and father (Uranus), in which the god/father figure, by his decree, causes the son to become a child once more.[12]

John J. White has similarly declared Georg's empirical existence a guilty one and demands its liquidation through the "absolute father", an embodiment of "absolute truth"; hence Georg dies in the name of a "more authentic world", reconciling himself with the "totality of being"—all this without the interpreter's once attempting to justify his thesis.[13] Erwin R. Steinberg sees Georg's suicide on the model of the Yom Kippur ritual, as even more explicitly aiming at divine reconciliation, whereas Kurt Weinberg's speculative, religious, allegorical reading—to which Ingo Seidler also by and large subscribes—works only when violently applied to the text.[14]

Meanwhile in all these readings the contradictory father figure is dissolved into a monolithic fact. Heinz Politzer rightly cautioned against moving "from the universal meaning of the story back to its psychological motivations".[15] The shortcoming of his explanation, however, lies in his too swiftly assuming that Kafka tried to seize in the paradox of the father's judgment the "indissoluble contradictoriness of human existence", that the story arises from his "never fulfilled desire for a genuine metaphysical orientation." Accordingly, Politzer is forced to draw from the text as its sole "discernible message" the "warning against the loss of bachelorhood." Politzer furthermore finds Georg guilty of "self-centeredness" and the loss of "purity."

Walter H. Sokel has investigated this dimension more explicitly, proposing the following dichotomy and antithesis: the friend becomes "the pure self," whereas Georg himself is assigned the function of a mere ego-facade. The "pure self" or "true existence" triumphs in the alliance with the father figure—the absolute authority—over the "false existence" which has violated its own "law", its innermost being.[16] Equally, Sokel sees the suicide as a reconciliation with forces transcending the limited ego, as a return, namely, to the "idyll which existed before the fall." Lawrence Ryan protests against this alleged misreading of Freud, arguing that the son's self-annihilation and return to the id cannot be a fulfillment of his innermost being.[17] Ryan considers Sokel's thesis incompatible with Freud's theory of ego-development, which is meant to serve the purpose of emancipation from, not submission to, the id.

For clarity's sake let us consider certain features of Kafka's own interpretation of the story. Kafka left a number of comments about this "work most dear" to him, which reveal its connection with his own life.[18] These remarks serve as a useful point of departure for a consideration of Kafka's own attitude toward "The Judgment." First of all they show that he doubted the existence in it of "any sort of straightforward, coherent, plausible meaning."[19] However, the materials which he adduced do point rather directly to his situation in 1912 and the all-pervasive problem of his relation to his father. The tension and abrasiveness of this relation struck him decisively when, after meeting Felice Bauer, he was confronted with the problem of marriage more acutely than ever before.

Kafka's original intention in writing "The Judgment" is quite revealing:

> When I sat down to write, after a Sunday so miserable I could have screamed..., I meant to describe a war; from his window a young man was to see a vast crowd advancing across the bridge, but then the whole thing turned in my hands into something else.[20]

It is evident how the inner pressure of the latent conflict dislocates the original realistic intent as it is found in the empirical, social treatment of the problem of self and world in the early works. Instead of a general critique of society, a story arises "full of abstractions, though they are never admitted." Kafka considers the story to be "a journey around father and son, and the friend's changing shape may be a change in perspective in the relationship between father and son."[21] Thus the friend is the "link between father and son, he is their strongest common bond."[22] Kafka's reference to Freud reveals that these unacknowledged "abstractions" structure an oedipal conflict, which arises through Georg's wish to marry and his attempt—following his success in business—to usurp the patriarchal power. The rivalry is staged through gestures, as when Georg carries the apparently invalid father to bed and tries to cover him up in an act suggestive of parricidal intent; the result is an unexpected peripety. The father, "still a giant",[23] is determined to settle accounts. The deceased mother becomes a mere pawn between the parties to this family quarrel. The friend is unmasked as an accomplice of the father, who strips his son—despite his recently acquired social skill and business power—of all his resources; he confronts him with his indubitable patriarchal authority, shattering his resistance, rebuking the allegation of clownishness and, in the role of a merciless judge, condemning him to death by drowning. The kind of repressive power employed by the father is in itself irrational and therefore gives the story an aura of inscrutability.

Kafka notes that Georg suddenly finds himself confronted by everything that formerly seemed to him held in common with his father, but in the form of something alien and independent of him, a sign of his self-estrangement. The father, as the more powerful, has deviously robbed the son of what was once part of him; and since Georg "has lost everything except his awareness of the father, the judgment, which closes off his father from him, does have so strong an effect on him."[24] The son capitulates before this unscrupulous use of power. The father as depicted in the story rejects Georg's life in society, which he brands as "devilish," in favor of the friend's mode of life. Here lies the real difference between him and Hermann Kafka, who had little but contempt for someone who, to judge by appearances, is a martyr manqué, the type of the alienated ascetic suggested by the east European actor Yitzchak Löwy, with whom at that time Kafka was closely acquainted. In many ways Löwy served as a model for the "friend" in "The Judgment." Kafka's father condemned him as a "useless relationship,"[25] illustrating his dominant mode of thinking and judging—according to social status. Kafka, however, failed to perceive or, at any rate, to indicate in his own interpretation the inversion of his father image.

In the interpretation proposed by most commentators, the friend is seen as the representative of a pure ascetic existence, divorced from all thinking according to social categories; this reading makes a good deal of sense. To stress the relation to the writer's existence, as Kafka understood this word, seems plausible, although the friend, precisely like Georg, is, however inept, a businessman. This means that in "The Judgment" Kafka defends the order of writing against the order of society and that of his real father: Georg's successful embourgeoisification does not take place; the father is not dislodged, and his position of power is not eliminated. Instead, this attempt at "parricide" is declared taboo, and the writer's existence (to be identified with bachelorhood) is simultaneously affirmed. Put radically, the action amounts to an aborted revolt against established power, ending in the total reduction of the self in suicide. The question, meanwhile, of whether any other solution is possible, whether the elimination of the father is indeed the sole form of emancipation, does not enter the horizon of the story. Moreover, there remains an indissoluble mood of ambivalence which arises from the paradoxical image of the father and the narrative perspective of the story.

Georg is at the same time the center of perception, the narrative focus, and a persona of the author. Georg reflects, remembers, acts. The father is seen through his perspective. This is, according to Friedrich Beissner, the *"Einsinnigkeit"* of Kafka's narrative mode—the single perspective constituting a unity of meaning. Georg's consciousness also determines how everything that happens, that comes to light, is evaluated and judged. Georg's phenomenological field shapes in advance the reader's perception. At the same time Georg is also depicted, and indeed in such a fashion that a judgment upon him as a figure is shaped by the author and communicated to the reader. Thus without the intrusion of the narrator the reader assumes an attitude of distance.[26] Georg, whose consciousness is that of the successful bourgeois, the man bent on career, comes to light as morally reprehensible, appearing, as he does, to represent that kind of man who—superficial, dehumanized, insubstantial—utterly lacks spiritual orientation and furthermore deceives his friend and neglects his father. To the same extent the father as judge is made into a quasi-divine agency of punishment or at any rate the representative of an absolute, superhuman order. The story encourages such an interpretation because through its particular portrayal of Georg, it casts a negative light on "normal" human existence and criticizes the bourgeois life and mode of consciousness from the standpoint of an ethical regorism. The procedure time and again adopted by the story's interpreters, that of legitimizing the father as a higher power, of turning him into an absolute or exponent of absolute truth, follows a tendency of the story.

This is contradicted however by an important detail which has often been noted, most recently by Heinz Politzer, Jörgen Kobs, and J.P. Stern[27]—the fact namely that after the father, as supreme judge, has delivered his verdict, he collapses back into his former state of miserable weakness, comes crashing down from the heights. As Politzer puts it, "The authority of the father dissolves into nothingness." Expressed differently, in the very moment in which he loses his son, and just before Georg kills himself, the father "as judge in his own cause is extinguished" (Kobs). Kafka thus denies him any sort of absolute, let alone divine status. Although the father's fall is heard only as a subjective impression by the son, as he goes rushing off, the fact is as such incontestable. Consequently, one can now argue, as indeed Kobs has argued, that—once the frequently assumed theory of the father's insanity has been excluded—"The Judgment" turns on the annihilation of two incompatible and irreconcilable adversaries who as subjects of equivalent status locked in combat can bring their struggle to a close only by mutual annihilation. The introduction of a metaphysical dimension (that of the father as "God" or judge) and a mythic dimension (that of the father as primordial patriarch, inviting parricide) dislocates what originally begins as a struggle of subjectivities in the social order. A social reality becomes a prop in a mythic scenario devoid of real social content. The friend is no longer a social being but rather one who—as Kafka puts it—is "unreal",[28] is in the Kafkan sense of a symbolic figure of highly personal significance, for that Russia to which the story alludes is a key metaphor in the poetic universe of the writer, signifying the domain of ascetic isolation, solitude, and suffering.[29] Kafka however is bent on the concrete dramatization of these things—on the one hand through gesture and on the other hand through symbols; the main thesis of Kafka's poetics speaks of the "embodiment of symbols,"[30] a process often indicated by the verbal sign "förmlich" ("downright", "actually").

It is therefore not right to conceive Kafka's narrated world as having a purely "psychic reality"[31] even when unrealistic elements encourage this idea. Thieberger for example asserts that Kafka "is happiest representing completely unrealistic things in a pseudo-realistic style."[32] Politzer likewise sees in the verdict of "The Judgment" a "paradoxical statement which can only be appreciated on the metaphysical level."[33] Ms. Beck denies any "commonsense perspective" in the story and refuses to see in any of the figures a valid norm of human behavior.[34] This is the difficulty which Herbert Kraft seeks to resolve by assuming "a direct confrontation of two levels of reality in the world—normality and paradox." Having taken into account the narrative structure of the story, he concludes: "The opposing world seems paradoxical in comparison with normality in the perspective of the hero."[35]

This leads to the question of consciousness. J.P. Stern asserts in the manner of earlier critics that Georg is guilty of self-centeredness, of "moral solipsism," and is therefore rightly condemned, although the authority is in itself questionable.[36] Cyrena Pondrom likewise considers Georg's limited horizon an epistemological problem and the sentence as self-imposed. The execution of the judgment is seen as an admission of guilt through which Georg acknowledges the world which he hitherto refused to recognize as compelling and real.[37] Herbert Kraft goes beyond this thesis, in declaring that the second part of "The Judgment" "puts into question empirical reality itself."[38] All of Georg's behavior consists of "a refusal of awareness, of falsity—in the discrepancy between being and seeming," and this leads to his admission of guilt. Through the process of coming to consciousness, Georg is said to achieve an insight into the necessity of carrying out the sentence. Kraft remarks:

Normality is unmasked in its amorality through Georg's admission of guilt, the insufficiency of its reality in the light of *this* reality is unmasked through his death. The admission of his guilt and death mean nothing less than the affirmation of paradoxicality with respect to normality: the second world is a paradox which discloses reality; normality is revealed as distorted reality.[39]

Kraft's argument seems plausible when he notes apropos of Ernst Fischer's notion of "distortion as method" that "the estrangement of reality is rendered recognizable 'through a second-order aesthetic estrangement,' the alienation of the paradox."[40] On the other hand, his views as to the "amorality" of the normal are not wholly convincing, for they miss the point that Georg's empirical existence is judged from a standpoint which from the start is concerned to show that his is a "devilish" existence. It would be prudent to question so total a condemnation of the empirical order, even if one detects in it, as Helmut Richter has done, the "reflection of a social order which either dehumanizes the man who cannot put up any internal or external resistance to it or else corrupts him precisely by imposing on him a blind quest for a truly human life."[41]

Thus we are led to the following conclusion: In "The Judgment" Kafka detects and embodies in a new and paradoxical form the insight that empirical reality is determined by laws which cannot be controlled or even perceived by the individual, principally those governing the struggle of subjectivities (as represented in the conflict of the generations, that oedipal conflict between father and son, which has, as it were, a mythical origin). Kafka registers the absence of alternatives within ordinary reality (to this extent Kafka was an intellectual alienated from the bourgeoisie), which frustrates every attempt at legitimate ethical emancipation, although there still remains the possibility of the economic "emancipation" of a career. The sole mode of autonomy lies in the estranged existence of the friend, that is to say, existence outside

the social order, in the confined circle of one's own individuality, which condemns the individual to isolation and asceticism;
whereas normal reality, on account of its dehumanizing social
structure and economic constraints, produces despicable, self-
estranged beings like Georg. "The Judgment" reflects this
reality. Here is a story whose action and developing perspective
suggest to the protagonist only one solution: the self-
destruction of normal existence. In this domain no emancipation could be possible, because "true" autonomy consists,
according to Kafka, in the insistence on an uncompromising
otherness, in an ethically rigorous isolation from the empirical
order which is perceived as "devilish". The escapism of the
early work has here established itself for the first time with the
authority of an existential imperative. With this the "proof of
the impossibility of living" of the "Description of a Struggle"
does appear to be elevated with the claim of complete generality
to the paradox of human existence as such. What is striking in
"The Judgment" is the negativity with which the normal,
empirical order is seen. Accordingly, a metaphysical dimension emerges, the question of man's culpability, of his
inexorable existential guilt. How true autonomy and emancipation might be possible without a fall into the negativity of
the friend and without a forced abandonment of the social
order—how in short self-realization might be possible within
human society—hardly enters the world of "The Judgment."
Georg's resistance to subjugation does not point to the
bourgeois element in him but instead to that will to
emancipation which sees through the father's "comedy,"
perceives all the archaic props of authority, and ridicules the
mercilessly imposed inevitability of the sentence.

"The Judgment" is the expression of a radically estranged
individuality, which elevates a specific historical (and
personal) experience to a universal law. The reader is therefore
not obliged to linger in the attitude of mere approbation of the
Kafkan paradox, as Cyrena Pondrom would have it, when she
says:

Georg is both *ein unschuldiges Kind* and ein *teuflischer*

Mensch (innocent and devilish). The paradox is the situation of man, inexplicable and in the context of generations, infinite.[52]

Against this sort of eternal reification of, the paradox, "The Judgment" should be examined with respect to its liberating impulse, its emancipatory perspective.[43]

Translated by Stanley Corngold
with the author

NOTES

1. D 1, 278.
2. Janouch: *Conversations*, 31 (1971 ed.). Kafka refers to the night of Sept. 22-23, 1912. See D 1, 275.
3. KS, 149-151.
4. Pinthus's review appeared in the *Zeitschrift fur Bücherfreunde*, XI (Feb.-Mar. 1918), Col. 559; rep. in KS, 151.
5. Benjamin: *Illuminations*, 113-114. Tauber: *F.K.I.*, 16.
6. Kate Flores: "The Judgment." FKT, 5-24, also elsewhere in the present volume. C.E. Magny: "The Objective Depiction of Absurdity." FKT, 75-96. Georg's friend has been subject to contradictory interpretations: for example, Kate Flores sees in him Georg's feminine self, whereas Ruth Tiefenbrun considers him to be the prototype of the Kafkan homosexual, and Werner Rehfeld speaks of the "admonishing and disquieting conscience." Tiefenbrun: *Moment of Torment*, 79; Rehfeld: *Das Motiv des Gerichts*, 39.
7. Binder: *Motiv und Gestaltung*, 372.
8. Falke: "Biographisch-literarische Hintergrunde," 174.
9. For the doppelganger-motif see Platzer: "Kafka's 'Double-Figure'," 7-12, and Wollner: *Hoffmann und F.K.*
10. Marson: "F.K's 'Das Urteil'," 167-178.
11. Edel: "F.K.: 'Das Urteil'," 216-225.
12. Ruhleder: "F.K's 'Das Urteil'," 13-22.
13. White: "F.K's 'Das Urteil'," 208-229.
14. Steinberg: "The Judgment in Kafka's 'The Judgment'," 23-30; Weinberg: *Kafkas Dichtungen*, 318-350; Seidler: "'Das Urteil'," 174-190.
15. Politzer: *F.K.*, 63, 61, 59 (1966 ed.).
16. Sokel: *F.K.*, 50, 82.
17. Ryan: "'Zum letzten Mal Psychologie'!", 162.
18. Br, 149. For Kafka's comments on "The Judgment" see Heller & Beug (eds.): *F.K.: Dichter uber Dichtungen. F.K.*, 19-30.
19. LFe, 265.
20. *Ibid.*
21. *Ibid.*, 267.
22. D 1, 278. Kafka mentions Freud in the entry for Sept. 23, 1912. Cf. D 1, 276.
23. CS, 81. Grotesque elements in "The Judgment" are discussed by Rehfeld: "Das Motiv des Gerichts," 87-92. See also Kassel: *Das Groteske*. The phenomenon of sudden,

unexpected peripety has been pointed out by Asher: "Turning Points," 47-52.
24. D 1, 279.
25. *Ibid.*, 125. For a closer analysis of Kafka's relationship to Lowy, see Beck: *Kafka and the Yiddish Theater*, 17-19, 87-89.
26. The concept of *"Einsinnigkeit"* was proposed by Beissner in *Der Erzahler F.K.*, partly translated in Gray: K, 15-31. Cf. also Kobs: *Kafka*. A differing view stressing the distancing elements of Kafka's narrative strategy in Beicken: *Perspektive und Sehweise*, and *F.K.*, 69-75.
27. Politzer: *F.K.*, 62; Kobs: *Kafka*, 342; Stern: "F.K's. 'Das Urteil'," 127.
28. "The friend is hardly a real person." LFe, 267.
29. Cf. D 1, 233. See also Sokel: *F.K.*, 51, 66. White in "F.K.'s 'Das Urteil'," 211, speaks of Russia as a metaphor for the infinite and the absolute. Evelyn Beck, on the other hand, considers it to be a synonym for eastern European Judaism *(Kafka and the Yiddish Theater*, 88). Ellis in "Kafka's 'Das Urteil'," rejects these interpretations, and views them as "pitfalls of assuming that Kafka always had one thing in mind whenever he thought of Russia." Instead he proposes: "Russia in 'Das Urteil' is primarily a symbol of openness, as opposed to the closedness of an existence at home." Ellis' critique rightly cautions against a one-dimensional reading of Kafka's symbols, but he fails to substantiate his contention. For Kafka, "Russia" is associated with loneliness, both in his *Diaries* and in "The Judgment," since Georg's friend is, indeed, exposed to an environment which he experiences as hostile.
30. For a discussion of *"förmlich,"* see Kobs: *Kafka*, 301-303, and Beicken: *Perspektive und Sehweise*, 429-436. Gesture or "Gestus, as Walter Benjamin pointed out *(Illuminations*, 121, 129), is a very important element in Kafka's depiction of narrative reality. Early in his career as a writer Kafka copied "cinematographic gestures," Cf. Jahn: "Kafka und die Anfänge des Kinos," 353-368. Also David E. Smith: *The Use of Gesture as a Stylistic Device in Heinrich von Kleist's "Michael Kohlhaas" and Franz Kafka's "Der Prozess"*. Stanford University, 1971 (typ dis).
31. Beissner: *Der Erzähler F.K.*, 62.
32. Richard Thieberger: "Moderne deutsche Prosa." *DU*, XVI (1964), 12.
33. Politzer: *F.K.*, 59.
34. Beck: *F.K. and the Yiddish Theater*, 78-80.
35. Kraft: *Kafka*, 39-44. Richard Thieberger speaks of "subjective" and "objective reality" in *Le genre de la nouvelle*, 72.
36. Stern: "F.K's 'Das Urteil'," 126: "heedless egocentricity."
37. Pondrom: "Coherence in 'Das Urteil'," 64.
38. Kraft: *Op cit.*, 41-42.
39. *Ibid.*
40. *Ibid.*
41. H. Richter: *F.K., 111.*
42. Pondrom: *Op. cit.*, 78-79.
43. *Ibid.* Aside from the studies quoted above, the following deal with "The Judgment": Baumer: *Sieben Prosastuke*, 101-109; Foulkes: *The Reluctant Pessimist*, 100-106; Greenberg: "The Literarture of Truth," and in his *Terror of Art*, 47-88; Pongs: *F.K.*, 50-55; Weber: " 'Das Urteil';" Zimmermann: "F.K.: 'Das Urteil'."

The various editions of "The Judgment" are discussed by Ludwig Dietz: "F.K. Drucke zu seinen Lebzeiten. Eine textkritisch-bibliographische Studie." *JDSG*, VII (1963), 416-457; "Drucke F.Ks. bis 1924. Eine Bibliographie mit ANmerkungen." *KS*, 85-125; "Die autorisierten Dichtungen Ks. Textkritische Anmerkungen." *ZDP*, LXXXVI (1967), 301-317. CF. Beicken: *F.K.*, 1-8.

For the genesis of "The Judgment" and Kafka's biographical situation in 1912, see Binder: *Motiv und Gestaltung*, 125-135; and, more extensively, Demmer: *F.K.*, although his conclusion about Kafka the man and Kafka the writer fails to go beyond a mere adumbration of the biographical situation in 1912. Corngold explicates much more rigorously the significance of the biographical elements in Kafka's poetic universe, interpreting Kafka's writings as allegories of his existence as a writer: See Stanley Corngold's ed. of F.K.: *The Metamorphosis*. N.Y.: Bantam Books, 1972, xi-xxii.

Recent critical attention has centered on Kafka's relationship to Freud: Murill/Marks: "Kafka's 'The Judgment'." The authors endeavor to corroborate the claim that Kafka was familiar with Freud's *Interpretation of Dreams*, but they fail to see, as Binder has shown, that Kafka up until 1912 had only a second-hand knowledge of Freud. The same is true of Beharriell who believes it is no longer necessary to prove Freud's influence on "The Judgment": Kafka's reference to Freud "means only that psychoanalytic ideas or methods played a key role in its composition." (28). A somewhat vaguer notion is introduced later when Beharriell speaks of Kafka's "new ability to give free expression to his feelings about his father and to his Angst-neurosis," or notes that "with 'Das Urteil,' his dream images become more recognizably Freudian. It is credible speculation too, that his study of Freud may have clarified his conviction that it was by objectifying 'spectres' in writing that he could maintain his hold on sanity." (31). Although Kafka confessed to these "thoughts about Freud" (D 1, 275), and to the "unacknowledged abstractions" (LFe, 267), he denied "any sort of straightforward, coherent, plausible meaning" in "The Judgment." This leads to the conclusion that Kafka did not have a clear, analytical insight into his relationship to his father based on the Freudian method; Kafka's mode of narrating his psychic experience was mainly mythological. For a similar view see Hillmann: *F.K.*, 214 (1973 ed.).

In his *Kafka-Kommentar*, 123-152, Binder gives a detailed commentary of the background of "The Judgment." For remarks on the "comedy à la Bendemann," see Bodeker: *Frau und Familie*, 42-45. A reading of "The Judgment" on the basis of the "autobiographical-psychological components" together with an interpretation of the religious symbolism alleged to transcend the story of a family conflict is given by Nagel: *F.K.*, 172-200. An interesting analysis which points out some fairy tales motifs, is presented in Ruf: *F.K.*, 11-51. Focusing on the division in Georg Bendemann's character, Rolleston in his *Kafka's Narrative Theater*, 42-51 investigates the protagonist as actor and comes to the conclusion: "If consciousness implies manipulation, then the collapse of the mental theater involves the extinction of every trace of consciousness . . . Georg had denied himself (as he denied his friend) to such an extent that his death does more than negate his life, it replaces it with an image—'innocent child'—of his father's choosing." Yet another key to "The Judgment" is proposed by Ellis: Kafka's 'Das Urteil',' 209, who states that "the explicitly Christian motifs underline the fact that in 'Das Urteil' the values of Christianity are thrown up in the air, and come down in an unfamiliar shape."

There can be no doubt, the strangeness of Kafka's story calls for renewed exploration of its unfamiliarity—calls for further judgment of "The Judgment."

Notes on Contributors

Peter U. Beicken, born in Germany, studied at the Universities of Cologne and Bonn; Magister Artium from the University of Munich (1968), and Ph.D. from Stanford (1971). Teaching German literature at Princeton University since 1971. Among his publications: *Franz Kafka. Eine kritische Einführung in die Forschung* (1974).

Charles Bernheimer, educated at Haverford College and Harvard (Ph.D., 1972). Has been teaching at SUNY (Buffalo) for the last few years and writing about Flaubert, Gogol and Structuralism. Now working on a book on Flaubert, Kafka and Beckett.

Hartmut Binder, born in Germany in 1937. Currently professor of German literature at the Pädagogische Hochschule at Ludwigsburg. Author of *Motiv und Gestaltung bei Franz Kafka* (1966) and the two-volume *Kafka-Kommentar* (1975 & 1976). Edited, with Klaus Wagenbach, Kafka's *Briefe an Ottla und die Familie* (1974). Now preparing a monumental *Kafka Handbuch* with the collaboration of leading scholars from all over the world.

Stanley Corngold, a Ph.D. in Comparative Literature from Cornell, is Associate Professor of German at Princeton. Author of *The Commentator's Despair: The Interpretation of Kafka's "Metamorphosis"* (1973) and of an annotated translation of *The Metamorphosis* (1972). Has also published essays on Rousseau, Mann, Frisch, Heidegger, Tarn, and Kosinski.

John M. Ellis, born in London (1936), studied at the Universities of London and Vienna, completing his Ph.D. at the University of London (1965). Now Professor of German literature at the University of California (Santa Cruz). In addition to his studies of Schiller's aesthetic theory (1970) and Kleist's *Prinz Fiedrich von Homburg* (1970), he is the author of *The Theory of Literary Criticism. A Logical Analysis* (1974) and *Narration in the German Novelle* (1974).

Angel Flores began his Kafka research in 1925 upon reading a

Spanish version of "The Metamorphosis" in the *Revista de Occidente*. Published Kafka homages in *The Literary World* (1934) and *QRL* (1947); three symposia: *The Kafka Problem* (1946, 1963, 1976), *Franz Kafka Today* (with H. Swander) (1958, 1959, 1976) and *The Kafka Debate* (1976). *A Kafka Bibliography 1908-1976* is the latest of a number of bibliographies compiled by him since 1942.

Kate Flores, born in N.Y. City; studied at New York University and the University of Wisconsin. Taught poetry at Queens College, CUNY. Besides interpretations of Emily Dickinson and Kafka, is known for translations of difficult poets including Góngora, Hölderlin, Mallarmé, Rilke, Valéry. Lately has been working on the applicability of Einstein's ideas to living nature. "Relativity and the Origin of Consciousness," which appeared in *Perspectives in Biology and Medicine* (University of Chicago), attracted worldwide attention.

Ronald Gray lectures on German literature at Cambridge University, where he is a Fellow of Emmanuel College. Has published *Goethe, a Critical Introduction;* an edition of Goethe's poems; *German Poetry, a Guide to Free Appreciation;* a study of Brecht; and a general work of criticism, *The German Tradition in Literature, 1871-1945.* To Kafka he has devoted *Kafka's Castle* (1956) and *Franz Kafka* (1973), and edited *Kafka: A Collection of Critical Essays* (1962). A new volume on Brecht will be published in 1976. He has in hand a study of Ibsen.

Malcolm Pasley, born 1926. A Fellow of Magdalen College, Oxford University, has encouraged the study of Kafka's manuscript texts, and is one of the editors of the forthcoming critical edition. Together with Klaus Wagenbach, he compiled a chronology of Kafka's works in *Kafka-Symposion* (1965). The first volume of his translations of Kafka into English (*Kafka: Shorter Works, Vol. I*) appeared in 1973. His other publications include *Germany: A Companion to German Studies* (1972).

James Rolleston, born in England (1939); educated at Winchester College, Kings College, Cambridge; University of Minnesota, and Yale (Ph.D., 1968). Taught French in Accra, Ghana (1962-4). On the Yale faculty (1968-1975) and now Associate Professor of German at Duke. Married Priscilla, 1962; Christopher born, 1967, Victoria, 1970. Among his books: *Rilke in Transition* (1970) and *Kafka's Narrative Theater* (1974).

Walter H. Sokel, born in Vienna, taught at Columbia and Stanford; now Commonwealth Professor of German literature and member of the Center for Advanced Study at the University of Virginia. Author of *The Writer in Extremis* (1959), a study of Expressionism, and *Franz Kafka: Tragik und Ironie* (1964) as well as monograph *Franz Kafka*, in the series Columbia Essays of Modern Authors (1966). Now engaged in a full-length study of Kafka: *The Myth of Power and the Self.* Editor of *An Anthology of German Expressionist Drama* (1963); together with Jacqueline Sokel, translated a number of German plays into English.

J.P. Stern, born in Prague and educated in Czech schools and at St. John's College, Cambridge. During the War served in the Czech army and the Royal Air Force. For many years Fellow and tutor of St. John's College and lecturer in the department of German at Cambridge University. Has been Visiting Professor at C.C.N.Y., the University of California (Berkeley), SUNY at Buffalo, the University of Virginia, and Gottingen University. Since 1972 has held the chair of German at University College, London. Among his publications: *Ernst Junger: A Writer of Our Times* (1952); *Re-Interpretations: Seven Studies in Nineteenth-century German Literature* (1971); *On Realism* (1972); and *Hitler: The Führer and the People* (1975). At present working on a book about Nietzsche.

John J. White, Lecturer in German at Westfield College, University of London, was educated at the Universities of Leicester, Alberta, London and the Free University, West Berlin. Author of *Mythology in the Modern Novel* (1971) and a volume of critical essays on the German Expressionist poet August Stramm. He is co-editor of *German Life and Letters.*

Key to References

Angel Flores: *A Kafka Bibliography 1908-1976,* Staten Island, N.Y.: Gordian Press, 1976, 200 pp., lists further references to all of Kafka's works.

Asher: "Turning Points..."
Asher, J.A.: "Turning Points in Kafka's Stories." *MLR,* LVII, No. 1 (Jan. 1962), 47-52.

Baumer: *Sieben Prosastücke*
Baumer, Franz: *Sieben Prosastücke.* Munich: Kosel, 1965, 101-109.
Beck: *Kafka and the Yiddish Theater*
Beck, Evelyn T.: *Kafka and the Yiddish Theater.* University of Wisconsin Press, 1971, 248 pp., 70-121.
Beharriell: "Kafka, Freud and 'Das Urteil'."
Beharriell, Frederick J.: "Kafka, Freud and 'Das Urteil'," in Manfred Durzak & Others (eds.): *Texte und Kontexte. Festschrift für Norbert Fürst.* Bern: Francke, 1973, 27-47.
Beicken: *F.K.*
Beicken, Peter U.: *Franz Kafka. Eine kritische Einführung in die Forschung.* Frankfurt: Fischer Athenaum Taschenbucher, 1974, 453 pp., 241-250.
Beicken: *Perspektive und Sehweise*
Beicken, Peter U.: *Perspektive und Sehweise.* Stanford University, 1971 (typ dis, 535 pp.), 409-465.
Beissner: *Der Erzähler F.K.*
Beissner, Friedrich: *Der Erzähler Franz Kafka.* Stuttgart: W. Kohlhammer, 1952, 51 pp.
Beissner: *Kafka der Dichter*
Beissner, Friedrich: *Kafka der Dichter.* Stuttgart: W. Kohlhammer, 1958, 44 pp.; tr. in part as "Kafka the Artist" in *GK,* 15-31.
Benjamin: *Illuminations*
Benjamin, Walter: *Illuminations.* N.Y.: Harcourt, Brace & World, 1968, 111-140 and 141-148.
Beutner: *Die Bildsprache*

Beutner, Barbara: *Die Bieldsprache Franz Kafkas.* Munich: W. Fink, 1973, 328 pp.

Bezzel: *Natur bei Kafka*
Bezzel, Christoph: *Natur bei Kafka.* Bonn: Bouvier, 1966, 406 pp.

BF   F.K.: *Briefe an Felice und andere Korrespondenz aus der Verlobungzeit.* Ed. by Erich Heller & Jürgen Born. Frankfurt: Fischer; N.Y.: Schocken, 1967, 784 pp.

Binder, Harmut: "Kafkas Schaffesprozess, mit besonderer Berucksichtigung des *Urteils.*" Euphorion (Heidelberg), LXX (1976), 129-174.

Binder: *Motiv und Gestaltung*
Binder, Hartmut: *Motiv und Gestaltung bei Franz Kafka.* Bonn: Bouvier, 1966, 406 pp., 125-135, 349-396.

Binder: *Kafka-Kommentar*
Binder, Hartmut: *Kafka-Kommentar zu samtlichen Erzählungen.* Munich: Winkler Verlag, 1975, 346 pp., 123-152.

BK   F.K.: *Beschreibung eines Kampfes.* Frankfurt: S. Fischer, 1954.

BM   F.K.: *Briefe an Milena.* Frankfurt: S. Fischer, 1952.

BO   F.K.: *Briefe an Ottla und die Familie.* Frankfurt: S. Fischer, 1974.

Bödeker: *Frau und Familie*
Bödeker, Karl-Bernhard: *Frau und Familie im erzählerischen Werk Franz Kafkas.* Bern/Frankfurt: Lang, 1974, 177 pp., 42-45.

Born: "F.K. und seine Kritiker"
Born, Jürgen: "Franz Kafka und seine Kritiker (1912-1924). KS, 149-151.

Br   F.K.: *Briefe 1902-1924.* Ed. by Max Brod. Frankfurt: Fischer, 1958, N.Y.: Schocken, 1958, 531 pp.; Frankfurt: Fischer Taschenbuch, 1975.

Brod: *F.K.*
Brod, Max: *Franz Kafka. Eine Biographie.* Prague: H. Mercy, 1937, 281 pp.; Berlin: S. Fischer, 1954, 360 pp.

Brod: *F.K.: A Biography*
Brod, Max: *Franz Kafka. A Biography.* N.Y.: Schocken, 1957, (2nd. enlarged ed., 1960, 267 pp.; paperback, 1963, 252 pp.

Brod, Max: *Über Franz Kafka.* Frankfurt: Fischer Bucherei, 1966, 416 pp. [Contains: F.K. Eine Biographie; F.Ks. Glauben und Lehre; and Verzweiflung und Erlösung im Werk F.Ks.].

C   F.K.: *The Castle.* N.Y.: Knopf, 1964.
Collins: "Kafka's Special Methods of Thinking"
   Collins, R.G.: "Kafka's Special Methods of Thinking." *Mosaic,* III, No. 4 (Summer 1970), 43-57.
CS   F.K.: *The Complete Stories.* Ed. by Nahum N. Glatzer. N.Y.: Schocken, 1971, 486 pp.
Czermak: *Kafka's "The Metamorphosis"*
   Czermak, Herberth: *Kafka's "The Metamorphosis" and Other Stories.* Lincoln, Nebraska: Cliff Notes Inc., 1973, 23-32.

D 1   F.K.: *The Diaries 1910-1913.* Ed. by Max Brod. N.Y.: Schocken, 1948, 345 pp.
D 2   F.K.: *The Diaries 1914-1923.* Ed. by Max Brod. N.Y.: Schocken, 1949, 343 pp.
Demmer: *F.K.*
   Demmer, Jürgen: *Franz Kafka, der Dichter der Selbstreflexion. Ein Neuansatz zum Verstehen der Dichtung Kafkas, dargestellt an der Erzählung "Das Urteil".* Munich: W. Fink, 1973, 203 pp.
DF   F.K.: *Dearest Father. Stories and Other Writings.* N.Y.: Schocken, 1954, 409 pp.; entitled *Wedding Preparations in the Country.* London: Secker & Warburg, 1954, 409 pp. [Contains "Letter to his Father," "Wedding Preparations in the Country, etc.]
Doppler: "Entfremdung und Familienstruktur."
   Doppler: Alfred: "Entfremdung und Familienstruktur. Zu Franz Kafkas Erzählungen 'Das Urteil' und 'Die Verwandlung'," in his *Zeit— und Gesellschaftskritik in der osterreichischen Literatur des 19. und 20. Jahrhunderts.* Vienna, 1973, 75-91.
DU   *Der Deutschunterricht* (Stuttgart)

DV   Deutsche Vierteljahrsschrift für Literaturwissenschaft und Geistesgeschichte (Stuttgart)

E   F.K.: *Erzählungen und kleine Prosa*. Berlin: Schocken, 1935, 280 pp.; N.Y.: Schocken, 1946, 287 pp.; Frankfurt: Fischer, 1952, 334 pp.
ed   edited
Edel: "F.K.: 'Das Urteil'"
    Edel, E.: "Franz Kafka: 'Das Urteil'." WW, IX, No. 4 (1959), 216-225.
Ellis: "Kafka; 'Das Urteil'."
    Ellis, John M.: "Kafka: 'Das Urteil'", in his *Narration in the German Novelle*. N.Y. & London: Cambridge University Press, 1974, 188-211.
Emrich: *F.K. A Critical Study*
    Emrich, Wilhelm: *Franz Kafka. A Critical Study*. N.Y.: Frederick Ungar, 1968, 561 pp.

Falke: "Biographisch-literarische Hintergrunde"
    Falke, Rita: "Biographisch-literarische Hintergrunde von Kafkas 'Urteil'. GRM, X, No. 10 (1960), 164-180.
F.K.   Franz Kafka
FKT   Angel Flores & Homer Swander (eds.): *Franz Kafka Today*. University of Wisconsin Press, 1958, 290 pp.; N.Y.: Gordian Press, 1976.
Flores, A.: *Bibliography*
    Flores, Angel: *A Kafka Bibliography: 1908-1976*. Staten Island, N.Y.: Gordian Press, 1976, 200 pp.
Flores, K.: "F.K. and the Nameless Guilt"
    Flores, Kate: "Franz Kafka and the Nameless Guilt. An Analysis of 'The Judgment'." QRL, III, No. 4 (1947), 382-405; "'The Judgment'." *FKT*, 5-24; "'La condena' de Franz Kafka." *Etcaetera* (Guadalajara, Mexico), V, No. 19 (Sept. 1956), 133-151 (Tr. by Miguel Rodriguez Puga).
Foulkes: *The Reluctant Pessimist:*
    Foulkes, A. Peter: *The Reluctant Pessimist: A Study of Franz Kafka*. The Hague: Mouton, 1967, 176 pp., 100-106.
Fürst: *Die offenen Geheimtüren*

Fürst, Norbert: *Die offenen Geheimtüren Franz Kafkas. Fünf Allegorie.* Heidelberg: W. Rothe, 1956, 86 pp.

Gibian: "Dichtung und Wahrheit"
Gibian, George: "Dichtung und Wahrheit: Three Versions of Reality in Franz Kafka." *GQ,* XXX (Jan. 1957), 20-31.
GQ   German Quarterly (Philadelphia)
GR   German Review (N.Y.)
Gray: *F.K.*
Gray, Ronald: *Franz Kafka.* N.Y. & London: Cambridge University Press, 1973, 57-66.
Gray: *K*
Gray, Ronald: (ed.): *Kafka: A Collection of Critical Essays.* Englewood, N.J.: Prentice-Hall, 1962, 182 pp.
Greenberg: "The Literature of Truth"
Greenberg, Martin: "The Literature of Truth: Kafka's 'Judgment'." *Salmagundi* (Flushing, N.Y.), I, No. 1 (1965), 4-22.
Greenberg: *Terror of Art*
Greenberg, Martin: *The Terror of Art: Kafka and Modern Literature.* N.Y.: Basic Books, 1968, London: Deutsch, 1971, 241 pp., 47-68.
GRM   Germanisch-Romanische Monatsschrift (Heidelberg)
H   Hamalian, Leo (ed.): *Franz Kafka. A Collection of Criticism.* N.Y.: McGraw-Hill, 1974, 151 pp.
Haas: "Differenzierende Interpretation"
Haas, Erika: "Differenzierende Interpretation auf der Oberstufe," dargestelt an Aichinger 'Spiegelgeschichte,' Musil 'Die Amsel Kafka 'Das Urteil'." DU, XXI, No. 2 (1969), 64-78.
Heller: *F.K.*
Heller, Erich: *Franz Kafka.* London: Fontana, 1975, N.Y.: Viking, 1975, 140 pp., 1-13, 27-28.
Heller & Beug: *F.K.*
Heller, Erich and Joachim Beug (eds.): *Franz Kafka: Dichter über ihre Dichtungen.* Munich: Heimeran/S. Fischer, 1969.

Hibberd: *Kafka in Context*
 Hibberd, John: *Kafka in Context*. London: Studio Vista,
 1975, 144 pp., 43-47.
Hillman: *F.K.*
 Hillmann, Heinz: *Franz Kafka: Dichtungstheorie und
 Dichtungsgestalt*. Bonn: Bouvier, 1964, 196 pp. (2nd. ed.,
 1973, 259 pp.)
Hoch   Hochland (Munich)
Honegger, Jurg B.: *Das Phanomen der Angst bei Kafka*. Berlin:
 Erich Schmidt, 1974, 320 pp., 223-232.
Hyde, Virginia M.: "From the 'Last Judgment' to Kafka's
 World," In G.R. Thompson (ed): *The Gorthic Imagina-
 tion*. Washington State University Press, 1974, 176 pp.
 128-149.
Ide: "Existenzerhellung"
 Ide, Heinz: "Existenzerhellung im Werke Kafkas." *JWB*,
 (1957), 66-104.
Janouch: *Conversations*
 Janouch, Gustav: *Conversations with Kafka. Notes and
 Reminiscences* London: Verschoyle, 1953 and N.Y.: F.A.
 Praeger, 1953, 109 pp., (enlarged ed., London: Deutsch,
 1971 and N.Y.: New Directions 1971, 219 pp.).
Janouch: *Gespräche*
 Janouch, Gustav: *Gespräche mit Kafka. Erinnerungen und
 Aufzeichnungen*. Frankfurt: S. Fischer, 1951, 138 pp.
 (enlarged ed., 1968).
JDSG Jahrbuch der deutschen Schiller-Gesellschaft (Stutt-
 gart)
JWB Jahrbuch der Wittheit zu Bremen (Bremen/Hanover)
Kassel: *Das Groteske*
 Kassel, Norbert: *Das Groteske bei Franz Kafka*. Munich: W.
 Fink, 1969, 176 pp.
Kemper: "Gestörte Kommunikation"
 Kemper, Hans-Georg: "Gestörte Kommunikation. Franz
 Kafka: 'Das Urteil'," in Silvio Vietta & H.G. Kemper:
 Expressionismus. Munich: W. Fink, 1975, 286-305.
Kobs: *Kafka*
 Kobs, Jürgen: *Kafka: Untersuchungen zu Bewusstein und*

Sprache seiner Gestalten. Ed. by Ursula Brech. Bad Homburg: Athenaum, 1970, 559 pp., 301*ff.*, 342*f.*

KP Angel Flores (ed.): *The Kafka Problem*. N.Y.: New Directions, 1946, 468 pp.; N.Y.: Octagon Books, 1963, 477 pp.; N.Y.: Gordian Press, 1976, 503 pp.

Kraft: *Kafka*
Kraft, Herbert: *Kafka. Wirklichkeit und Perspektive.* Bebenhausen: Rotsch, 1972, 82 pp., 39-44.

KS *Kafka-Symposion.* Contributions by Jürgen Born, Ludwig Dietz, Malcolm Pasley, Paul Raabe, and Klaus Wagenbach. Berlin: Verlag Klaus Wagenbach, 1965, 189 pp.

Kuna: *F.K.*
Kuna, Franz: *Franz Kafka: Literature as Corrective Punishment.* Indiana University Press, 1974, 196 pp., 42 f., 143 f.

LFe F.K.: *Letters to Felice.* Ed. by Erich Heller & Jurgen Born. London: Secker & Warburg, and N.Y.: Schocken, 1974, 592 pp.

LM F.K.: *Letters to Milena.* Ed. by Willy Haas. London: Secker & Warburg, and N.Y.: Schocken, 1953, 238 pp. (2nd printing, 1954).

Magny: "Objective Depiction"
Magny, Claude-Edmonde: "The Objective Depiction of Absurdity." *KP*, 81-87 (ed. 1976).

Marson: "F.K.'s 'Das Urteil'."
Marson, Erich L.: :Franz Kafka's 'Das Urteil'." AUMLA (University of North Queensland), 16 (1961), 167-178.

Memmi: "Motivations inconscientes..."
Memmi, Germaine: "Motivations inconscientes et formes dans 'Le Verdict' de F.K." *Revue de l'Allemagne* (Paris), 5 (1973) 785-800.

MFS Modern Fiction Studies (Purdue University).
Miyai: "Motiv..."
Miyai, Toyo: "Motiv zu F.Ks. Erzählung 'Das Urteil'." *Jahresbericht des germanisch-romanischen Instituts von Kwanseigakuin Universität,* II (1968), 41-44.

MLN Modern Language Notes (Johns Hopkins University).
MLR Modern Language Review (King's College, London).

Monatshefte   Monatshefte fur Deutschen Unterricht (University of Wisconsin)

Mosaic   Mosaic (University of Manitoba)

Murrill/Marks: "Kafka's 'The Judgment;...'"
> Murril, V. and W. S. Marks: "Kafka's 'The Judgment' and *The Interpretation of Dreams.*" GR, XLVIII (1973), 212-228.

Nagel: *F.K.*
> Nagel, Bert: *F.K. Aspekte zur Interpretation und Wertung.* Berlin: Erich Schmidt, 1974, 398 pp., 172-200.

PC   F.K.: *The Penal Colony.* N.Y.: Schocken, 1948, 320 pp.

Platzer: "Kafka's 'Double-Figure'"...
> Platzer, Hildegard: "Kafka's 'Double-Figure' as a Literary Device." *Monatshefte,* LV, No. 1 (1963), 7-12.

Politzer: *F.K.*
> Politzer, Heinz: *F.K.: Parable and Paradox.* Cornell University Press, 1962, 376 pp., 53-65; (2nd, ed., 1966, 398 pp.).

Pondrom: "Coherence in Kafka's 'The Judgment'."
> Pondrom, Cyrena N.: "Coherence in Kafka's 'The Judgment'," *SSF,* IX, No. 1 (Winter 1972), 59-79.

Pongs: *Im Umbruch der Zeit.*
> Pongs, Hermann: *Im Umbruch der Zeit. Das Romanschaffen der Gegenwart.* Göttingen: Göttinger Verlangsanstalt, 1956, 2nd. ed., 66-95.

Pongs: *F.K.*
> Pongs, Hermann: *Franz Kafka: Dichter des Labyrinths.* Heidelberg: W. Rothe, 1960, 136 pp., 105-112.

QRL   Quarterly Review of Literature (Princeton, N.J.).

Rehfeld: *Das Motiv des Gerichtes*
> Rehfeld, Werner: *Das Motiv des Gerichtes im Werke Franz Kafka. Zur Deutung des "Urteils," der "Strafkolonie," des "Prozess."* Frankfurt: J. W. Goethe University, 1960 (typ dis, 212 pp.), 87-92.

Richter: *F.K.*
> Richter, Helmut: *Franz Kafka. Werk und Entwurf.* Berlin: Rutten & Loening, 1962, 348 pp., 105-112.

Rolleston: *Kafka's Narrative Theater*

Rolleston, James: *Kafka's Narrative Theater.* Pennsylvania State University, 1974, 165 pp., 42-51.

Ruf: *F.K.*

Ruf, Urs: *Franz Kafka: Das Dilemma der Söhne.* Berlin: E. Schmidt, 1974, 103 pp., 11-51.

Ruhleder: "F.K.'s 'Das Urteil'."

Ruhleder, Karl H.: "Franz Kafka's 'Das Urteil': An Interpretation." *Monatshefte,* LV, No. 1 (Jan. 1963), 13-22.

Ryan: "'Zum letzen Mal Psychologie!'"

Ryan, Lawrence: "'Zum letzen Mal Psychologie!'": Zur psychologischen Deutbarkeit der Werke Franz Kafkas," in Wolfgang Paulsen (ed.) *Psychologie in der Literaturwissenschaft.* Heidelberg: L. Stiehm, 1971, 157-173.

S   F.K.: *Das Schloss.* Frankfurt: S. Fischer, 1935.

Sautermeister: "Sozialpsychologische Textanalyse"

Sautermeister, Gerd: "Sozialpsychologische Textanalyse. Franz Kafkas Erzählung 'Das Urteil'," in Dieter Kimpel & Beate Pinkermeil (eds.): *Methodische Praxis der Literaturwissenschaft.* Kronberg/Ts.: Scriptor Verlag, 1975, 179-221.

Schneeberger: *Das Kunstmärchen*

Schneeberger, Irmgard: *Das Kunstmärchen in der ersten Hälfte des 20. Jahrhunderts.* University of Munich, 1960 (typ dis, 17-46).

SE   F.K.: *Sämtliche Erzählungen.* Ed. by Paul Raabe. Frankfurt: S. Fischer, 1969 and 1972; Frankfurt: Fischer Bücherei No. 1078, 1970, 406 pp.; Frankfurt: Taschen Buch No. 1078, 1975 (10th ed.), 448 pp.

Seidler: "'Das Urteil': 'Freud natürlich?'"

Seidler, Ingo: "Das Urteil': 'Freud natürlich?' Zum Problem der Multivalenz bei Kafka," in Wolfgang Paulsen (ed.): *Psychologie in der Literaturwissenschaft.* Heidelberg: L. Stiehm, 1971, 174-190.

Sokel: *F.K.T.I.*

Sokel, Walter H.: *Franz Kafka: Tragik und Ironie.* Munich/ Vienna: A. Langen/G. Muller, 1964, 586 pp., 44-76.

Sokel: *F.K.*

Sokel, Walter H.: *Franz Kafka*. Columbia University Press, 1966, 48 pp., 19-21 (Columbia Essays on Modern Writers, No. 19).

SSF   Studies in Short Fiction (Newberry College, S.C.).

Spann, Meno: *Franz Kafka*. Boston: G.K. Hall, 1976, 205 pp., 50-63 (Twayne's World Authors Series).

Steinberg: "The Judgment in Kafka's 'The Judgment'."
Steinberg, Erwin R.: "The Judgment in Kafka's "The Judgment."" MFS, VIII, No. 1 (1962), 23-30.

Stern: "F.K's 'Das Urteil'."
Stern, J.P.: "Franz Kafkas's 'Das Urteil': An Interpretation." GQ, XLV (1972), 114-129.

Szanto: *Narrative Consciousness*
Szanto, George H.: *Narrative Consciousness: Structure and Perception in the Fiction of Kafka, Beckett and Robbe-Grillet*. University of Texas Press, 1972, 189 pp. 15-68.

T   F.K.: *The Trial*. London: Secker & Warburg, 1956 (definitive ed); N.Y.: Knopf, 1957 (definitive ed); Penquin Books, 1970.

Tag   F.K.: *Tagebücher* N.Y.: Schocken, 1946, 351 pp. 1951, 737 pp.; Frankfurt: Fischer, 1967, 737 pp.

Tauber: *F.K.: An Interpretation of his Works*
Tauber, Herbert: *Franz Kafka. An Interpretation of his Works*. Yale University Press, 1948, 12-17.

TB   F.K.: *Tagebucher und Briefe*. N.Y.: Schocken, 1946, 351 pp.

Thalmann: *Wege zu Kafka*
Thalmann, Jörg: *Wege zu Kafka*. Frauenfeld/Stuttgart: Huber, 1966, 298 pp., 52-55.

Thieberger: *Le genre de la nouvelle*.
Thieberger, Richard: *Le genre de la nouvelle dans la litterature allemande*. Paris: 1968, 74-78.

Thorlby; *Kafka*
Thorlby, Anthony: Kafka: A Study. London: Heinemmann 1972; Totowa, N.J.: Rowman & Littlefield, 1972, 101 pp., 28-34.

Tiefenbrun: *Moment of Torment*
Tiefenbrun, Ruth: *Moment of Torment. An Interpretation*

of Kafka's Short Stories. Southern Illinois University Press, 1973, 160 pp., 79-110.

tr   translated

TuK   *Text und Kritik* (Munich)

Wagenbach: *F.K.*

Wagenbach, Klaus: *Franz Kafka. Eine Biographie seiner Jugend, 1883-1912.* Bern: Francke Verlag, 1958, 345 pp.

Walser: *Beschreibung einer Form*

Walser, Martin: *Beschreibung einer Form. Versuch über Franz Kafka.* Munich: Hanser, 1961, 156 pp.

Weber: "'Das Urteil'."

Weber, Albrecht: "'Das Urteil'," im A. Weber & Others (ed): *Interpretationen zu Franz Kafka.* Munich: Oldenbourg, 1968, 140 pp., 9-80.

Weinberg, K.: *Kafkas Dichtungen*

Weinberg, Kurt: *Kafkas Dichtungen: Die travestien des Mythos.* Bern/Munich: Francke, 1963, 509 pp., 318-350.

White: "Franz Kafka's 'Das Urteil'."

White, John J.: "Franz Kafka's 'Das Urteil': An Interpretation." *DV,* XXXVIII, No. 2 (1964), 208-229.

Wöllner: *E.T.A. Hoffman und F.K.*

Wöllner, Günter: *E.T.A. Hoffmann und Franz Kafka. Von der "fortgeführten Metapher" zum "sinnlichen Paradox."* Bern/Stuttgart, 1971 (Sprache und Dichtung, N.F. Bd. 20).

WW   Wirkendes Wort (Dusseldorf)

ZDP   *Zeitschrift fur Deutsche Philologie* (Berlin)

Zimmermann: *Deutsche Prosadichtungen*

Zimmermann, Werner: *Deutsche Prosadichtungen der Gegenwart.* Dusseldorf: Schwann, 1954, 174 pp.; enlarged ed., retitled *Deutsche Prosadichtungen unseres Jahrhunderts,* 1966, 189-208.

Other books on Kafka edited by Angel Flores

THE KAFKA PROBLEM

FRANZ KAFKA TODAY
co-editor Homer Swander

THE KAFKA DEBATE

A KAFKA BIBLIOGRAPHY 1908-1976

All published by Gordian Press
85 Tompkins Street
Staten Island, N.Y. 10304